Israel's Most Wanted Man

Rabbi Eliezer Berland

Ben Brito

 Published by Matronita Press

Canada House, Morasha, Jerusalem, Israel

To contact Matronita Press directly, email our Customer Care Department at: info@matronitapress.com

Brito, Ben
Israel's Most Wanted Man: Rabbi Eliezer Berland / Ben Brito – First edition

ISBN: Trade Paperback: 978-965-7739-17-4
ISBN: eBook

FIRST EDITION

Printed in the USA

When a holy man does not have enemies, he cannot draw people to God.

- Rabbi Nachman of Breslov

"Ultra-orthodox extremism has darkened our lives. This is more dangerous than Ahmadinejad."

– Former Mossad Chief Efraim HaLevy,
speaking in June, 2012

Contents

INTRODUCTION

The year is 2010 and the state of Israel is waking up to a new reality which the secular elites who run the country can't accept: by 2030, most people will be ultra-orthodox. The continuing explosion in the *haredi* population is threatening to engulf the country and bring the emerging global powerhouse back into the dark ages.

Ultra-orthodox Jews don't believe in serving in the army. Most value learning the Bible over working in hi-tech in Israel's Silicon Valley. And most would place their allegiance to God far above their allegiance to the secular State.

And their numbers are growing exponentially.

From the 1990s, the secular media in Israel began ringing the alarm bells loud and clear about the coming demographic nightmare threatening to flood the country with a wave of righteous darkness.

Writing in the Financial Times in 2013, journalist John Reed summed up the problem succinctly:

"Although there were only about 30,000 *haredi* Jews in Israel at its founding in 1948, they now account for about 10 percent of the 8 million-strong population because of their high birth rates. With their large families and low median age of 16, the community's demographic profile has more in common with those of poor sub-Saharan African countries than mainstream communities in upper-income Israel."[i]

The Israeli media were far less polite in their assessment. In 2012, popular journalist Yaron London wrote an article for the Ynet website where he compared the growing *haredi* population to a "malignant body part", and stated: "We should aim to reduce the number of their grandchildren. This is not an impossible mission. It is not an abusive mission either. This is a mission of salvation."[ii]

This statement was not unusual. Many in Israel's media took it upon themselves to 'stop the rot' of this growing population of Jews who they believed were threatening to take over and ultimately destroy their country. In 2011, London's fellow writer on the Ynet news site, Assaf Wohl, took aim at the people he blamed for causing this unacceptable situation to develop: *the rabbis.*

In a piece entitled 'Why the rabbis are hated', Wohl wrote: "The Rabbinate has become the 'military wing' of the *haredi* community. Through it, the *haredim* abuse the rest of the population. Through the Rabbinate they force Israel's citizens to get married, divorce, convert and set their clocks the *haredi* way."[iii]

The poster child for this outpouring of fear and hate against the *haredi* community in Israel was Yair Lapid, a popular TV journalist who created a new political party called *Yesh Atid* ('there is a future') in 2012, with the catchphrase: *Sharing the burden.*

Yesh Atid benefitted from strong support in the media and from the State of Israel's secular institutions. It was

[i] John Reed, Financial Times, February 13, 2013 Israel's ultra-Orthodox at heart of furor.
[ii] 'Say no to Jewish Hezbollah' appeared on Ynet on 28.2.2012: https://www.ynetnews.com/articles/0,7340,L-4195684,00.html
[iii] https://www.ynetnews.com/articles/0,7340,L-4078068,00.html

going to force *haredim* to serve; it was going to slash the State's financial support towards the *haredi* world; and most of all, it was going to break the power of the rabbis who were the identified root cause of the problem. *Yesh Atid* succeeded in joining the Israeli government in January 2013 and wasted no time in implementing their policies.

The story of Rabbi Eliezer Berland unfolds against this backdrop.

Rabbi Eliezer Berland is a *haredi* rabbi. For more than 5 decades, he has been bringing tens of thousands of people back into the world of orthodox Judaism and back to the *haredi* way of life. Rabbi Berland is also no stranger to politics. He's clashed directly with the State over access to Jewish holy sites, and he enthusiastically and publically promotes an emphasis on peace and prayer, in place of confrontation and war.

It is perhaps, then, not so surprising that by 2012, Rabbi Eliezer Berland had become Public Enemy #1.

Over the next four years, Rabbi Berland became the most wanted man in Israel, as the State of Israel chased him and his followers across three continents, spending more than 10 million shekels in the process. Lurid slanders filled the press as one of the most successful 'trials by media' ever known played itself out across the world's television and internet screens.

But the tale of Rabbi Eliezer Berland, Israel's most wanted man, goes far beyond the individuals involved. Really, it's the story of modern-day Israel, and a microcosm of the battle that is currently being waged for the soul of the country.

This book lifts the curtain on the persecution and incarceration of Rabbi Eliezer Berland, and explains what really happened from those on the inside. It reveals a torrid saga of media malice, petty jealousies and political persecution. But far more is hidden under the surface.

You are about to enter a world where the spiritual holds sway, where miracles are possible, and where problems are solved with penitence and prayer.

And where nothing is really as it seems.

ALWAYS UNUSUAL

"From the establishment of [Israel's] statehood, opposition to the ultra-orthodox became a permanent characteristic of the secularists. And it also came along with suppressive measures."
- Dr Amnon Raz-Krakotzkin, Professor of Jewish History at the Ben Gurion University of the Negev.

"We're encountering significant numbers of those who are religiously-observant amongst our youngsters, especially amongst the youth counsellors and in the transit camps for new immigrants.

"Obviously, our goal is to make them aware that their faith in God is illogical and unreasonable, since religion is the result of living under a reactionary dictatorship, and has no place amongst those who are fighting to establish a progressive regime...

"Counselors should use patience and try to belittle religiosity as a socially-disturbing factor in the movement. After briefing a youngster in this way, which does not directly attack religion but undermines it, the youngster will independently come to the conclusion that there is no God, and will abandon his religious faith."
- Excerpt of the Shomer HaTzair[i]'s Guide on How to Deal with Religious Youngsters, printed in Israel in 1956.

---

[i] From the official Hashomer HaTzair website: "Hashomer Hatzair was founded in Europe in 1913 as the first Zionist youth movement for the Jewish people, and today it is the oldest Zionist youth movement still in existence... The movement founded hundreds of Kibbutzim across the country where new immigrants could find a home and a community.

On December 27, 1937 Chaim and Etia Berland became the proud parents of their second son, Eliezer. The couple had recently escaped pre-War Europe to settle in the Northern Israeli city of Haifa. Chaim Berland, a Polish Jew, had made every effort to get to Israel because he said he could see a Holocaust coming. He worked as a partner and baker at one of Haifa's cooperative bakeries, while Etia Berland worked for a coffee wholesaler.

The Berland family was unusual, even then. Most of their neighbors were diehard Labor Socialists who celebrated Labor Day instead of Yom Kippur, Judaism's holiest day of the year. In stark contrast, the Berland household was that rare oddity: a family who still believed in the Torah. As a three year old boy, the young Eliezer was mocked by his friends for being the only religious boy in his playgroup.

In his Bnei Akiva high-school, Eliezer was the only boy who insisted on wearing his hat to school, which raised the ire of the head teacher and nearly earned him a beating. "Why are you insisting on being different from the other pupils?!" the head demanded, angrily. No-one else was making such a fuss about covering their head. But Eliezer Berland was never a person for half-measures. If he was going to do something, he was going to do it 100%.

The young Eliezer was unusual in other ways, too. While the other children would spend their time playing and swimming, he spent his time learning through books of religious law, and would even stay up all night learning Torah. His friends were struck by how seriously he behaved, even as a young teen, and his strange way of praying in the local

---

"Further Hashomer Hatzair took part in the founding of the Palmach, the IDF, in the development of a new Hebrew culture in Israel and the Diaspora... and educating hundreds of thousands of children and youth in Israel and the Diaspora." - http://www.hashomer-hatzair.net/cgi-webaxy/item?181

Vizhnitz shul – where he would bend down almost to the ground, engrossed in his prayers - drew all the neighborhood children to come and watch him.

At the age of 17, he went to study at the Knesses Chizkiyahu yeshiva, which had just opened up in nearby Kfar Chassidim. His unusual conduct was noticed by the staff and students alike, who'd never seen any other student, learn for 20 hours a day, even on fast days, when everyone else was melting in the heat. (This was in the days before air-conditioning).

They also noticed that his prayers so often seemed to get answered. Whenever another student fell ill, the students would run to ask Eliezer to pray for him, and he would then shut himself in his room, with his book of psalms, and come out again a couple of hours later with eyes red from crying. And the student would so often recover.

One of his contemporaries at the yeshiva, Rabbi Jacob Moshe Shpitzer recalls: "I never once saw him teasing anyone, or heard him speak badly about another person. I never once saw him sitting with the other boys outside the yeshiva after our studies and spending his time simply chatting. I only saw Rabbi Berland engaged in holy matters and Torah learning. He really threw himself into his learning with an enormous amount of energy."

There was no question that the young Eliezer was unusual, and that his strange behavior made a deep impression on people, wherever he went. When he was 21, he left Haifa to learn in the Ponevezh Yeshiva in Bnei Brak. Around that same time, he was set up on a date with Tehillah Shaki, daughter of Rabbi Shalom Abraham Shaki, a Yemenite immigrant and member of Israel's National Religious Party.

Before the date, he wrote a question to one of the most senior Rabbinic figures in Israel at that time, Rabbi Yaakov Yisrael Kanievsky (also known as the 'Steipler Gaon'), to ask him if he could keep his eyes closed during the meeting[i]. The Steipler responded with his customary sharpness: 'If you're going to keep your eyes closed for the rest of your life," he told him, "then it's also permitted for you to close your eyes during that meeting.'"

After the wedding, the young man moved from the Ponevezh Yeshiva to study with the Steipler, at the Volozhin *kollel*. He was the Steipler's study partner for more than three years, and Rabbi Jacob was clearly taken with his young prodigy. In one letter, he referred to him as: "The precious young student, a genius in Torah and [full of] fear of heaven, our master and teacher Rabbi Eliezer Berland."

As news of the Steipler's special treatment of the unusual young man from Haifa spread, another of the young men studying Torah in Bnei Brak, David Chaim Stern, plucked up the courage to ask the Steipler what he saw in Eliezer Berland.

"He was a very young man, while the Steipler was the leading Rabbi of the generation, and so much older than him. They were study partners, learning many hours together each day, so I was interested in finding out what he had to say about him," explains Rabbi Stern[ii]. "The Steipler told me, 'You should know, he is an expert in the entire Torah, a holy man and a *tzaddik* (saint)!' That was the testimony from the mouth of the generation's leading Rabbi."

But while he was very happy with the Torah learning at the Volozhin yeshiva, Rabbi Berland was still feeling something lacking in his religious devotions. He discussed this with the Steipler, and asked him: "What's going to be

---

[i] Rabbi Berland actually had more than 10,000 written responses from the Steipler Gaon over the course of their correspondence, sadly most of which have been lost.
[ii] Today, Rabbi David Chaim Stern is one of the most important kabbalists and religious figures in Israel.

with my praying?" The Steipler responded, "If you want praying, you need to go to the *Chassidim*."

Over the coming months, Rabbi Berland went to a number of different *chassidic* synagogues, prayer houses and yeshivas, to see where he felt most inspired. In the end, he came across the Breslov yeshiva almost by accident, on the night of Purim, 1961. He was returning home from the Lelov synagogue in Tel Aviv when he suddenly felt inexplicably tired, so he turned into the Breslov Yeshiva in Bnei Brak[i], to sit down for a while, and started learning a copy of *Likutei Moharan*, which he found there.

The place appeared to be deserted, so when the yeshiva's administrator, Rabbi Nachman Rosenthal, showed up, Rabbi Berland asked him where all the students were. He was informed that everyone was in bed, asleep, so they could wake up at midnight in order to go out to the fields and pray. Reb Lazer responded: "What?! There are other people who go out to the field to pray?! This is exactly what I've been looking for!"

But it wasn't so easy to make the jump instantly into the Breslov way of life, not least because the Breslov chassidic group, which was nicknamed the 'dead *chassidus*' by the other chassidim[ii], had been decimated by the Russian Revolution, and the post-World War II community was both tiny and in much disarray. For the next two weeks, returning to the Breslov yeshiva slipped Rabbi Berland's mind, until he bumped into Rabbi Nachman Rosenthal late one Friday afternoon, and agreed to come and visit him again at the yeshiva that Friday night. When he heard the praying, and

---

[i] Located on Am HaDerech Street, between Chazon Ish and Vizhnitz Streets.

[ii] After Rabbi Nachman of Breslov, the founder of Breslov *chassidut*, died in 1810, no child or follower took over the mantle of leading the movement, as usually occurred in the other *Chassidic* dynasties.

the way the cantor was repeating the same word over and over again for 15 minutes, Rabbi Berland was sold. Finally, he'd found the spiritual path he'd been searching for.

But first, he returned to the Steipler, to ask for his understanding regarding all the unusual ideas Breslov seemed to teach, especially about the concept of the "Tzaddik" – a superlatively holy individual - who exists within every generation. He sat with Rabbi Jacob and went through every detail.

When he got up to the comment where Rebbe Nachman of Breslov stated that the Tzaddik could even take his students out of hell, he asked the Steipler: "Can you get me out of purgatory?" The Steipler laughed, and told his young learning partner that it was only with great difficulty that he could get himself out of purgatory. Who'd ever heard of such a thing?!

But the Rabbi wasn't to be put off. He asked again: "But, what if you found a tzaddik who could get you out of purgatory?" The Steipler responded, "If that's the case — run after him!" So that's what Rabbi Berland did, with every last iota of his strength.

Very quickly, he became a legend in the Breslov yeshiva in Bnei Brak. No-one could keep up with him, as he spent whole nights talking to God in the fields, praying for hours on the roof of the yeshiva, at full volume, dancing for hours in order to sweeten harsh judgments, getting up for the midnight prayers, and sleeping just an hour every night, in the process.

Whatever advice he found in the Breslov books, Rabbi Berland made every effort to fulfill it in every detail. He sought out the Breslov elders in Jerusalem, and spent months and even years as their attendants, building close relationships with luminaries including Rabbi Israel Ber Odessa, Rav Hersh Leib Lippel, Rav Tzvi Aryeh Rosenfeld, and Rav Binyomin Zeev Cheshin, Rosh Yeshiva of the 'Shaar Hashamayim' Kabbalistic yeshiva in Jerusalem.

Rabbi Berland's reputation as a miracle worker was also growing exponentially, and the Steipler and other rabbinic luminaries at that time, like the famous Sephardi kabbalist Rav Mordechai Sharabi, started sending people to Rabbi Berland for a blessing.

"Go to the Lederman synagogue in Bnei Brak," Rav Sharabi told one of his petitioners. "There, you'll see a student of the Torah who prays with a lot of enthusiasm and different movements. Ask him to give you a blessing that you should get your miracle — and don't take no for an answer! Even if he tells you he's nothing and speaks disparagingly about himself and tells you he's not on the level to give you a blessing."

★   ★   ★

But not everyone in Bnei Brak was thrilled with their strange neighbor, who would often disappear for weeks at a time to pray in the wilderness, like a Biblical prophet of yore. "There were times when the Rav would disappear for whole weeks, or even whole fortnights," recalls Abish Dickshtein, one of the Berlands' old neighbors. "Some of the Lithuanian Jews who lived on Rashbam Street in Bnei Brak used to laugh at the Rebbetzin and tell her, 'You see! Your husband has run off and disappeared!' Rabbi Berland used to go away to pray, so I used to go and talk to the Rebbetzin to give her some encouragement, so she shouldn't be broken by the things her neighbors were saying."

Even then, Eliezer Berland was a polarizing figure. But love or hate him, no-one could really ignore him, or the dramatic events that always seemed to surround him.

When the Berlands' only son, Nachman, was four months

old, he fell out of his pram and sustained a severe head injury that left him a coma for almost six weeks. The doctors told the distraught parents that he had a one in a thousand chance of surviving, and recommended very high risk brain surgery, as the only possible course of action.

But Eliezer Berland told the doctors that his son would live, even though he needed an open miracle. He immediately left the hospital, and went straight to sell his apartment in Bnei Brak for 10,000 Israeli liras.[i] He then distributed all the money from the house sale to charity.

Miraculously, Nachman Berland woke up, and completely recovered.

★ ★ ★

Over the next few years, Reb Lazer started to make a lot of friends within the still relatively closed circles of Breslov chassidus – but also a few enemies. Over time, he'd grown closer to the Breslov elders, including Rav Shmuel Shapira, and Rav Levi Isaac Bender, who in his quiet way had become the *de facto* leader of Breslov chassidus, after the Second World War.

One year, Reb Lazer had astounded the Breslov Chassidim gathered together in the Northern Israeli town of Meron for *Yom Kippur* by standing rooted to the spot, in prayer, for the full 25 hours. When Reb Lazer finally made it onto the bus returning to Jerusalem, he broke his fast with a drop of grape juice, and then launched into a three hour Torah class, which only ended when he decided to get off the bus in the Jerusalem forest, to spend the rest of the night praying in the fields.

The next morning, he appeared for morning prayers in the Breslov shul in Meah Shearim, and again he just stood

[i] Roughly equivalent to around 500,000 shekels, in today's money.

there praying for hours and hours. When the service was over, he went up to the roof to continue his prayers, and at that point, some of the congregants went over to Rav Shmuel Shapira. "What do you say, about this Rav Lazer Berland?" they wanted to know. Rav Shmuel replied, "It's already known to us that this is not a person, it's an angel!'"

But not everyone agreed with that assessment. Some people within Breslov eyed the newcomer, and his strange habits and boundless enthusiasm, with a lot of suspicion. They referred to him as the *meshugganer*, the crazy man – and Reb Lazer did everything he could to encourage them.

Ben Zion Grossman explains that this wasn't an accident, and that Reb Lazer would actively seek out ways for people to disparage him. "One of his spiritual devotions is to bring shame upon himself," begins Rabbi Grossman. "It's not just that he doesn't go after honor, he literally encourages people to insult him and humiliate him."

And the more positive attention he was starting to garner for his erudition and sincerity, the more Reb Lazer was looking for ways to cool all the adoration down. From a young age, it seems that Reb Lazer decided to take a leaf out of King David's book, and to turn himself into a 'fool', who didn't appear to know or understand anything.

Moshe Yosef Haas first met Reb Lazer at the Vizhnitz yeshiva in Bnei Brak, where he was routinely called 'Reb Lazer the *Meshugeneh*.' People would mock him and laugh at his funny practices and strange ways – and Reb Lazer heartily encouraged them to continue. It was only a few years' later, when Rabbi Haas got interested in Breslov *chassidus* that he discovered that 'Reb Lazer the Meshugeneh' was actually a Rosh Yeshiva in his own right, and a highly accomplished scholar.

"That's when I realized that Rabbi Berland had fooled a whole city for decades," says Rabbi Haas. "It was really a miraculous thing, because he was already a Rosh Yeshiva and also the Steipler's regular learning partner. Yet despite all that, people in Bnei Brak believed he was crazy.

"I started to understand that as well as being part of his spiritual work to deliberately seek out humiliation, it had also been a strategy to get people to leave him alone so they wouldn't argue with him about the new path he'd chosen. Now, when I think about it, it's truly a wondrous thing: How could someone run his own yeshiva, learn with the Steipler, and still get people to believe he was crazy? The Rav is simply a genius at hiding his greatness from other people."

When members of the community used to approach Rabbi Bender with negative comments about his young protégé, he told them, "What can I tell you? What I see in Reb Lazer, I don't see in any other person." But not everyone was willing, or able, to see through the disguise.

★　★　★

After a couple of years of learning the ropes of Breslov *chassidus*, one of his mentors, Rav Lippel, took him to one side, and told him that he couldn't teach him any more Breslov Torah until he'd made the trip to Uman. Back then, in the late sixties and early seventies, the USSR was totally barred to citizens of Israel. The Soviet Union had broken off diplomatic ties with Israel after the Six Day War in 1967, and they weren't minded to do any favors for religious Jews.

While most people faced with the challenge of getting to Uman would have given up before they ever really began, Rabbi Berland was not most people. In 1972, he traveled to America and stayed there for six months, hoping to get the Green Card that would unlock the gates of Uman, as American citizens could still get permission from the Soviets to visit.

But successfully getting into the former USSR was only the first obstacle. While the Soviets permitted foreign tourists to visit the cities of Odessa and Kiev[i], Uman itself was totally off-limits, because it was home to a Soviet army base. Any foreigner caught visiting illegally would be interrogated, imprisoned — and perhaps even killed.

It was the height of the cold war, and no-one was taking these threats lightly. The first few attempts Rabbi Berland made to get to Uman ended in failure, when he was caught by Communist officials and prevented from even crossing the border into the Ukraine. But he didn't give up, and kept trying different routes until nine attempts — and many tens of thousands of dollars later — he finally made it in. The gates to Uman were open.

By the early 1970s, Rabbi Berland was making the hazardous trip to Uman every two weeks, each time taking a different route and using a different counterfeit passport, and bringing tens of new visitors with him. On each trip, Rabbi Berland would give all his fellow travelers careful instructions on what to say and do at the border, and also how to deal with the Communist officials and give them the runaround so they wouldn't make any further trouble or succeed in their repeated attempts to arrest the 'illegal tourists'.

Back in the alleyways of Meah Shearim, not everyone was happy about these trips to Uman. At various points in the 1970s, dissenting voices were heard within the Breslov community that Rabbi Berland was taking unnecessary risks, endangering people's lives with his clandestine visits to Uman, and charging way too much money for the trips.

While the trip was certainly dangerous and expensive – not least because securing counterfeit documents didn't come

---

[i] Both these cities are a couple of hundred miles away from Uman, but the closest big cities in the vicinity.

cheap, and it was impossible to take a direct route into Uman – the careful observer could also detect a hint of festering jealousy from some of the old-school Breslov *chassidim*, who'd been pipped to the post on getting to Uman.

True, Reb Lazer was taking risks to get to Uman, but there really was no other way of doing it, and it was widely known that he would fast the whole day of the trip, until his group had successfully crossed the border into the Ukraine. The dangers involved were very real, no-one denied that. But what was the alternative?

On one occasion, Rabbi Levi Yitzchak saw Rabbi Berland in the street, and started screaming at him that he was endangering people's lives. Before World War II, Rabbi Bender himself had famously risked his life to attend the last Rosh Hashanah gathering in Uman in 1938, where he'd only narrowly escaped being caught and executed by the murderous Soviet authorities. That was the last time he'd been in Uman, and he was keenly aware of the risks involved.[i]

Rabbi Berland wasn't fazed by the accusation. He asked Rabbi Bender: "And what about when you went to Uman, to the grave, [in 1938] and the [Soviet] informer was running after you? How did you get there? Wasn't that endangering people's lives?' Rabbi Levi Yitzchak started laughing and accepted the answer. As Rabbi Bender himself used to say, the only thing more frightening than the idea of going to Uman is the idea of staying away.

So the clandestine trips continued for the best part of two decades, before they finally became legal for Israeli citizens in 1989, when the former Soviet Union imploded, and the Iron Curtain disintegrated.

In 1977, on the way home from one of these trips, where

---

[i] See *Words of Faith*, Volume II, #53, The Last Rosh Hashana in Uman.

he'd been caught, interrogated, and finally released by the KGB, Rabbi Berland finally decided the time had come to open his own yeshiva, for all the hundreds of people he was steadily attracting to the Breslov way of life.

This yeshiva would put the focus on in-depth Torah learning; lengthy, heartfelt prayers, including hours spent talking to God in the fields around Bnei Brak, and getting up for the midnight lamentation every single night; visits to holy grave sites; personal holiness – and accepting criticism and humiliation with love.

And when it came to that last piece of 'spiritual devotion', it would quickly become clear that no-other yeshiva in the world would be able to hold a candle to Reb Lazer, now Rabbi Eliezer Berland, and his 'Shuvu Banim' yeshiva.

In the meantime, young Jews were starting to throng to Rabbi Berland in their hundreds and even their thousands, as he criss-crossed the country giving Torah lessons anywhere he believed he could find these secular 'lost' Jews. Way before the concept of ' religious outreach' became popular and acceptable, Rabbi Berland was spending his days and nights in anti-religious kibbutzim and bars in Tel Aviv, where he'd close his eyes, and just start talking Torah.

He often went door to door for days at a time in the big cities, with no sleep, trying to talk to the people society had rejected, and to find the traumatized, searching people who had a big, black hole which only God could fill. Many of the people who were attracted to Rabbi Berland at this stage were hippies, who were searching for an alternative to non-stop materialism and the emphasis on making money.

The Berlands' neighbor from Bnei Brak, Abish Dichter recalls that the Berland residence became like a second home for many of these hippies. "He used to travel down to Eilat, and he'd even meet the hippies on the bus and bring them back to Bnei Brak," he recalls. "And that's how he started Shuvu Banim."

Of course, many of the neighbors were less than impressed about what was going on, which is when Rabbi Berland collected another nickname, this time as the "Rebbe of Wayward People". 'Pious' people were gossiping about what was happening at the Berland home, and the shame and the 'filth' all these irreligious hippies were bringing into the holy environment of Bnei Brak.

Some residents on the increasingly prestigious Rashbam Street were so upset about all the "outreach" going on at the Berland home, they decided to take matters into their hands. Some of the neighbors started a petition to have the Berland family kicked out of Bnei Brak. The petition was taken around to the important people in the neighborhood – some of whom even signed it – but when it reached the door of the Steipler Gaon, he gave the organizers a scathing look, and killed their petition stone dead.

In Yiddish, he told them 'Reb Lazer *az ir agroiser, groiser yarai Shamayim!*' (Reb Lazer is a tremendous God fearing Jew) and refused to listen to another word. So the neighbors had to back down, but some of them weren't done with trying to get Rabbi Berland out of their neighborhood just yet. They'd just have to be more *creative.*

★ ★ ★

Just as Rabbi Berland was coming up to the grave of Shmuel HaNavi, in the Jerusalem suburb of Ramot, the two thugs struck. Some of Rabbi Berland's neighbors had received permission from a 'rabbi' in Bnei Brak to hire people to beat up the Rav and teach him a lesson, and they wasted no time in following the ruling they'd been given.

When Rabbi Berland went out to the field that night

and began to walk into the forest near Shmuel HaNavi, two ruffians jumped out of the bushes where they'd been hiding in wait for him, and started to beat him up. The Rav had some students with him, but everyone was too shocked to react. As the beating continued, one of the thugs prepared to deliver the message from the man who'd sent them.

Before he could say the name, Rabbi Berland got back onto his feet, and held out two 100 shekels[i] notes to his assailants. "Thank you, thank you," he told them. "If you do it again, I'll pay you another 100 shekels each!"

The two thugs were so bewildered and embarrassed by this bizarre turn of events, they ran off. Later, they showed up on Rabbi Nachman Horowitz's doorstep, and told him that they'd been paid 20 shekels each by a neighbor, to beat up Rabbi Berland. The Rav's response made such an impression on them, one of them subsequently joined Shuvu Banim.

Another time, the people who owned the local *mikveh* (a special pool of water that religious Jews immerse in to cleanse themselves spiritually) in Bnei Brak decided to super-heat the water, to stop Rabbi Berland bringing all his hippies, drop-outs and irreligious hangers-on from using it. When the Rav and his followers showed up at the *mikveh* at 3am, after a long night of praying in the fields and reciting the midnight lamentations, they found the water was at boiling point. No-one could use it. No-one, that is, except Rabbi Berland, who simply carried on as usual and immersed in the water.

One of the people who witnessed this firsthand said: "There's no way of explaining what happened according to the laws of nature. I still have no idea how the Rav did that." But finding a yeshiva that would accept his new followers

---

[i] 100 shekels was obviously worth way more then, than now.

was proving resistant to even Rabbi Berland's very powerful brand of magic.

In a fundraising letter that Rabbi Berland wrote to a potential donor in July 1976, he explained:

"We have tens and tens of people who are returning to the Jewish faith coming to us, and we have nowhere to place them. And they want to come and learn with us, and to be drawn closer [to God] by us, but many of them are being lost, because there is no yeshiva that is suitable for them.

"We tried to get them into other yeshivas, but they weren't always received so nicely, and experienced whatever they experienced. Last year, I had one person with me in my home for two whole months, eating and drinking by me. Afterwards, he enrolled in a yeshiva where he was treated so badly, that he ran away and completely disappeared from the scene. We've been looking for him for a few months, and we still have no idea where he is.

"Tens and tens of people, and in truth it's already close to 200 people, if not more [are coming to us], and if we had a suitable institution, with God's help we could save hundreds and even thousands of people... as every Jewish returnee immediately attracts another, and another."

The Shuvu Banim yeshiva officially opened its doors in the summer of 1978, in Bnei Brak, and from the very beginning, it charted a unique course. Even newly-observant students were obliged to wake up for the midnight prayers, and there was a strong emphasis placed on praying with feeling, and serving God sincerely, and with self-sacrifice. Torah learning was also strongly stressed, as Rabbi Berland emphasized over and over again that Breslov teachings could only really grow in the soil of long hours spent toiling over a Tractate of the *Gemara* (the codified Oral Torah).

Not everyone was convinced. When they heard that Rabbi Berland was refusing to run his yeshiva the way 'everyone else' was, he quickly lost the support of his main backers. Unperturbed, Rabbi Berland explained: "We want to found a yeshiva that follows Rebbe Nachman's path, and Rebbe Nachman's path is talking to God in your own words and getting up for the midnight prayers. Whoever can't do it doesn't need to stay here. There are lots of other yeshivas in Bnei Brak."

And many of those first students who enrolled and stayed on have become some of the leading lights of the Breslov community today. Rabbi Michael Lasry, Rabbi Shalom Arush, Rabbi Moshe Tzanani, Rabbi Michael Goll, Rabbi Ofer Erez, Rabbi Shmuel Stern, Rabbi Meir Malka, Rabbi Eliyahu Meirav and Rabbi Eliyahu Succot, to name but a few, are all household names today, in Israel and often beyond.

As the yeshiva continued to grow, Rabbi Berland sent groups of his students out on more 'outreach' missions across Israel, and many more people, numbering into the thousands, returned to the fold of observant Judaism as a result, including top soldiers in the IDF, fighter pilots, and many other highly-talented individuals.

At this point, even the secular establishment started to hear about this "dangerously charismatic" rabbi who could persuade promising officers in the IDF to turn their backs on the base and leave, after just a short conversation. The secular media started to come up with all sorts of strange theories and bizarre ideas about how Rabbi Berland was exerting so much influence over otherwise 'normal' people – and as the years passed, their negative feelings and antagonism towards Rabbi Berland only deepened.

★ ★ ★

By 1982, things were getting a little out of hand. Shuvu Banim had exploded in popularity, and so a new branch of the yeshiva had opened in Jerusalem, while the yeshiva also continued to operate in Bnei Brak. Also, Rabbi Berland was still spending large amounts of time learning at the knee of the Breslov elders in Meah Shearim, and bringing his students with him.

On Thursday nights, seven taxis would leave from Bnei Brak to Jerusalem, filled with students from Shuvu Banim who were coming with the Rav to attend Rabbi Levi Isaac Bender's Torah class, which was reinvigorated by this influx of newcomers. At first, Rabbi Bender continued to speak in Yiddish, but agreed to have a Hebrew translator for the Shuvu Banim students.

Then, as the number of Yiddish speakers attending started to be dwarfed by the Hebrew-speaking returnees to religious observance being brought in by Rabbi Berland, Rabbi Bender announced that he was henceforth switching to Hebrew – and not everyone in Meah Shearim was happy about that. Some of the old-school Breslov community were so *unhappy* about that, that they decided to lock Rabbi Bender out of his own Breslov synagogue, known as 'The Shul' in Meah Shearim, to prevent him from giving the class.

When Rabbi Levi Yitzchak saw this, he told the Shuvu Banim students who were stuck outside on the pavement, "Why are you just standing there?! Bring some crowbars and break down the door!" That was the first of many subsequent occasions when the religious extremists based in the Breslov Shul tried to prevent Rabbi Berland and his students from entering. But all that was still in the future, and for now, Rabbi Berland was far more preoccupied with the question of what to do with his yeshiva.

Despite the Rav's great willingness to sacrifice himself for his students, the fact of the matter was that with the yeshiva in two separate locations, he had no time to sleep, no time to eat, and was constantly traveling back and forth between Bnei Brak and Jerusalem. It was obvious to everyone that things couldn't continue like that for much longer, so the Berlands started to look for a suitable building in Jerusalem where the whole yeshiva could be reunited.

By the Passover holiday in 1982, they still hadn't found anything suitable, but then, shortly after the holiday, the sea parted for Shuvu Banim. One of the yeshiva students called Rabbi Dachbash, was down by the Western Wall that morning, in the Old City of Jerusalem, when he heard a man crying his eyes out nearby. Rabbi Dachbash went over to him to see if he could comfort him, and discovered that the man, a rich Syrian industrialist by the name of Abraham Dwek, had been double-crossed by the State of Israel.

Dwek had donated money to purchase a half-ruined building called the *Chaye Olam* courtyard, on *Maale Haladia* Street in the Muslim Quarter of the Old City of Jerusalem. He'd been promised by the quasi-governmental *Atara L'Yoshna* organization that if he put up the funds, they would turn the building into a synagogue, to honor the memory of Reb Dwek's grandfather, Rabbi Shaul Dwek HaKohen. But Dwek had just discovered that they were planning to turn the place into residential apartments instead, and he was heart-broken.

Rabbi Dachbash asked Dwek if there was anything he could do to help, Dwek answered: "If you could bring me a *kollel* of at least 25 or 30 students, we could house them there today and establish our rights to the building. That's the only way of saving the situation." Shuvu Banim had found its new home.

But the State of Israel, and particularly Teddy Kollek, the then mayor of Jerusalem, were very unimpressed with this turn of events, and sent in the army to boot out the yeshiva. But they met their match in Shuvu Banim, many of whom had been elite soldiers in the IDF. After months of threats and scuffles – and even a failed petition that Kollek made direct to then Prime Minster Yitzhak Shamir, to use his executive power to force Shuvu Banim to leave their premises in the Muslim Quarter - eventually, even Teddy Kollek had to admit defeat. Shuvu Banim were in the Old City to stay – and the people in the defense establishment started to sit up, and take notice.

Rabbi Berland was also creating some powerful enemies in the secular world by continuing his emphasis on Jewish outreach, which is what he saw as the main role of his Shuvu Banim yeshiva. Shuvu Banim had been created for outreach, and to help more people discover the path of Rebbe Nachman, and Breslov *chassidus* – and it was proving highly successful.

So much so, that Israel's newspapers in the 1980s were filled with headlines and stories about secular parents complaining their child had been 'brain-washed' by all these Jewish religious 'cults', with Shuvu Banim frequently being cited as one of the most popular destination for disaffected secular young Jews.

But despite the exponential growth in the number of people joining his community, Rabbi Berland continued to stress that he didn't want a yeshiva where people would start think they were better than others, just because they had long beards and side curls. He said:

"I would prefer to sit here with just five students who have simplicity and innocence, because with those five students, I could get a lot more done in the world than if I had the 24,000 students of Rabbi Akiva, who were obsessed with their own honor and status, and thought they were better than other people."

Who would have thought that Shuvu Banim could ever get close to numbering 24,000 students? But within a decade, Rabbi Berland found himself the head of an organization that comprised a number of Talmud Torahs, kindergartens, nurseries, boys' schools, girls' schools, yeshivas and women's seminaries in Jerusalem and many other locations around the country. And his enemies within the Breslov community of Meah Shearim couldn't stand it.

★   ★   ★

Shuvu Banim's arrival in Jerusalem announced the beginning of a worldwide Breslov revival that had slowly been gathering steam for years. The move to Jerusalem's Old Quarter brought many of the Rav's students in much closer contact with the existing Breslov community of Meah Shearim, and this clash of cultures lead to a lot of resentment and hard feelings on both sides.

On the one hand, there was Rabbi Berland's formerly secular, often Sephardi, Hebrew-speaking "new" Breslovers, some of whom were still sporting long, hippy hair, who sincerely tried to fulfill every word that Rebbe Nachman spoke, to the best of their abilities. These guys were making maximum effort to spend Rosh Hashanah in Uman; they were getting up to pray at midnight, going out to the fields to talk to God every night, going to the *mikveh* every day, learning Torah, praying with feeling and guarding their eyes.

But to the Yiddish-speaking group of Breslov extremists centered on the Breslov Shul in Meah Shearim, these newly-observant Jews were anathema. Whenever students from Shuvu Banim would try to pray in the Breslov Shul, these extremists would yell at them, insult them, and even physically bar them from entering. More than one of the Rav's newly-religious students left the Breslov shul in tears, stunned at the hostile reception they'd been given by these Breslov zealots.

The obvious aggression at the Shul was paired with a growing campaign of slander and gossip in the back streets of Meah Shearim. The extremists would go to Rabbi Levi Yitzchak's house and come to him in shul, to try to turn him against Rabbi Berland and his followers. Their non-stop slander once prompted Rabbi Levi Isaac to say: "What do they want? I get to shul before dawn and who do I find there? Rav Lazer's people. Who goes to the field [to talk to God]? Rav Lazer's men. Who do I meet in the *mikveh* before dawn? Rav Lazer's men. What do they want?'"

It looks like the extremists wanted Breslov *chassidus* to stay small and effectively "dead" forever. What they definitely didn't want was for Rabbi Berland to bring in a flood of outsiders whom they viewed as trying to take over "their" synagogue and "their" customs. And they were particularly possessive over Uman.

Over Succot in 1989, the year the Soviet Union finally crumbled, Rabbi Michel Dorfman, a leading Breslov figure and Soviet *refusenik,* who'd spent many years behind the Iron Curtain, publicly praised Rabbi Berland for blasting open the gates to Uman for everyone. It seems that was the last straw.

For years, Rabbi Berland's enemies in Meah Shearim had been muttering about the "outsider" and the "usurper" who was taking over Breslov and filling it with hippies and Sephardim. As long as Rabbi Berland continued to have the backing of the Breslov elders, there was nothing they could really do against him openly. But when Rabbi Bender, the last of the three Breslov elders who'd been shielding the Rav from his opponents, died, the hatred against the Rav and Shuvu Banim erupted into the open.

People started complaining that Rabbi Berland had taken too much money for the clandestine trips to Uman. Then they started arguing against the Breslov idea that there is a "true tzaddik" in every generation, who had been given the unique ability of passing Rebbe Nachman of Breslov's teachings on to the next generation. Either, they said that Rebbe Nachman was the only "tzaddik" required, or they took umbrage at the suggestion that Rabbi Berland could be the "true tzaddik" of our generation – even though he seemed to have all the necessary credentials.

Who else had hundreds of people beating a path to their door to ask for a blessing? Who else had inspired tens of thousands of people to come back to God and observant Judaism, and to travel to Uman? Who else was trying to follow Rebbe Nachman's path as sincerely and whole-heartedly, as Rabbi Berland?

After Rabbi Shmuel Horowitz and Rabbi Velvel Cheshin passed away, Rabbi Bender had become increasingly concerned about what the Breslov zealots would try to do to harm Rabbi Berland and his community after his own passing. A month before he passed away from cancer on July 25, 1989, Rabbi Bender made a final attempt to pull the community back together, and to stop all the in-fighting being stoked by the extremists.

Rav Bender said then: *"When I begin to speak about the topic of love, people don't understand what I'm referring to, they have no idea what I'm talking about, but we need to know that this is what's lacking, this is what's lacking by us!!! ... Even if I don't agree with the other person I still need to love him!*

"We have to be very careful not to lose or even lessen the love between all the Breslov Chassidim. When I'm talking about how we need to hold ourselves together in unity, people have no idea what I'm talking about! It seems to them that I'm talking in a different language...!

"Rebbe Nachman said: 'I judge everyone to the side of mercy, apart from people who instigate strife and communal discord.'... [T]here is always a punishment for the sin of speaking evil words about others. Whether the punishment

will occur immediately or be delayed — this is a decision made Above, but certainly a punishment will come!

"God has mercy on us. We have Rebbe Nachman, a merciful Rebbe, a true merciful leader! Rabbeinu judges everyone favorably. Nevertheless, WATCH YOURSELVES! Watch yourselves with this one point, because about this he is not silent. You will get punished for this [slandering other people] no matter how great you are!

"We have no idea about the secrets of the arguments between the tzaddikim, therefore, DON'T GET INVOLVED! It seems like they are arguing, but in reality, they are working together in a way that's deeper than we can imagine... All of a sudden, a third person gets involved and gives his opinion — 'this one is good, that one is bad...' He's messing up the whole thing!"

Rabbi Bender was giving a stark warning that whoever came after him, Breslov *Chassidus* should pull together and unite behind him. But the Breslov zealots were too far gone in their hatred and jealousy to heed him.

Following Rabbi Bender's passing, the zealots' antagonism against Rabbi Berland only intensified. Rabbi Berland had maintained the custom of praying the Breslov Shul in Meah Shearim on Friday nights, and also on Yom Kippur, even after Shuvu Banim moved to the Old City. That year, on the first night of the *selichos* service, the Breslov shul was packed to the rafters.

As soon as Rabbi Berland entered, the zealots started yelling at him and cursing him. Some people even stood on tables to throw things at him and there was a tremendous commotion as they screamed themselves hoarse, yelling at the Rabbi to leave. Yosef Assulin was with him at the time, and he recalls:

"Throughout the whole ordeal, Rabbi Berland just stood completely still, with a serene, pleased look on his face. After the storm died down, Rabbi Berland left to meet his wife outside the shul, and he was still wearing a look of amazed delight, as if he'd just experienced the best thing in the world. The Rebbetzin asked him: 'How was it?' And the Rav replied: "It was great! I prayed for this for so long. But one thing bothered me, I was hoping it would go on for 2 hrs, why only 20 minutes?!"

As the poisonous storm in Meah Shearim Breslov's community continued to rage, Rabbi Yehuda Zerachia HaLevi Segal, a leading Jerusalem kabbalist of the previous generation, decided to intercede, to try to end the poisonous complaints. On November 11, 1991, he wrote a letter to Rabbi Jacob Meir Shecter, the official head of the community in the Breslov shul, where he emphasized how important it was to have peaceful relations within the Breslov community.

Rabbi Segal wrote: "*The very high level of piousness and commitment to God's work of the Torah genius and tzaddik Rav Eliezer Berland, shlit"a, is well known to me. It's forbidden to harm an angel of God... and Rabbeinu HaKadosh (Rebbe Nachman) is extremely upset about recent events... The honor of Rabbeinu HaKadosh forces me to intercede and protest about what is going on.*"

Thanks to the pressure they came under from Rabbi Segal and a number of other Rabbis and spiritual leaders to end their attacks against Rabbi Berland and his followers, the Breslov extremists in Meah Shearim ultimately had no choice but to stop their open persecution of Shuvu Banim.

But these people's hatred of Rabbi Berland and his students never really disappeared, it just quietly festered underground, watching and waiting for the next opportunity to burst out into the open. Over the next few years, one of their ranks would quietly infiltrate himself into Shuvu Banim, and attempt to destroy the community from within. And he very nearly succeeded.

A HOLOCAUST EVERY 70 YEARS

"TEHRAN — Iran's conservative new president, Mahmoud Ahmadinejad, said Wednesday that Israel must be "wiped off the map""
— New York Times, October 27, 2005[i]

"Iran is continuing to advance as a military nuclear capability, and it has a radical regime. The combination of the two and a high desire to achieve nuclear capability…is an existential threat against the state of Israel,"
- Former Israeli Defense Minister Shaul Mofaz, speaking in 2009.

"The Iranians actually wrote on one of the missiles: "Israel must be removed from the earth." These are missiles that are designed to carry - and deliver - nuclear warheads. I call on the Security Council to take action."
– Israel's UN Ambassador Danny Danon, speaking to the Security Council on March 14, 2016.

★   ★   ★

---

[i] Wipe Israel 'off the map' Iranian says - https://www.nytimes.com/2005/10/27/world/africa/wipe-israel-off-the-map-iranian-says.html

In 1981, Rabbi Berland told his daughter that there was a Heavenly decree that there should be a holocaust against the Jewish people every 70 years, but, that it was possible to sweeten this decree via accepting insults and humiliation. Rabbi Berland said that if there had been a tzaddik at the time of the Holocaust who would have been prepared to accept terrible shame and humiliation upon himself, the Holocaust wouldn't have occurred.

★ ★ ★

In 2012, sixty-seven years after the Holocaust, the Bushehr Nuclear Power Plant had reached its full capacity, and the Iranians were very close to obtaining a full-fledged nuclear arsenal – and everyone knew where those war heads would be aimed.

The Jewish year 5772 (corresponding to 2011-2012) had long been touted as a very likely date for the redemption of the Jewish people to begin. The late Rabbi Yitzchak Kaduri had publicly stated on a number of occasions that *Moshiach* (the Jewish messiah) would come during the month of *Av* (August) 5772.[i]

Rabbi Yitzchak Shlomo Zilberman also publicized the tradition he'd received from a Lithuanian Rabbi named Elijah ben Solomon Zalman (also called the Vilna Gaon, 1720-1797), who had hinted that 5772 was the year of the 'End of Days', as had other descendants of the Vilna Gaon's students.

Meanwhile, Rabbi Yosef Scheinberger publicized the story he'd heard directly from Rabbi Grosnas, the student of another very famous holy man called Rabbi Israel Meir HaCohen Kagan. Rabbi Kagan, known as the 'Chofetz

---

[i] Rav Kaduri stated this directly to Rav Yehuda Moalem and Rav Yosef Chai Zakkai.

Chaim' (1838-1933) had said in 1932 that it wouldn't take more than another 80 years for *Moshiach* to come—again, bringing us to the Jewish year 5772, or 2011-12.

Then there were all the sources from the *Zohar* and other holy works, and all the *gematrias* and all the anecdotal traditions which all seemed to be pointing to the year 5772, as the year of redemption. As more and more of this information came to light, the religious public waited with bated breath to see *what will be* in 5772.

Back in the 1980s and 1990s, the saying "We want Moshiach NOW!" became very popular in certain sections of the Jewish community, and there were many who believed that the Jewish people had already begun the redemption process, and that all that was left was to wait to greet *Moshiach.*

A senior student of the Rav, Rabbi Shlomo Gefen, recalls that when Rabbi Berland first heard this, he commented, "It's not so simple to say that we've already begun the redemption process. Blood is still going to be smeared on the walls of our cities, and the Jewish nation still needs to undergo the selection and clarification process associated with the nuclear bomb."

★　★　★

Before *Moshiach* could come and redeem the nation, the world would first have to undergo the difficult test known as the "birth pangs of *Moshiach*," including the War of Gog and Magog. These were known to be such difficult tests that some of the Jewish Sages who had redacted the Gemara had said, "Let the *Moshiach* come, but let me not be there to see him!"[i]

---

[i] Other sages said: "Let me see him, even if I sit in the dung of his donkey."

If the Jewish people would merit it, the *Moshiach* would come the sweet way. If they didn't merit it, *Moshiach* would come with enormous wars, suffering, and loss of life. As 5772 approached, the papers were full of headlines screaming about Iran's imminent nuclear bomb, and many of the nation's leading kabbalists and Rabbis began to issue detailed warnings about the terrible events they could foresee in the near future.

At this crucial juncture, three of the Jewish nation's holiest men got together to try to avert the coming disaster, by sweetening the awful judgments at their spiritual root. It's taught that there are three things that can sweeten even the harshest judgments, namely: death, shame, and exile.

Rebbe Nachman of Breslov writes that the embarrassment of losing one's good name and reputation is akin to dying. It's taught elsewhere that when a person has no home of his own and is forced to wander from place to place, on some level that's also considered akin to dying.[i]

THE TZADDIK SACRIFICES HIS SOUL TO SAVE THE JEWISH PEOPLE

In Lesson I:260 of *Likutei Moharan*, Rebbe Nachman describes how the one *Tzaddik* who takes upon himself exile, shame, and suffering will save the whole generation from suffering terrible things. And by doing so, this holy man will enable the redemption to come with mercy, and without wars. He writes:

Sometimes a vast number of Jews need to be killed, God forbid, in order to facilitate a certain spiritual unification.

A person can be famous but not really be famous—that is, everyone knows about him and speaks about him, but he is not

---

[i] Lesson I: 260 of Likutei Moharan.

really famous, since he is not respected at all. Or, there is the person who against his wish loses his fame, which is a loss of the name, which is the soul…

But there is one person who does this intentionally and consciously, surrendering his soul for the sanctification of God's Name. He surrenders his fame—his 'name,' corresponding to the soul—and on account of this, although he is renowned, he is not famous at all.

On the contrary, everyone talks against him, conjuring stories about him that he would never have dreamed of doing. He experiences this as if he was literally being killed. He does this all intentionally, because it is a literal self-sacrifice of [his] soul… and he experiences it as death.

But in this way, he saves the Jewish people from what would have happened to them in order to facilitate this unification, as said, and by thus sacrificing his name, which is his soul, he spares them.

★   ★   ★

On the evening of July 28, 2011, Rabbi Elazar Abuchatzeira (also known as the Baba Elazar) was stabbed to death in the waiting room of his *yeshiva* in Beer Sheva. His killer was an outwardly observant ultra-orthodox man from the city of Elad who had come to speak with the Baba Elazar many times before. Eyewitnesses said that the Baba Elazar seemed to have known in advance what was about to happen and rushed over happily to meet his attacker, who then drew a knife and repeatedly stabbed him.

The Baba Elazar was rushed by ambulance to the Soroka Medical Center in Beer Sheva, but was pronounced dead on arrival. The murder of this holy man shocked the nation to its core, and many thousands of people attended his funeral the following day, when he was buried on the Mount of Olives in Jerusalem.

Shortly before this, in December 2010, Rabbi Eliezer Berland's exile from Jerusalem and the Shuvu Banim *Yeshiva* began. From Jerusalem, the Rav went up to the Galilee for a period of time before returning to live in the ultra-orthodox city of Beitar Illit, located to the south of Jerusalem.

The next part of the deal—being publicly shamed, insulted, humiliated, and losing his good name—only began two years' later. But the most important thing to remember is that *Rabbi Berland wanted to be shamed and exiled, in order to atone for the Jewish people and to bring their redemption the sweet way.*

Even many years ago, he knew that he would be shamed and exiled, and spent a lifetime preparing himself—and his *yeshiva*—to pass the test.

ACCEPTING AN INSULT LOVINGLY PROTECTS A THOUSAND JEWS

The following excerpt comes from a Torah class Rabbi Berland gave more than 20 years ago:

"It says in *Likutei Moharan* that when a person accepts an insult lovingly, he saves tens of thousands of Jews from getting killed... When a person lovingly accepts insults upon himself, he can save the entire Jewish people....

"Those people who chase after insults, who are looking for people to insult them and disgrace them at every moment, and who are trying to give others a reason to disgrace them and insult them, these people are saving the whole nation of Israel! Not just hundreds and not just thousands, they are saving *all the Jewish people!*

"A regular person is afraid of getting insulted, because

he doesn't know that through every single insult he merits rising up ten levels.

"The students want an explanation! They ask, "Why are you bringing all this controversy down on yourself!? It's hard for us!" So [the Rebbe] says, 'It's your life insurance! It would be harder for you to be blown up in a terrorist attack or end up missing an eye, or who knows else could happen to you."

THE NEW START

"There are those who are convinced that the entire aim of Haredi society is to bring about the collapse of the Zionist State of Israel."
- Professor Menachem Friedman, Professor of the Sociology of Religion at Bar-Ilan University, writing in Ha'aretz on September 17th, 2001[i]

"Stop sweeping their streets, cut off their electricity and water, let's give up on their taxes (which they usually don't pay). They are useless; they don't produce anything, don't contribute anything, they don't plant a tree or a tomato, don't manufacture high-tech. They are parasites of the worse kind, and as far as I am concerned – if it was realistic – I would pack [the haredim] up in one package and send them to their primitive brothers in the dark courtyards of Brooklyn, Queens and all the other places they should live in; let Americans handle them."
– Non-Stop Radio Host Gabi Gazit, speaking on air, May 7, 2010

★ ★ ★

B etween 2000 – 2010, a number of problematic individuals rose to positions of authority within the Shuvu Banim community, and started throwing

---

[i] https://www.haaretz.com/life/books/1.5397433

their weight around. Some of these individuals demanded large sums of money from anyone who wanted to speak to Rabbi Berland or ask for a blessing. Others started to play "power games" within Shuvu Banim, demoting and promoting students on a whim, drawing up lists of those people who would be allowed access to the Rav privately, deciding who could attend the Rav's weekly Torah classes and even, deciding who would be allowed to pray with the Rav on Shabbos, the Jewish Sabbath.

Anyone who was "caught" recording or photographing Rabbi Berland's classes would be blacklisted, as would anyone who tried to talk to the Rav or get a blessing without paying a large sum of money to the people who'd effectively seized control of the *yeshiva*.

The Rav and his family were greatly pained by these developments, and in private, they begged the people responsible to stop. But in public, Rabbi Berland kept silent.

So, he became a virtual recluse in his home for more than ten years. He stopped praying with the Shuvu Banim community in the Old City. He barely gave classes or attended public events. This continued until December 2010, when, with the help of two students and one grandchild, Rabbi Eliezer Berland finally managed to escape.

At that time, Rabbi Berland recorded a message for his followers where he told them:

"After I ended up being admitted to the hospital three times in just four weeks... after I saw that this is now a situation of saving a life, and that I was on the cusp of a complete physical breakdown, I decided to leave [Jerusalem]...

"It pains me to leave my family and especially my beloved wife, beloved children and my beloved grandchildren. But [understand] I left because I care for them; I care for my son

that he should have a father, and for my grandson that he should have a grandfather.

"When I used to leave my wife for long periods of talking to God, I would say to her that I left in order to bring you back a husband who is a Rosh Yeshiva, so now I left in order to bring you a Rosh Yeshiva who is alive, not a Rosh Yeshiva who is in the hospital every two weeks, and who every three or four days has a heart attack (God forbid).

"I don't want them to eulogize me in the newspaper, saying what a holy person I was, so I decided to lengthen my days...

"Now I'm in the North talking to God and going to the graves of our holy tzaddikim. I wish you could all be here with me. I learned more Torah on one Shabbos [up North] than I learned in almost all the last ten years...

"*If I can't return to Jerusalem, where the threats against me are very serious and terrible, I can't go into details about them here, but the threats being made against me are increasing each moment. The situation in Jerusalem is only getting worse with each passing moment, so there may be no choice except to reopen the yeshiva in the Galilee.*

"If the terror continues, so we'll build a yeshiva here so we can all be together, and serve God, a yeshiva that will accept all different kinds of people, an elementary school for all different kind of boys, and girls school for all different kind of girls so that there will no longer be a possibility that a boy or girl is asked to leave or not accepted because they don't fit a certain criteria.

"There will be a place in Shuvu Banim for everyone, for every type, so we can once again raise up the glory of Torah. That's the goal of Shuvu Banim, my goal all my life, to raise up and glorify the Torah...

"I want to make a new start now. The Rebbe [Rebbe Nachman] wrote in Lesson 64 that every controversy leads *to a new creation of the world... Everything that has been done until now, it's for the best... The Rebbe explains that it's forbidden to condemn anyone, or to put anyone down, or to take vengeance against them. Now, we're getting ready to create the world completely anew. Shuvu Banim is going to get a new lease of life...*

THE TROUBLE BREWING
IN BEITAR

"Long-sleeved shirts instead of bikinis? Synagogues instead of nightclubs? Pessimistic researchers say growth rate within haredi community may lead to the end of the State of Israel as we know it. "If trend continues we will no longer be part of the Western World," one of them warned."

– Secular Public's Demographic Nightmare,
Ynet Magazine, published October 31ˢᵗ, 2010[i]

"As haredi education rejects a life of work and participation in defending the homeland, and as we cannot imprison tens of thousands of yeshiva students (and those pretending to be such,) and as national service would hold justice in contempt, and as purely haredi regiments are a recipe for an armed civil war, and as the haredi community mushrooms as result of natural growth – the national majority has no choice but to embark on a determined cultural war.

Time is of the essence. Should the majority lose this war, the Zionist enterprise would be remembered as a short-lived historical episode."

– Israeli Journalist Yaron London writing
for Ynet.com, February 28ᵗʰ, 2012[ii]

---

[i] Secular Public's Demographic Nightmare - https://www.ynetnews.com/articles/0,7340,L-3977159,00.html
[ii] *Say no to Jewish Hezbollah* - https://www.ynetnews.com/articles/0,7340,L-4195684,00.html

★ ★ ★

In March 2011, the Rav and his wife, Rebbetzin Tehillah Berland, moved into an apartment on Kedushas Levi Street in the ultra-orthodox town of Beitar Illit, a 20-minute drive south of Jerusalem. After years of being inaccessible to many of his followers and the general public, hundreds of Rabbi Berland's followers joyfully followed him out to Beitar Illit, with many of them even renting apartments close by.

Crowds of people lined up outside his home 24/7, as Rabbi Berland gratefully stepped back into his public role. Difficult as the last 10 years had been, it was hoped that the worst was now behind the Rav and his community. It was time to rebuild. It was time to renew. It was time to look forward to different and better times. Shortly after he'd left Jerusalem to go up to the North of Israel, Rabbi Berland had recorded a message for his students, where he told them:

"I want to make a new start now.... "It could well be that we will have to continue wandering. We learn in the Gemara, Tractate Rosh Hashanah that after they burned down the Jewish Temple the Shechina experienced 10 different exiles... After they burned down the Temple, I started my exile in Jerusalem [by leaving the Old City]. Now, I'm already in my third exile.

"On Shabbos I was in Chanita, and now I am in Amirim, and I intend to continue wandering onward...we are living on wheels now...until we bring to fruition the vision that we had at the creation of Shuvu Banim, and that vision finally moves from potential to actuality, 'For My House will be called a House of Prayer, for all the nations[i]...'

"We're now on the cusp of creating a completely new framework...Just strengthen yourselves, and pray for me, that all the different communities should be reunited, and through

[i] A quote from *Isaiah* 56.

being unified the verse will be fulfilled: '[And it will happen at the End of Days:] The mountain of the House of God will be [firmly established as] the head of the mountains and it will be exalted above the hills, [and all the nations will stream to it].'"[1]

On another occasion, Rabbi Berland returned to the theme of rebuilding the Third Jewish Temple. He said:

"Here in the yeshiva, we've also experienced such tests and difficult situations in recent years. But you should know that we had to go through all of these things, as it's the only way we could acquire for ourselves the spiritual vessels we need for the Third Temple, may it be built speedily in our days."

Around this time, the State of Israel was preparing for another election, and some of Rabbi Berland's students asked him which of the religious parties they should vote for in the ballot. Rabbi Berland replied, "It doesn't really matter who you vote for, either Shas or Agudas Yisrael. In terms of the [proposed law to conscript ultra-orthodox Jews into the Israeli army], it's already been decided in Heaven what's going to happen with that, and the elections aren't going to change anything."

No one really understood what the Rav meant, but after the elections it became crystal clear.

On January 22, 2013, a new government was elected in the State of Israel, which prompted many of our Torah leaders to hint that this was yet another sign that *Am Yisrael* had reached that point in history known as the End of Days, just prior to Moshiach revealing himself.

The new government included the openly 'anti-haredi' Yesh Atid party, but no religious parties, and it quickly went about the business of trying to change the law that had enabled yeshiva students to receive a deferment from the Israel Army. Yesh Atid proposed that a maximum number of 1800 yeshiva students each year should be exempted from serving in the army – while the rest would face financial penalties and even prison sentences, if they failed to enlist.[i]

On March 12, 2014, the Knesset approved a new law that stated that non-exempt yeshiva students either had to enlist in the army or face imprisonment.

This laid the foundation for the next stage of the onslaught against the *hareidi* world in Israel, when the government tried to pull the plug on government funding to yeshivas. Many religious organizations had to close their doors, while others — and the families who relied on them — faced the harshest economic conditions in years.

Against this backdrop, Rabbi Meyer Maimoni asked Rabbi Berland during one of his Torah lessons, "[What does it mean that] Moshiach will only reveal himself in a generation where everyone is either worthy, or everyone is unworthy[ii]?" Rabbi Maimoni pointed out the obvious problem with this statement, namely, that no generation is ever completely "only good" all of the time, or completely "only bad." There will always be some *tzaddikim* even in the most evil generations, and some evildoers even in the most righteous generations.

Rabbi Berland explained that the true meaning of this passage is that before the coming of Moshiach, there will be a period of tremendous clarification and sorting out, where people will be forced to choose whether they want to go down the path of holiness, or the opposite - because they won't be able to sit on the fence anymore.

The Rav continued that it was going to be the same sort of clarification process that had occurred many centuries earlier, when the Prophet Elijah had told the people of Israel: "How long are you going to continue to jump between two

---

[i] https://hamodia.com/2014/01/07/setting-record-straight/
[ii] A famous statement from the *Gemara*, in *Maseches Sanhedrin* 98.

camps?! If the Baal is god, then follow him. And if *God* is God, then follow Him!"

This test — of following wholeheartedly after God and believing wholeheartedly in Him, even when we are beset with doubts and troubles — would be the final test before Moshiach comes. And Rabbi Berland and his followers were about to find themselves smack bang in the middle of it.

★ ★ ★

One of the first things Rabbi Berland did when he moved to Beitar was begin a regular round of visits to the holy graves in the area. Night after night, he'd lead a convoy of cars to Hebron, to pray at the Tomb of the Patriarchs, and sometimes, he'd also stop in at the radically Islamised town of Chalchul, where the Prophets Nathan and Gad were buried underneath the local mosque.

After the failed Oslo Accords, many Jewish holy sites had effectively been given away to the Palestinians, and barred to Jews. Both the secular government and the secular media viewed the holy Jewish graves located in the heart of Palestinian towns and villages as a massive security problem and were only too pleased to prevent Jews from visiting them. But while this view perhaps seemed "logical" from the purely secular standpoint of the Israeli government, from a spiritual and religious viewpoint it was akin to national suicide.

Before, during and also after Oslo, Rabbi Berland and many other religious leaders continued to stress that while the IDF chose not to protect these holy graves, the *Tzaddikim* buried in these places were actually the ones protecting the IDF and the people of Israel in general. If the secular government succeeded in making it impossible for

Jews to legally visit these graves, the implications for Israel's national security would be very grave.

So Rabbi Berland and many others, including Rabbi Shalom Abergel, Rabbi Golan Mor, and Rabbi Mordechai Gross, fought hard to maintain Jewish access to these sites. Rabbi Berland continued to encourage his students to visit these holy sites and to visit them himself at every opportunity, eventually forcing the Israeli government into a partial compromise about allowing Jewish access to these graves.

These visits were roundly condemned in the secular press and also angered many of the leading figures in the army, intelligence agencies and Israeli government, who didn't want this Rabbi and his followers forcing their hand on security matters and dictating policy to *them*. For as long as Rabbi Berland had been out of action, the defense establishment didn't care so much. But now he was back, and he was encouraging hundreds of people to visit the holy graves of *Tzaddikim* like Joseph the son of the Patriarch Jacob in Shechem, and Jacob's wife Rachel on the outskirts of Bethlehem, and the Prophet Natan and many other holy sites that were officially in 'Area A', the area placed under Palestinian control.

On July 31, 2011, shortly after another fatal shooting during an unauthorized visit to Joseph's tomb in Shechem (Nablus), Rabbi Berland was visited by the Head of IDF Central Command, who asked the Rav to stop his students from making any more unauthorized visits to Joseph's tomb and the other Jewish holy tombs in the West Bank. Rabbi Berland agreed on condition that the army chief would start arranging more authorized entries to these sites.

Also in 2011, the IDF Commander of Yehuda and Shomron met with the late Rabbi Yosef Shalom Elyashiv to try to convince him to issue a statement forbidding any more unauthorized visits to Joseph's tomb and other Jewish holy sites. The IDF was clearly very serious about trying to stop the unauthorized visits.

Two years' later, following a rock attack on the Rav and his followers' cars in Chalchul in 2013, the Head of the IDF in Samaria made another visit to Rabbi Berland, to try to persuade him to stop visiting Chalchul.

Rabbi Berland showed the army chief many of the passages in the holy books that describe how all the protection of Israel is only due to the tombs of the *Tzaddikim*. He told him that all the miracles that Israel experienced in the Six-Day War and the Yom Kippur War were in the merit of the holy *Tzaddikim* buried in Israel.

"You are saying it's a danger to go into Chalchul, and I'm saying it's a danger not to go into Chalchul!" the Rav remonstrated. But the army chief was not impressed by Rabbi Berland's words and left.

Shortly after Rabbi Berland's encounter with the IDF chief — and many months still before the first slanders surfaced in the Israeli press — the Rav mentioned in one of his classes that he suspected that there were people in Israel who wanted to create a libel against him so he'd end up dying in jail.

Soon afterwards, Rabbi Berland left the country.

★   ★   ★

On June 28, 2012 Rabbi Berland appeared at a huge rally

that was held at Tel Aviv's Winter Stadium. A sell-out crowd of eight thousand people showed up at the venue, with many more thousands of people tuning in from their homes. Back then, the disastrous civil war in Syria that would go on to claim more than 560,000 lives, and destroy two million homes was only just beginning.

As well as speaking about peace and *teshuva* the whole night, the Rav also demanded that the world should intervene to stop the bloodshed happening in Syria, where women and children were being slaughtered daily. But Rabbi Berland's plea to end the violence in the Middle East was a message that did not go down so well with the defense establishment.

EXCERPT OF RABBI BERLAND'S SPEECH AT THE WINTER STADIUM, JUNE 28, 2012

"The Talmud teaches us that we need to do acts of kindness to Arabs; it does not matter what kind of Arab! Other than a terrorist, we need to help and assist every single Arab in every way possible; with money, with encouragement, in every way possible, even to split the sea for him!

All the more so when we see the horrible massacre that is happening two hours from here [in Syria], right under our noses! And the entire world is silent! Kofi Annan says we'll take Ahmadinejad to make peace! He will stop the terrible massacre!

This past Thursday 170 children were killed, two days ago 107 children, every day they are slaughtering right under our noses, and Kofi Annan says, "We'll take Ahmadinejad!" He will make peace! He who creates all the weapons of mass destruction? He will make peace?! What have we come to?! What kind of merciless world have we come to?!

The nations of the world are silent. And we? the Israelite

Nation, the Nation of Justice, the Nation of Conscience, the Nation of Fairness, the Israelite Nation is the conscience of the entire world! The entire world lifts up their eyes to the Israelite Nation, the entire world believes in the Israelite Nation, the entire world knows that the Israelite Nation will bring the redemption, only the Israelite Nation will bring the Moshiach!...

Beloved is man for he was created in God's image.[i]" Every person is in the image of God! Every person is composed of sparks of Godliness! God created them all! All of mankind! Seven billion people! For "Beloved is man who was created in God's image."

When we go pray at Joseph's tomb and I see Israeli soldiers standing there with M-16s, I say to them, "Are you not ashamed?! Here lies Joseph the Tzaddik! What are you afraid of?! Why are you standing here with M-16s?! I used to walk here alone when I lived in Bnei Brak, I walked here by foot! Who needs these M-16s?!...

When we went to war with Ammon and Moab, the prophet got up and said, "Just play music! Just sing! Throw away all your instruments of war! Throw away all your weapons! Begin singing! Just sing!" ...

"If you believe in the words of the prophet then you can win over all your enemies just through song and music." Because all our victories and all the wars that we won with weapons are not considered "victories!" Any war that is won with weapons is not eternal; they also have weapons, they have the atom bomb, and one day everything can turn around.

"Victory" is only what we win through the power of song and music which awakens the Jewish spark in every nation, in every gentile, in every single Arab, for there does not exist an Arab or gentile that does not have within him a Jewish spark.

---

[i] Pirkei Avot (Ethics of the Fathers) Chapter 3, Mishnah 14.

We just need to arouse that spark, and then automatically there will be peace in the entire world!"

Rabbi Berland's peace and *teshuva* rally was widely covered by the media, both in Israel and abroad, and garnered a great deal of attention in both the secular and religious press.

For many of the months that the Rav had been living in Beitar, certain individuals had been demanding large sums of money from him, and threatening to spread outrageous slanders against him if he didn't comply. The highly publicized event at the Winter Stadium gave the Rav's opponents new impetus to act. Just two and a half weeks later, the first slanderous lies began to be reported in the Israeli media.

The next stage of Rabbi Berland's deal to atone for the Jewish people had come due.

THE TZADDIK IS LIKE A MIRROR

The Baal Shem Tov[2], the founder of *chassidus*, once taught that the Tzaddik is like a mirror: Whatever a person sees when he looks at the Tzaddik is simply a reflection of himself. The Tzaddik shows the person who he really is. If he comes with a negative attitude and outlook, that's what he'll see reflected back at him. And if he comes with a positive attitude and outlook, then that's what he'll see when he looks at the Tzaddik. This is one of the tests involved in coming close to the Tzaddik.

THE ACCUSATIONS BEGIN

In the generation when the Moshiach comes, there will be terrible persecution against the Torah scholars.
                    – Commentary to Likutey Moharan

"It is clear to everyone that the hareidim currently constitute a significant portion of Israeli society and the non-haredi population is concerned they will 'take over.'"
                    – Ilan Gael-Dor, Gesher, 2010[i]

"You won. There was a competition in Israel for 'Israeli-ness' that lasted over 100 years, since the second wave of immigration. And in the end, you won. We lost, and you won."
                    – Yair Lapid speaking to a group of Haredi college students in Kiryat Ono, 2011[ii]

★ ★ ★

For all that Israel is nominally a democratic State, many influential public figures on the political right, and many rabbis in the orthodox world have been

---

[i] Poll: Secular Public Believes Chareidi Majority Endangers Israel - https://dev.matzav.com/poll-secular-public-believes-chareidi-majority-endangers-israel/ May 6th, 2010.
[ii] See the video of Yair Lapid speaking with English subtitles here: https://www.youtube.com/watch?v=jNwAv6zpmh4

investigated by the police in Israel, and even temporarily jailed, solely on the basis of a story in the media. The media wields tremendous political power in Israel; the Israeli media can initiate a police investigation by the sheer force of its will; and the Israeli media, for the most part, doesn't like hareidi rabbis with large followings.

At the beginning of 2013, when the first incredible stories started to pop up in the press, the battle against drafting *hareidim* into the Israeli army was at its peak, and the political environment in Israel was charged and toxic. Some secular journalists were keen to publish any 'hareidi bashing' story they could find, regardless of whether it was actually true.

A month before the first stories about Rabbi Berland started to run, an Israeli journalist published a very controversial piece claiming that a five year old girl had been violated in a synagogue in Modiin Illit, and that the community had covered the incident up.

In the wake of that awful accusation, the Modiin Illit municipality and the police went to every effort to verify the details of the report, and to provide the family and girl in question with help and support. Their efforts turned up something very interesting: the story wasn't true. There was no victim. Nothing had happened.

But that didn't stop the media from trying the same trick, again.

Rabbi Eliezer Berland left Israel of his own free will on February 21, 2013, three weeks before the first false allegations against him began to appear. He flew to Miami, in the United States, where he'd started a new branch of Shuvu Banim a few months' earlier, before moving on to Switzerland.

Back in Israel, a number of senior Rabbis including Rabbi Isaac Meir Morgenstern and Rav Yehuda Sheinfeld convened an informal Rabbinic Court to examine the accusations that had surfaced against Rabbi Berland. They questioned Rabbi Berland's persecutors and determined that the evidence being presented was a total web of lies and deceit.

"When Rabbi Berland was in Switzerland, I spoke to him and he told me that he'd been given a holy mission to do, but that not everyone believed that," Rabbi Yehuda Sheinfeld later explained. *"Instead, they believed the testimony of a lone witness[i], and the things that they read on the internet and in the secular media."*

Once it became clear that the allegations were completely false, a number of the nation's leading Rabbis, including Rabbi Shalom Arush, Rabbi Meir Sirota and Rabbi Shechnazi, undertook to inform the Israeli public of the true facts of the matter.

But, when Rabbi Berland found out that Rabbi Arush was attempting to clear his name, he immediately called him from Morocco and urgently requested that Rabbi Arush should stop what he was doing, and not get involved in the matter. Rabbi Berland explained that he'd worked very hard to procure all these insults, and he didn't want the whole thing to be ruined prematurely.

So Rabbi Arush's letter, together with many other letters that were written at the time by other notable Rabbis in defense of Rabbi Berland, were never published, and stayed hidden within the Shuvu Banim community.

As you can tell from the following letter of support that was written by Rabbi Aharon Tzvi Rompler, head of Tehillos Israel, who had no prior connection to Rabbi Berland or the Shuvu Banim community, if these letters had been widely

---

[i] Jewish religious law requires a minimum of two witnesses to bring a case to court.

circulated when they were first written, back in March, 2013, it would have totally changed the whole picture.

We have translated a few excerpts from this letter from the original Hebrew and made some very minor adaptations to include it in this book. (Note: Some of the footnotes can be found at the back of this book, and are also part of the original letter written by Rabbi Rompler):

"We are dealing with someone who is an awesome Torah Scholar; who labors in Torah day and night; who has been known from his childhood to be a servant of God, serving God with tremendous self-sacrifice; who is completely abstinent from all mundane worldly matters[3]; and who is known to tens of thousands of people to be a Tzaddik of tremendous stature...

[T]he person who is talking and spreading the rumors is someone who is known to be [*text omitted for legal reasons*], and whose wife is also [*text omitted for legal reasons*]...

[I]t is understood by anyone with any intelligence that this evil speech has no basis in truth whatsoever.

....Instead of denying the rumors against him, even though he certainly has what to say, as explained, on the contrary, [Rabbi Berland] admits and disgraces himself, and gives the impression that he is the biggest, notorious criminal...

Therefore, this kind of behavior proves the awesome level of the tzaddikim, who hear their disgrace and do not respond, (and even strengthen the disgrace)...T]hose who know him and know how he has spoken throughout all the years....know full well that this is his way of insulting himself in public, and to lower his honor in very extreme ways. No-one else can compete with him in this regard, and there is no one else who does this like him[4]....

[T]here is no doubt that [the people who are speaking against Rabbi Berland] have some kind of agenda, and a grudge in their hearts, and that their portion is with the arrogant ones of the generation...

This is even more so, because they are defiling the name of Heaven in a horrible, awful, terrifying way. In particular, that they sent all this to the media and news outlets, and helped the evil doers who are always looking for ways to speak badly against religious people, religion in general and about God. They have caused others to revile the Torah-observant community, and to destroy them, by standing against the holy Torah and the safeguarding of religion. They have given up everyone, big and small, for disgrace and abuse in a public way before all the Nations and all the people under the sun....

I have no connection with this Rav [Berland] and his community at all, nevertheless, after I heard these rumors, [I] was sickened to my stomach by them.

Rabbi Moshe Mordechai Karp, the Rabbi of Kiryat Sefer and one of the successors of RavbbiShalom Elyashiv, Rabbi Dov Kook of Tiberius, and Rabbi Shalom Arush also signed onto the letter.

Next to his signature, Rabbi Karp added the following words:

"According to the Holy Torah.. it is forbidden to have evil thoughts about someone who is known to be a Torah Scholar and a Tzaddik, and we shouldn't accept or listen to lashon hara. And this certainly applies to someone who also has turned the masses to teshuva.

And even more so in this case [with Rabbi Berland], where it's known that people who hold a grudge against him for monetary reasons and the like are coming against him...

Anyone who is pulled after this nonsense testifies about himself that he himself is stuck in these impure activities. Woe to the generation that this has happened in their days! This is certainly the last process of clarification before the coming of Moshiach, when "chutzpah will be common" in public against God and His Torah, without fear and without shame.

They are the arrogant of the generation..."

When Rabbi Dov Kook was given the paper to sign he was standing at the gravesite of Rabbi Akiva in Tiberius. After he read over the letter he signed it and said "May the *Erev Rav* disappear!"

But none of these letters, none of these protestations, were allowed to reach the public. Rabbi Berland stopped them all. Later on, Rabbi Chaim Reicher, one of the Rav's grandsons who is closely connected with many of the generation's leading Rabbis, shed a little more spiritual light on why Rabbi Berland did this, and why so many of the nation's spiritual leaders appeared to do very little to openly help the Rav against his persecutors throughout his three years of exile.

"[The nation's] leading Rabbis speak to me privately and tell me that they have explicit instructions from the Rav not to support him openly," explained Rabbi Richter, *"except for some things he permits because of the desecration of God's name [that would otherwise be involved]. The Rav feels that he must take on himself this disgrace in order to mitigate decrees and ignite the light of teshuva in all of the Jewish people."*

So all the Rabbis' early public protestations against the terrible calumnies being spread about Rabbi Berland were silenced by the Rav himself. This made the spiritual test of who to believe infinitely more difficult.

> *"Believe me, if I wanted to I could end all the controversy against me, and there would not be a single person against me. But what can I do? There are levels that cannot be reached without controversy".*
> — Rebbe Nachman of Breslov

MIRACLES IN MOROCCO

Those who serve in the army are not taken care of, while those who don't serve are given money. Isn't that backward? Those who pay the most taxes get the least education from the state. It's all backward. The middle class, those who work the hardest, will never be able to buy an apartment. Those who don't work get apartments at half-price. I'm telling you, it's backward. So I ask, isn't it about time to turn things around?

– Yair Lapid, talking in an election ad for his new political party 'Yesh Atid' in 2012

"Lapid Tells Haredim 'Go Work' as Child Subsidy Cuts Go into Effect. Israel's social security administration objected to these cuts, arguing that they expect them to send some 35,000 new children below the poverty line."

– Headline in the Jewish Press, August 20th, 2013[i]

★   ★   ★

---

[i] https://www.jewishpress.com/news/breaking-news/lapid-tells-haredim-go-work-as-child-subsidy-cuts-go-into-effect/2013/08/20/

During September 2012, Rabbi Berland had been in Uman for Rosh Hashanah, where he'd met one of his followers, Rabbi Nachman Biton, who'd moved out to Morocco some five years earlier.

Reb Biton came over to the Rav to ask for a blessing, but before he left, the Rav called out to him that when he got back to Morocco, he should start to make arrangements to hire a couple of vans — one to transport all of the Rav's books from the airport, and the second to transport all of the Rav's students.

At the time, Reb Biton thought Rabbi Berland was joking, as the persecution of the Rav hadn't even begun. Reb Biton couldn't imagine that just a little while later, Rabbi Berland — together with his books and some of his students — would be with him in Morocco, just as the Rav predicted on Rosh Hashanah.

Throughout the long years of exile, the Rav's attendants confirmed that the decision of 'where to go next' nearly always occurred spontaneously. There was no fixed plan, there was no special strategy. Just as the Jewish people followed the Divine presence across the desert, resting when it rested, and traveling onwards when it started moving again, Rabbi Berland's moves were also decided by the word of God.

So despite his comments to Nachman Biton, the decision

to travel to Morocco occurred to the Rav spontaneously, while he was staying in Switzerland. From the time he first set foot in Morocco, the Rav himself made it clear to the people who were closest to him that he'd be in exile for three years, and so it came to be. But what was unclear was whether Rebbe Berland would stay in just one place.

When he first came to Morocco, the Rav spent some time with his follower Nachman Biton in Casablanca, before moving to the small Jewish community in the Moroccan city of Marrakech.

The Rav explained that Morocco contained some of the holiness of the land of Israel, because around 3,000 holy *Tzaddikim* were buried there, and as Rebbe Nachman taught, wherever a *Tzaddik* is buried, he creates a spiritual atmosphere around his tomb that's permeated with the holiness of Israel.

Throughout the seven months that he spent in Marrakech, Rabbi Berland frequently visited many of the holy gravesites of *Tzaddikim* buried in Morocco, including the grave of Rabbi Amram Ben Diwan.

In a class he gave over the phone from Morocco before May 2013, Rabbi Berland made a point of encouraging all his students to make the trip to the grave of Rabbi Shimon Bar Yochai in Meron, for the annual *L'ag B'Omer* celebration. He explained that all the difficulties involved in making the trip up to Meron would atone for their sins and reassured them that the community was passing through the final test now. "Don't worry!" he said. "I'm with every single one of you, and everyone needs to believe that I could be there with you again in a split second. Don't worry! Everything will work out for the best!"

But it was hard for everyone. When one of his students saw how deeply Rabbi Berland was suffering, he asked the Rav about it. The Rav told him: "What can I do? No one else could have taken on so much suffering in order to atone for the sins of the generation."

★ ★ ★

As more of his followers started to make the trip out to Morocco to be with him, Rabbi Berland tried to put more of a communal infrastructure in place. The community in Marrakech welcomed the newcomers warmly. The old synagogue had been struggling to find the 10 men required for a *minyan* during the week, but with a regular influx of guests from Shuvu Banim, it was enjoying a new lease of life.

Very early on, Rabbi Berland asked the President of the Moroccan Jewish community, Jacky Kodesh, to help him establish a *kollel* in the city, which was even able to provide its students with a modest stipend. Next, the small Jewish community of Marrakech agreed to help the Rav establish his own Shuvu Banim community there, and to contribute toward its upkeep.

In a phone call he made to Rabbi Moshe Binenstock back in Israel, Rabbi Berland explained, "When I started on my journey, I thought I'd have a maximum of five students with me here in Morocco. But with God's help, I see that my students are following me even to here."

When Rabbi Berland had been in Beitar Illit, many of his students made the four hour walk out from Jerusalem to come and pray with him on Shabbos. And now, they were starting to make the trip out to Morocco, too, and despite the stressful circumstances, there was almost a party atmosphere going on around the Rav.

When one of Rabbi Berland's grandchildren traveled to Morocco to celebrate their marriage with him, the Rav said that he hadn't felt so free in 40 years. In his latter years in Jerusalem, Rabbi Berland had been accompanied by guards everywhere he went, who prevented his community from interacting with him, and vice versa. "But now," continued the Rav, "I finally feel free and able to connect to you again [i.e., his community], as though you were my own family."

★ ★ ★

Around this time, word first reached the Rav's attendants that the Israeli police were seeking to question the Rav as a result of all the media instigation that had occurred back in Israel.

The police in Israel cannot make an extradition request simply in order to question someone, so the Rav's attendants contacted the Lahav 433 police unit that was responsible for dealing with Rabbi Berland's case and offered that Rabbi Berland would return to Israel to clear his name, on condition that he would be dealt with respectfully.

The attendants had a key requirement that Rabbi Berland should only be questioned in his own home and that he shouldn't be imprisoned without a trial, as had happened to other individuals in the past. They were concerned about the lack of transparency, honesty and goodwill being shown by the Israeli police.

Later events would prove their concerns to be well-founded.

The two sides (Rabbi Berland's attendants and the Israeli police) were about to come to an agreement that would see Rabbi Berland voluntarily returning to Israel to clear his name when one of the Lahav 433 police chiefs stepped in and nixed the deal. "I don't care if he's a Rabbi or not a Rabbi," he told the attendants. "I will bring him here with handcuffs!"

According to the Jewish calendar, a year to the day after Rabbi Berland left Israel, on March 14, 2014 this man resigned from his position. The following year, on July 5, 2015 — the same time that Rabbi Berland disappeared from Holland — this police chief sadly committed suicide.

While all of these negotiations were continuing behind the scenes, more of the miracle stories involving Rabbi Berland started trickling out of Morocco. As the news of the miracle-worker in their midst spread, more people from the local Jewish community, and also from Israel and further afield, and even some of the local Moroccans, started to flock to the Rav to receive a blessing. One of the people who visited the Rav in Morocco at this time told the following story:

"On one of the occasions that Rabbi Berland left his house, there was a group of his supporters waiting outside to speak to him. As soon as the Rav came out, one woman came over to him from the group and asked the Rav if he remembered her. He said, 'Yes, I do. You came to me in Israel and asked me for a blessing that you would be able to find your husband [the woman's husband had disappeared without giving her a divorce]. I told you which country he was in, which city, which street, and the number of the house where he was staying.'

The woman replied excitedly that she'd found her husband exactly where the Rav had told her that she would, and that he'd been so shocked that she'd been able to find him, that she'd been able to encourage him to return to the family home. Now they were living together in peace once more as husband and wife.

Upon hearing this, the Rav turned to his followers who were standing there and told them, 'You see, I know where everyone is! And I also know who's upsetting their wife by coming to see me without asking her permission first!'"

As the summer stretched on into August, the Rav's thoughts turned to *Rosh Hashanah*, and the first days of the Jewish new year. Rabbi Berland hadn't missed being in Uman for Rosh Hashanah since the fall of Communism in 1989, but there were many obstacles in the way of the Rav traveling to Uman this year.

The Rav decided to visit the grave of Rabbi Daniel HaShomer at midnight and spent many hours there dancing and singing. He was overheard praying: "Master of the

World, You brought us all the way to here, please take us to Uman, too!" This was the same song of longing for Uman that the Rav had composed many years earlier, when the path had been blocked by the Iron Curtain.

Afterwards, the Rav remarked that he'd fervently prayed that he would be able to spend the coming Rosh Hashanah by Rebbe Nachman, which began on September 5th 2013. "Who knows what could happen in the world this coming year if I don't get to Uman," he said. "The judgments on the world are continuing to pile up and they need a lot of sweetening."

At this time, in August 2013, the Arab world was in an uproar, as part of the so-called 'Arab Spring'. Egypt was in the middle of a revolution; the conflict against Syrian dictator Basher Assad had officially degenerated into a civil war; in March of that year, former Turkish Prime Minister Recep Tayyip Erdogan had said that "Zionism is a crime against humanity" during a speech at the UN; and Iran had just announced that it now had the sixth biggest stockpile of rockets in the world, and that its plans to develop atomic weapon were coming along nicely.

Meanwhile, the Torah world in Israel was also coming under unprecedented attack as the Israeli government instituted swinging budget cuts, with Finance Minister Yair Lapid leading the charge.

Rabbi Berland told his students that the tremendous financial difficulty that they and many others had experienced that past year was part of the birth pangs of Moshiach. He said, *"I really hope that next year, 5774, we'll see the coming of Moshiach, as it says in Rashi's commentary on Sanhedrin 98: 'Everyone will say, just let the son of David come already!' because we'll already be so tired, and we'll realize that there's nothing more we can do to change or improve the situation. No one will have the strength to do anything anymore, not the secular people and not the religious people, and that's why everyone will want Moshiach to come right now."*

With Rosh Hashana fast approaching, a small group of around 30 of Rabbi Berland's followers tried to organize a flight to Uman. There were no direct flights from Morocco to Kiev, but the Rav's attendants had managed to find a Ukrainian tour group who had chartered a private plane with spare seat, and who were flying back to the Ukraine a day before Rosh Hashanah.

When they got to the airport, they discovered that the airport's flight booking system wasn't recognizing the tickets that had been purchased for Shuvu Banim, and the airport staff also couldn't register any new ticket purchases.

The offices of the tour group who'd chartered the plane were now closed for the day, and the Rav's attendants had no other way of getting in touch with the organizers of the flight. When all this became clear, Rabbi Berland told everyone to return to Marrakech, and to start saying the relevant prayers for the eve of Rosh Hashanah. Despite their best efforts, Rabbi Berland was not going to be in Uman, that year.

The next morning, a number of trucks started arriving outside Rabbi Berland's lodgings, bringing all types of different kosher food that had been donated by some of the wealthier members of the Jewish Moroccan community. Then, word arrived that someone had paid for the Rav and his followers to spend Rosh Hashanah in a vacation resort.

A number of taxis showed up, to take the students and Rabbi Berland to their temporary lodgings, and the small entourage of Breslovers had a 'three day' Rosh Hashana at the resort that was described as 'unforgettable'.

But when the news hit Uman that the Rav wouldn't be joining them for Rosh Hashanah, many of his followers were devastated. What was this going to portend, for the coming year?

★   ★   ★

From September 7, 2013 on, the number of people who decided to fly out to see Rabbi Berland in Morocco began to rise exponentially. The Rav called one of his students, Rabbi Naftali Biton, to tell him that as many as 1,000 of his followers had been given permission to fly out to Morocco to spend the remaining festivals with him. He asked Rav Nachman Biton for his help in arranging accommodations for them all.

In the end, around 300 people spent Yom Kippur with Rabbi Berland in Marrakech, while another 400 flew out to celebrate the Jewish holidays of *Simchas Torah* and *Sukkos* with him, totaling 700 people altogether. This was still more than enough to start garnering a lot of attention from the local Muslim population, who began to wonder why so many hundreds of Jews in traditional *Chassidic* garb were openly walking around the streets of Marrakech while the "Arab Spring" was in full swing everywhere else in the world...

After the High Holidays were over, the Rav decided to take a break from his teaching schedule and routine in Marrakech and have a few days "vacation" in Morocco's capital city, Casablanca.

While in Casablanca, Rabbi Berland stayed at the home of one of the influential members of the Jewish community. Over the course of Shabbos, tens of citizens and businessmen flocked to this man's home, to visit the Rav – including a number of local Moroccans. They were joined by a few of the Rav's own students, who'd flown out from Israel after the High Holidays to be with him, and who spent the nights learning Torah with him.

So it continued the whole week that the Rav spent in Casablanca, where he prayed in the Chabad synagogue of Rabbi Shalom Eidelman.

Among the many different people who came to visit Rabbi Berland in Morocco, one in particular stood out. This man had recently been told by the doctors that he had a cancerous growth in his throat. After he received this shocking diagnosis, he went to get a blessing from one of the most famous and well-respected rabbis in Israel, called Rabbi Chaim Kanievsky. Rabbi Kanievsky asked him who he had been speaking badly about, and after a long pause for thought, the man responded that he'd spoken negatively about Rabbi Berland – but that he'd only been repeating the things he'd heard on the news.

Rabbi Chaim Kanievsky then told that he should go immediately to ask forgiveness, and that if he did that, he'd be healed. The man took Rabbi Kanievsky's words to heart and called the Rav to ask for his forgiveness, which was very freely given. The growth subsequently disappeared all by itself.

★　★　★

For a couple of months, it felt like the good times had returned. Anyone who wanted could come and see Rabbi Berland in Morocco, and the Rav and his followers had developed a framework and routine for life in Morocco. But this state of affairs wasn't to last. On top of the "Arab Spring" a number of terrorist organizations including Al-Qaida were known to be operating in Morocco at that point in time, and the government was wary of adding any more fuel to what was already a potentially explosive domestic situation.

The remaining Jews in Morocco had learned to keep a low profile. By contrast, the Breslover newcomers were drawing an awful lot of attention to themselves, and the greatest attraction of all was Rabbi Berland.

As rumors of his holiness and abilities as a miracle-worker spread, even the non-Jewish Moroccans started lining up in the street outside his house to ask for blessings, and would mob him every time he came out of his home. Even some of the King's own advisors came to pay a courtesy call to the Rav. But as Rabbi Berland's fame continued to spread, and as the number of his followers who were coming to Morocco continued to grow, the King of Morocco was told by his advisors that something had to be done to nip this potential problem in the bud.

Back in Israel, the people who'd been persecuting Rabbi Berland started to realize that instead of clipping the Rav's wings, silencing him and destroying his community, his exile to Morocco had actually had the opposite effect. Rabbi Berland had been rejuvenated, his followers had been flocking to see him by the hundreds, and new life had been breathed back into Shuvu Banim.

This was not at all the state of affairs they'd been hoping for, and so began the pattern of "persecution by media" that continued throughout Rabbi Berland's exile.

The Rav's persecutors decided to send the Moroccan press a translated copy of some very negative news stories that had appeared about Rabbi Berland back in Israel. They posed as innocent bystanders with no hidden agenda, and no connection to the Rav and his followers, who just wanted the good people of Morocco to know 'the truth' about who the Rav really was.

Their ruse was discovered when members of the Shuvu Banim community contacted the Arabic-speaking Moroccan journalists who were running negative stories about the Rav to ask them how they'd come by their information. One reporter told them about the translated articles he'd received, and gave over the name of the person who'd sent it him. It was one of Rabbi Berland's main persecutors within the Breslov community.

Then, the local Moroccan press started publishing stories quoting complaints about the Rav's followers from the head of the Marrakech Jewish community, Jackie Kadosh. Jackie Kadosh was quick to respond that no one should believe the story, and that hosting Rabbi Berland was a tremendous privilege.

But that story was only the opening shot in the "media war" that was waged against Rabbi Berland in every country he fled to during his exile.

As the false stories about the Rav started to appear in the Moroccan papers, the King of Morocco found himself caught in a furious dilemma about what action, if any, he should take.

After a long, painful deliberation, the King of Morocco came to a decision. His aides contacted Rabbi Berland's host and passed on the following ultimatum: "The King of Morocco can no longer guarantee the safety of Rabbi Berland's followers. Around a thousand Jews are now in the country visiting the Rav, and it is beyond the King's ability to guarantee their welfare. All of Rabbi Berland's followers must leave Morocco immediately."

When he heard the King's ultimatum, Rabbi Berland made it clear that he couldn't stay in Morocco if his followers would no longer be able to visit him and learn with him.

After the Rav decided he had to leave Morocco, one of his students came over to him and asked him, "What do we do now? What should we tell everyone to do?" The Rav replied, "We have to believe that God is running the world. Whatever will be — will be! But our job is to carry on busying ourselves with our prayers and with our service of God, in whatever place we find ourselves next. Tell everyone to carry on studying the Torah portion of the week."

And that was that. The Rav was very relaxed, and he sent a very clear message to his students that no matter where the next part of the journey was going to take them all, the main concern should be just to simply carry on studying the Torah, learning its laws and living according to Jewish law, and not to let themselves get confused by anything that was going on around them.

While his followers scrambled to pack their belongings, Rabbi Berland stayed calm and focused on spiritual matters at all times, even though it appeared that no one had any idea where the Rav would go next.

After the Rav left the country, the King of Morocco had a change of heart and contacted the Rav to request that he should return. The King promised him full honor and protection, on the condition that the Rav would return alone, and keep a low profile. Again, Rabbi Berland refused. If he couldn't be with his beloved students, he wasn't interested in going back to Morocco, even if he could live there in luxury and peace.

Rabbi Berland left Morocco on November 7, 2013. It was time for the next leg of his exile.

DEFUSING A NUCLEAR BOMB

"Unlike you, who believe we can pray from morning until night, the rest of Israeli society (left wing and right wing, Sephardi and Ashkenazi, secular, religious and many from within the ultra-Orthodox community itself) understands that prayer alone cannot sustain a country. For a country to survive it needs to defend itself – its borders and its citizens. That defense comes at a terrible price, the highest price. It can't be that only some pay that price while an entire sector receives an exemption from it."

– Yesh Atid MK and former Major
General in the IDF, Elazar Stern,
writing in the Times of Israel.[i]

★   ★   ★

A week before Rabbi Berland ended up leaving Morocco, he sent one of his attendants back to Israel with instructions for him to gather as many high-level university books he could find on the topic of nuclear engineering, as well as any books describing the physics and other scientific knowledge required to build a nuclear bomb.

The attendant returned to Morocco with these books very shortly before the Rav left, and later traveled with them

---

[i] https://blogs.timesofisrael.com/ultra-orthodox-mks-should-be-thanking-us/, published September 13th, 2017.

to Johannesburg. One of the students who moved with the Rav heard him say: "I'm going to make a big disturbance in the nuclear reactor!" - referring to disrupting the Iranians' plans at the spiritual level.

★   ★   ★

While hasty arrangements were being made for Rabbi Berland to leave Morocco, over in Geneva the heads of the G6 nations were meeting, under orders from the President of the United States, Barack Obama, who wanted to explore a way of "making peace" with the Iranians.

This historical meeting ended with an agreement being signed that would in practice enable the Iranians to create a nuclear missile within a very short period of time. And everyone knew which country the Iranians would be aiming at first.

In 2008, when Obama first became president, Rabbi Berland commented in one of his public lectures that a modern-day *Achashverosh*[i] had just been elected in the United States and that his government would be a terrible thing for the Jews, as he was one of the most evil people to have been elected to power for a very long time.

The Rav explained that Obama wasn't only the Jewish people's problem. He would also turn out to be the American people's problem, too, as he was only interested in how best to destroy the country he'd just been elected to lead.

When Obama had first been elected President, Rabbi Berland sent one of his senior students, Rabbi Eliyahu

---

[i] Achashverosh was a Persian monarch who'd decreed total annihilation of the Jews living in his Empire around 355 B.C.E. The Jews were saved after three days of fasting and repentance, and they memorialized their miraculous rescue in the festival of Purim, which is still celebrated today.

Meirav, on an emergency mission to the United States. He tasked Rabbi Meirav with the job of passing on an urgent message to new President Elect, urging him to travel to the grave of Rebbe Nachman of Breslov in the Ukraine, and to say the 10 verses of psalms that make up the *Tikkun HaKlali* prayer.

Rabbi Berland promised the President Elect that if he would do this, he would be remembered as the best president in the history of the USA, and that he would make a number of instrumental, positive changes that would be engraved in the history books. But, if he didn't make the trip, then Rabbi Berland warned Barack Obama that he would go down as the worst president in the country's history. This message was passed on to the President Elect by his brother, but unsurprisingly, it was ignored.

In subsequent years, President Obama had been posing as the concerned "friend" of Israel, warning them away from neutralizing the Iranian nuclear program themselves because he, Obama, was going to take care of the problem himself. He made a lot of promises to Israel and other concerned countries that he would ensure that Iran would never be in a position to develop a nuclear bomb.

The world took Obama at his word — until, in 2013, the point was reached where alarm bells started to ring throughout the international community that the Iranians had already passed the point of no return with their uranium enrichment program, and that it was no longer possible for Israel — or anyone else — to bomb their nuclear reactors. At this point, the American president revealed his true colors and convened an international meeting that appeared to have an agenda designed to ease the passage of the Iranian nuclear bomb into the world.

★ ★ ★

When Rabbi Berland spoke at the gathering of 8,000 people in the Winter Stadium in Tel Aviv, at the peace rally he held in June 2012, he compared Achmadinejad, the then-president of Iran to a modern-day Haman[i]. The Rav said then: "The leaders of the world have been telling each other that it's a shame that Hitler, may his name be blotted out, didn't manage to finish off the Jewish people, but don't worry — now we've got the president of Iran to complete the job! But," the Rav reassured the crowd, "The Jewish People will prevail in the end!"

The Rav explained that Obama, the American president, wasn't at all bothered by the fact that the Iranians were developing a nuclear weapon. He was only making a big show about wanting "peace" with the Iranians in order to tie Israel's hands and prevent them from making a preemptive strike. Now, in Geneva, the mask was finally off, and Obama was busy encouraging the world's leaders to "make peace" with the genocidal leaders of Iran.

But all this had been foreseen by Rabbi Berland and by many of the other holy Jewish Rabbis many years earlier. Rabbi Yehuda Bracha, for example, published a Hebrew pamphlet around this time called "The Last Chance," which contained many ancient Torah sources that describe what would occur in the end of days, including references to what can be understood as referring to a nuclear bomb.

Whatever spiritual work had already been done by that point was still not enough to tip the scales in the favor of the Jews. Obama and Ahmadinejad were coming ever closer to developing a nuclear bomb, and now a group of the world's leaders were poised to sign on the Geneva Agreement, which would officially permit Iran to go nuclear.

---

[i] An archetypical persecutor of the Jews, who wanted nothing less than their total annihilation.

Throughout his stay in Morocco, Rabbi Berland had returned to the theme of Iran's nuclear bomb on many different occasions. Rumors had abounded in the media for months that despite all the international sanctions and pressure, Iran had nevertheless managed to produce enough fissile nuclear material to produce seven atomic bombs. Many weeks before the Rav left Morocco, he'd left his students in no doubt about where the Iranians were holding with their nuclear program:

"In two more months, the Iranians will have a nuclear weapon!" he'd declared to his shocked students. And subsequent events showed that his warning wasn't unfouded.

In December, when Rabbi Berland decided to leave Morocco, the king of Saudi Arabia had just flown out to the United States to urgently discuss the Iranian bomb, exactly as predicted in an ancient Jewish text called the *Midrash Yalkut Shimoni.*

The *Midrash Yalkut Shimoni (Yeshiya* 60) says the following:

"Rabbi Yitzchak said: The year that the King Moshiach will be revealed, all the kings of the nations of the world will provoke each other. The king of Persia will threaten the king of Arabia and because of this *the king of Arabia will go to the king of Edom [identified as the West] for advice.*

"Afterwards, the king of Persia will destroy [most of] the world. The remaining nations will be hysterical and frantic and fall on their faces and will be seized as if by birth pains.

"And the people of Israel will be frantic and hysterical and they will say, where will we come and go? Where will we come and go? And God will say to them: Do not fear, My children, do not fear. All that I have done I did only for you. Why are you afraid? The time for your redemption has come!"

The Associated Press at this time reported that Obama's administration had been conducting secret bilateral negotiations with the Iranians for months, without anyone else being any the wiser about what was really being discussed or agreed to.

Meanwhile, a French newspaper reported on November 20, 2013 that the French Foreign Minister Laurent Fabius had privately complained of the discrepancy between official multilateral negotiations and "a detailed accord John Kerry had negotiated in parallel with Iran." When it came to the Iranians and the nuclear bomb, Obama had pulled the wool over everyone's eyes, exactly as Rabbi Berland had predicted many years earlier.

The Israeli government was in a panic, and the papers were full of headlines screaming that the Israeli prime minister was begging someone to intercede and stop the Geneva Agreement from being signed.

The last day of the Jewish festival of light, Chanukah, found Rabbi Berland deep within Africa, where more trials, self-sacrifice and miraculous occurrences were awaiting him.

ZIMBABWE

"[Israel's] Channel 10 initiated a series of reports titled "Government by the Rabbi," playing on the Hebrew "Government by majority" by replacing the Hebrew word "rov" – majority – with "rav" – rabbi. The reporter, Avishai Ben-Chaim, tried to bring home the fear that the population explosion within the haredi community will turn the secular segment of Israel's population into a minority by the year 2030.

The implications were no more mixed swimming but stringent Shabbat and kashrut observance for everyone. Photos of a third-grade haredi teacher who was interviewed for the program are all shot with the reporter Ben-Chaim behind bars, as if in a jail, looking outside toward the free haredi world…

Two weeks ago, Avishai Ben-Chaim also exposed on Channel 10 an IDF lieutenant-colonel, Nurit Lamay, who stated in an answer to a phone call, "I get a rash from the haredim, I hate haredim, I want all haredim to die." Knesset Member Aryeh Deri demanded that Defense Minister Moshe Ya'alon force the resignation of the officer, but to the best of our knowledge, nothing has happened."

– Yisrael Medad and Eli Pollak of
Israel Media Watch, writing in the
Jerusalem Post, December 11th 2013[i]

---

[i] https://www.jpost.com/Opinion/Columnists/Media-Comment-The-ignorant-fear-of-haredim-334730

One of the unsung heroes of Rabbi Berland's time in exile was the Israeli diamond mine millionaire, Yaron Yamin. As Rabbi Berland started on the next leg of his exile, in deepest Africa, Yaron Yamin began to play an increasingly prominent role in the events surrounding the Rav.

Yamin, a self-described secular businessman, and Rabbi Berland, have known each other for 20 years, from the time they first met in Uman. Yamin recalls about their first meeting: "Suddenly, I found myself next to him [Rabbi Berland], and he was giving me a blessing, and I didn't even know who he was. Someone told me afterwards that he's one of the biggest *Tzaddikim* there is, but as I'm not a religious man, I didn't think it was a particularly big deal."

Nevertheless, their relationship began to develop, and the Israeli businessman would occasionally go to the Rav for advice and encouragement. Yamin continues: "Ten years ago, I had a big business failure, and the Rav told me to go to Africa, to Zimbabwe, and to dig. There, I was going to find a fortune.

"I thought to myself, 'How can I begin anything?!' All I had in my pocket was $10,000, and by the time I got to Zimbabwe it was $4,000... So I got there, and I wondered what the Rav wanted from me, and why he'd sent me there. Why here? Why Zimbabwe? It seemed completely unrealistic."

To cut a long story short, Yamin miraculously managed to purchase a plot of land in Zimbabwe practically for free from an old Jew. Rabbi Berland advised Yamin to start digging — and he discovered an enormous diamond mine that instantly catapulted him into the ranks of the super-wealthy. Overnight, he went from being almost bankrupt to being one of the wealthiest people in the world.

To this day, Yamin becomes very emotional when he

tells the story of how Rabbi Berland literally transformed his whole life. "I met with him at a very difficult point in my life," he says." "I have a letter that I wrote to the Rav that I keep in my phylacteries from the time I got there [to Zimbabwe], and the whole letter is soaked with tears. In terms of my finances, I never even dreamed that I'd get to the level I ultimately reached. I keep the letter so I'll never forget where I was, so I'll remember everything that the Rav did for me."

As a result of his African diamond mine, Yamin became a multimillionaire before the age of 30. Today, he's known as one of the most successful businessmen in Israel.

When Rabbi Berland had to leave Morocco, one of the first people he called was Yamin. "The community didn't want the Rav to stay with all of his followers," he explains. "It was very difficult for them to host everyone and provide what they needed, like kosher meat and so forth. So then it got to the papers, and then to the King of Morocco, and they decided to publicize what the King of Morocco said: 'Either you leave, or your followers leave.'"

Yamin continues: "The Rav would never prevent his students from coming to visit him — his *chassidim* mean everything to him. I had a conversation with him and he asked me to come and see him [in Morocco]. The Rav told me, 'By tomorrow, we won't be here already.' The Rav wanted to continue the institutions he'd established. The subject upset him, and sometimes he'd cry over what was happening to the institutions he'd founded."

Once the decision was made to leave Morocco, Rabbi Berland and the small group of people accompanying him moved fast. They first took a plane from Morocco to Cairo, on the same day that the leaders of the G6 nations in Geneva continued to discuss well into the night what to do with Iran.

Egypt at that time (November 8, 2013) was hardly a

welcoming place for an obviously Jewish, elderly *chassidic* man. At the time of the Rav's flight from Morocco, Northern Africa was in turmoil, with civil war, political unrest and Muslim terrorist groups sprouting up in practically every corner[i]. A few short months before the Rav's detour via Egypt, the country had voted the radical Muslim Brotherhood into power and was now in the grip of what was threatening to become a nascent civil war, as the Egyptian army had overthrown the Muslim Brotherhood and seized control of the country.

As the Egyptian army continued its crackdown on the Muslim Brotherhood, Egypt continued to be a hotbed of terrorism, intrigue and unrest. And into this chaotic, anti-Semitic and violent atmosphere flew... Rabbi Berland.

When the passport clerk at Cairo Airport asked the Rav who he was, the Rav jokingly told the clerk that he was part of Al-Qaida. The Rav repeated this statement twice, and the Egyptian clerk smiled broadly and welcomed him into the country to await his connecting flight.

The Rav and his traveling companions, including Yaron Yamin, safely caught their connecting flight from Egypt to South Africa. At the passport control in South Africa, when the clerks saw him wrapped in his customary, striped Jewish prayer shawl and wearing his phylacteries on his head and arm, they came over to take a closer look. The Rav started singing a Jewish song — and the African clerks joined in.

The Rav arrived in Johannesburg in time for Shabbos, just as the political leaders in Geneva continued trying to iron out their agreement with Iran.

Just after that Shabbos, on November 9, 2013, the French

---

[i] The so-called 'Arab Spring' had begun in neighboring Tunisia in December 2010, and subsequently spread to many parts of North Africa and the Middle East, including Algeria, Morocco, Libya, Egypt and Syria.

President Francois Hollande stormed out of the meeting in Geneva and broke the injunction of silence that had been laid on all of the participants by revealing to the world what exactly had been going on behind closed doors. He disclosed that all the other countries, including the U.S., Russia, Britain, Germany and China, had already consented to sign the agreement that would give Iran unfettered access to developing a nuclear bomb.

If the agreement went through, Iran could have a nuclear weapon within two weeks.

At the last minute, shockingly, the French president balked at the idea of giving Iran carte blanche to become a nuclear power and pulled out of the talks, refusing to sign the agreement. As the talks disintegrated into bitter recriminations and a swift face-saving operation by the Obama administration, no one could understand why the French president had pulled out in such a dramatic fashion, at the very last minute.

A couple of weeks later, on November 24, 2013, a short-term pact was signed in Geneva with Iran which specified that the Iranians would freeze crucial parts of their nuclear program in exchange for a number of economic sanctions being lifted. In the meantime, all the parties involved committed themselves to ongoing talks to reach a longer-term agreement.

At least for the moment, the immediate danger seemed to have passed.

★　★　★

On December 13, 2013, the city of Jerusalem was hit by the heaviest snowstorm in more than 20 years. Much of the city, including the areas where many of Rabbi Berland's followers lived, was without electricity for three days and largely cut off from the outside world, as the country scrambled to deal with the severe weather.

From South Africa, the Rav gave a *Torah class* to the Shuvu Banim Yeshiva via a live hookup where he began by saying: "Everything will become white, white, and all the sins will be erased, as though it was Yom Kippur[i]." Israel's worst winter storm for decades happened at exactly the same time that the Israeli government started imprisoning *yeshiva* students who refused to enlist in the army, as well as others for protesting against the new draft laws.

The Israeli radio station Kol B'Rama reported that after the snowstorm, one of the Knesset members had calculated how much the storm had cost the Israeli economy, and found that it came out to exactly the same amount that the government had cut from the Torah world's budget and family allowance.

★   ★   ★

When Rabbi Berland first arrived in Johannesburg, Yaron Yamin escorted him to his home with full honors, and also arranged for the Rav to be flown around South Africa in his private jet. But the Rav's first visit to South Africa was very short. Already by December 2, 2013, the sixth day of Chanukah, the Rav had contacted some of his students at Shuvu Banim back in Israel and asked them to increase their prayers for his success. He told them that there was another city in Africa that he needed to travel to, located near the southern part of the Sahara desert.

There, the Rav explained, there would be enough place for everyone, and all of his followers and students could start to visit him again.

Shortly afterwards, Rabbi Berland took up residence in

---

[i] Referring to a verse in *Yeshayah* 18.

the city of Bulawayo, in Zimbabwe, where Yamin took it upon himself to ensure that the Rav's needs were completely taken care of. He arranged and paid for the Rav's lodgings in a luxury hotel in Bulawayo, organized a *mikveh* for him to use, and even took it upon himself to travel out to Israel and bring the Rav all of his holy books, so he could maintain his learning schedule. Yamin went to the Rav's home in Jerusalem and ordered a shipment including two and half tons of books.

But perhaps the biggest kindness that Yamin tried to do for Rabbi Berland at this point was attempting to clear his name. The wealthy businessman went to the media in Zimbabwe and Israel and gave two emotional interviews where he described the Rav's daily schedule, his non-stop service of God, and also tried to explain a little of who Rabbi Berland actually was:

"Do you know who the Rav really is?" Yamin asked the journalist from Israel. *"I'm going to try and explain and define him to you,"* Yaron tears up, *"and not as a 'religious' person."*

"There are a lot of Tzaddikim in the nation of Israel, all of whom learn Torah and keep mitzvos, etc. But the Rav is above all of them for one reason. He believes himself to be absolutely nothing. And this is the trait that these people [referring to the group of people who were libeling and persecuting the Rav] used for their own personal interests and gain.

It's known throughout all the generations — look at the seven shepherds[i] of Israel. All of them were in exile. All of them were imprisoned. All of them were at the center of controversy. There's no Tzaddik that didn't experience opposition, not even Rebbe Nachman."

Yamin then started to describe a little of the Rav's daily

---

[i] The Seven Shepherds are: Abraham, Isaac, Jacob, Joseph, Aaron, Moses and King David

schedule: *"The Rav seems to be living in two realities at once. In some ways, it's the best time of his life. He himself says that he prayed for this for the last ten years, to go and do his talking to God alone in the fields; to use the mikveh as much as he wants; to pray as much as he wants..."*

The interviewer interrupted at this point, to ask Yamin about reported plans to build Rabbi Berland a "dream house" in Zimbabwe.

"The Rav doesn't need a 'dream house' or anything like that!" replied Yamin. *"He's the epitome of modesty, as anyone who knows him can testify. He's happy to wear the same pair of shoes for years. You give him a plate of food and he just picks at it and eats two spoonfuls at most. He barely sleeps; one to two hours a night, no more. I've witnessed this with my own eyes!*

He dips in the mikveh 20 to 30 times a day. Prays for three to four hours. And when he's not praying, dunking or talking to God, he's in a Torah book — and not just one book, but many of them."

The interviewer interjected that, nevertheless, people had made some serious claims about the Rav...

Yamin was visibly upset at this point in the interview, and close to tears.

"Look, I've been with the Rav for 20 years, and the Rav is never by himself with a woman," he replied. *"He's never even so much as touched a woman's hand, okay."*

"The people who spread these stories and libels about the Rav, I want to ask the Israeli police one thing. Do you even have a single piece of real evidence? Do you have any recordings? Do you really have anything at all in your hands? Or do you just have someone who was trying to get out of being prosecuted for attempted murder, and who decided to bring his wife along in order to slander Rabbi Berland? Is that all you really have in your hands?

Then a few other unhappy, destructive individuals joined

in, people who are known to be emotionally disturbed, and that's all you have against him."

An impassioned Yamin continued:

"The Rav is not a criminal, the Rav is not a fugitive, and he's not running from place to place, as they describe it in the media. The Rav despised the way [certain people in the community] treated him, the way they controlled him... and certainly there is no need to mention what the media did — you read it every day.

There is no warrant for his arrest, nothing on Interpol, no reason to detain him at any border. I myself crossed four borders with the Rav, and as a successful business man I wouldn't dream of helping a criminal or fugitive from justice. Everything they are saying against the Rav, all the people involved in this, it's a group, a handful of people who are working against the Rav. There is absolutely no evidence."

In a separate interview, Yamin reiterated that Rabbi Berland could return to Israel of his own free will whenever he chose. There was no warrant for his arrest, no case against him, and he'd left the country as a completely free man — all indisputable facts that the media and the Israeli government had been hiding from the general public, keen as they were to perpetuate the myth that the Rav was a "fugitive from justice."

For now, Yamin's efforts to set the record straight appeared to be enough to get the media to leave Rabbi Berland and his followers in peace.

While Yamin and the Rav's assistants continued with their plans to build a residential complex and study hall for the Rav and his followers, including a number of guesthouses for the Rav's followers and anyone else who wanted to fly out to Zimbabwe to see him, the Rav himself was being housed in an unusual luxury hotel that was known as a hunting resort, located in the middle of the African jungle.

"We want that the Rav should be available to all of the Jewish people," concluded Yaron Yamin. "He doesn't belong to just his *chassidim*, or just his community, or to you or me. He's the Rabbi of the whole nation of Israel. Every person can go speak to the Rav, visit him, consult with him — he's the Rav of the Jewish people. He's the Tzaddik of the generation."

Yamin had arranged for the Rav to stay in a private villa on the grounds of the hotel that was located in the middle of the African jungle. From the safety of the hotel grounds, which was surrounded by an electrified fence and had a security team on duty 24/7, the guests could see every type of wild animal and creature pass by them, including monkeys, giraffes, zebras and elephants. The more dangerous animals could also be seen, including lions, tigers, crocodiles and hyenas.

The hotel guests could also hear the sounds of the wild animals very clearly from the hotel grounds, particularly at night. It was a beautiful sight to behold, but it was also very dangerous to get too close. While guests could order a special jeep to take them deeper into the forest, accompanied by armed rangers, no one, not even the native Zimbabweans, dared to venture into the forest without their jeeps and their weapons.

When Rabbi Berland arrived, he started leaving the hotel grounds to go and talk to God, alone and unarmed, in the African jungle. The hotel management was initially incredulous that someone would want to do something so apparently dangerous and didn't know what to say to him. Later on, they were even more amazed when the Rav repeatedly returned to the hotel after hours spent alone in the forest, completely unharmed.

On another occasion, Rabbi Berland was walking in the jungle in Zimbabwe amongst a pride of lions, when suddenly a jeep appeared with five soldiers in it, who started screaming at him: "Where did you go?! Where are you going?! These lions killed a buffalo here just two days ago — you can see how they preyed on it!"

When the Rav told them that he was doing some *hisbodedus*, talking to God, in the forest they were stunned. "So, you're not coming back with us?" they asked him. Rabbi Berland responded: "No! You can go on without me...'"

Every day, the Rav would ask the guards by the hotel gates to open them, to enable him to go and pray alone in the jungle. And every day, they would spend quite a lot of time trying to dissuade him, sometimes even bringing his family members along to try to talk him out of it. "At least stay close to the hotel!" they tried to persuade him, but Rabbi Berland ignored them and headed out deep into the jungle until the guards couldn't see him anymore.

Then, after three or four hours of talking to God, he'd return as though nothing unusual had happened. The Rav explained to the hotel staff that he'd waited 77 years for the opportunity to pray in a place like this, a forest like this, in the same way that King David had done, many centuries earlier. Once the security guards saw this miracle for a few days in a row, they developed a profound respect for the Rav and where overheard telling each other, "This is not a human being, this is an angel!"

Once, the Rav invited one of his followers to join him in his "jungle *hisbodedus*," but the man demurred. He'd been out into the jungle already in an armored jeep, and what he'd seen then had been frightening enough. He told Rabbi Berland that he was scared to join him, because he didn't have the same Heavenly protection that the Rav was obviously enjoying. The Rav replied simply, "But you're with me!"

So then the student agreed to come, but as they reached the gates and all the sounds of the jungle filled their ears, he had a change of heart and decided he just couldn't accompany the Rav after all.

On a different morning, Rabbi Berland asked his student to come and dip with him in the stream that was near the hotel, which the Rav was using as a natural *mikveh*. Again, the student demurred, because he was scared of being attacked by crocodiles. The Rav told him: "You have nothing to fear." The Rav went over to the stream, immersed, and then returned — while the amazed student looked on, because he'd just seen a hippo emerge from the stream a few seconds after the Rav had exited. In Africa, it's well known that hippos kill more human beings than any other animals.

When the kabbalist Rav David Chaim Stern heard from one of the *yeshiva* students how Rabbi Berland had been praying alone for hours in the African jungle, in places where no other person would come without an armored jeep and a gun, Rav Stern said, "It's because of his incredible holiness!

The animals don't have permission to harm him — not the animals, and also not the human beings!"

Throughout his stay in Zimbabwe, Rabbi Berland spoke a great deal about King David, and how he'd continued to sing to God despite being chased and in danger of losing his life. "The more they chased King David, the more he sang," he remarked. "A person needs a lot of merit to see the song that's contained in everything, in all of creation. That was the strength of King David, who turned everything he experienced into the songs contained in the Book of Psalms, and that will also be the strength of Moshiach, too."

★   ★   ★

Very soon after Rabbi Berland moved to Zimbabwe, his followers from Israel started flying out to visit him again. If Morocco was like a different world for an Israeli *chassid*, then Zimbabwe was a completely different planet.

One of the Rav's followers flew out to visit the Rav in Zimbabwe, but ran out of money halfway through the trip... He didn't even have enough money to hail a taxi once he arrived at the airport in Zimbabwe to take him to where the Rav was staying. He also hadn't told anyone he was coming, so there was no one who knew about his visit and no one who could help him.

This follower decided to take a cab to the Rav's hotel anyway, hoping that someone at the hotel where the Rav was staying would help him pay for it once he got there. As the cab drove up to the gates, the Rav came out with a $100 bill in his hand and gave it straight to the taxi driver, without saying a word – even though the follower hadn't been in touch with the Rav at all, beforehand.

Rabbi Berland then asked the taxi driver to take the newly-arrived follower, together with one of the Rav's grandsons, to a different, specific hotel, where they could check in and leave their suitcases, before immediately bringing them back to the hotel where the Rav was staying. In the meantime, the follower didn't have a suitcase with him — only an item of hand luggage — but he knew better than to question the Rav's instructions, so he settled in for the drive.

This second hotel was located quite a few kilometers away, and throughout the drive they passed a number of other hotels that were much closer to where Rabbi Beralnd was staying. They simply couldn't understand why the Rav had told the taxi driver to take them to a place that was so far away, to drop off the luggage they didn't even really have. But as soon as they arrived, the mystery was solved — because they found two other students from the *yeshiva* in the hotel, who were as shocked to see them as they were.

None of these other students had told anyone else about their travel plans, yet the Rav had still known they were coming. One of the *yeshiva* students explained that they'd landed in Zimbabwe and headed straight over to the Rav's hotel. However, they been unable to find him, so they'd continued on to their own lodgings — the cheapest hotel they could find, which they'd booked ahead of their trip. It was only when they got there that they realized that instead of the hotel they thought they were coming to, they'd actually ended up at a seedy, bad-smelling B&B that was full of dangerous-looking locals.

The heat in Zimbabwe was unbelievable, and their hotel didn't even have a single air-conditioning unit. The *yeshiva* students were actually feeling a little down about their situation. As they sat in the hotel lobby feeling depressed about the way things had turned out, all of a sudden they spotted these two other followers of the Rav — who had apparently been sent expressly to them, via taxi, by the Rav himself! Not in a million years did they think that other religious Jews would ever show up in that place, let alone people they actually knew from the *yeshiva*.

Rabbi Berland had once remarked when he was in Morocco: "At the very same instant that someone thinks about me, I'm also thinking of them" — and this experience seemed to bear that out.

When the taxi brought the first two students back to Rabbi Berland, the taxi driver told the Rav that after everything he'd just witnessed, he didn't want to take the Rav's money, and he tried to give it back. "You're a big saint!" he told the Rav. "I don't want to take your money." Then, he got out of the car, gave the Rav a big hug, asked the Rav to give him a blessing, and snapped a selfie of himself standing next to the Rav.

Rabbi Berland gave the taxi driver a blessing, and then asked him to start keeping Shabbos. By this point, the students were truly shocked, as it hadn't crossed their mind that their driver could be Jewish. He certainly didn't look Jewish, and nothing in his conversation or behavior had suggested the possibility, yet the Rav seemed to know otherwise.

Before his exile, the Rav had once explained that the Ten Tribes had originally been dispersed and "lost" on the African continent, and that many of the locals in the places where he was staying in Africa had a "spark" of Jewishness in them, retained throughout all the years, because the people had continued to only marry each other.

(Three hundred years earlier, another Jewish tzaddik called the Ohr HaChaim had also passed through the same part of Africa, and attested that he'd also discovered remnants of the Ten Tribes there.) Rabbi Berland continued that you could see which of these people truly had a Jewish soul by the way they honored the Jews.

Having reassured his distant students that he knew about them, even in their dumpy hotel that was miles away, he now told the other two students that they could stay with him in his hotel, and arranged lodgings for both of them.

On another occasion, a group of zebras came right up to the electrified fence where the Rav and one of his students were praying the morning service. The Rav jokingly commented that they'd come to make up the 10 men required for a *minyan*, and were already wearing their prayer shawls (the black and white stripes resembled the Jewish prayer shawl, called a *tallis*). As soon as the prayers were over, the zebras disappeared back into the forest.

The student laughed, but the next day the same thing occurred again, and continued to happen each of the subsequent days that this student was with the Rav. Rabbi Berland would take him down to the field to pray the morning prayers and each morning as they were beginning, eight zebras would appear and stay there for the duration of the prayers, before quickly dispersing. The student noticed that each time, exactly eight zebras appeared.

Rabbi Isaac Luria Ashkenazi, (also known as the Arizal) founded the modern Kabbalistic tradition 450 years ago. The Arizal wrote that sometimes, souls are reincarnated into animals, and that these animals then seek out a *tzaddik* to help them achieve their spiritual rectification. This didn't just occur with evil people; sometimes, even *tzaddikim* themselves would petition for permission to return in animal form, in order to achieve some minute rectification that they hadn't managed to complete previously[i].

★　★　★

Rabbi Berland was thrilled with his new lodgings, and he told some of his followers: "What a miracle, that they threw us out of Morocco and that we came to a place like this!" He then quoted a saying from Rebbe Nachman, to the effect that while many people say that the old days were better, he believed that God was actually running the world in a better way each day.

Later, he explained that the Talmudic dictum that "a Jew who lives outside of Israel, it's as though they don't have a God" only applied when someone chose not to live in the land of Israel. But when they had to leave Israel against their will, then, the Rav explained, "The opposite is true. Every place he goes, it's Israel; every place he goes, it's Jerusalem. Here, it's Israel! Here it's Jerusalem!"

That's not to say that the Rav wasn't yearning to return to Israel proper. At around this time, Rabbi Berland asked his

---

[i] There is a famous story from modern times about how the Klausenberger Rebbe in Boro Park told a cat who was sitting under the table during one of his lectures that he could leave, since he'd now received his rectification. Immediately, the cat left the room.

followers back in Jerusalem to start arranging a number of big public prayer rallies at the Kotel, the remnant of the Temple's Western supportive wall in the Old City of Jerusalem.

The first rally was held on February 12, 2014, and Rabbi Berland hoped that these prayer gatherings would achieve a number of big spiritual aims, including saving Israel from its enemies, as well as giving the Rav himself the spiritual merit he needed in order to return to the Holy Land. Rabbi Berland was still very concerned about the Iranian plans to drop a nuclear bomb on Israel, and he returned to this theme on many occasions during his stay in Zimbabwe, but particularly over the Purim festival of 2014.

On one occasion, he sent his students a recorded message that said: *"Just as God enabled Mordechai to triumph over Haman, so He's also going to help us to triumph over all our 'Hamans' too, and all the enemies of Israel, like Al-Qaida and Hamas. And with that help from God, we're going to be able to save Am Yisrael from all of the terrible harsh decrees, including their desire to drop a nuclear bomb on us next month [April 2014]."*

He continued: *"They already have everything they need to do that; all the necessary raw material and components. That's why we're holding a huge prayer gathering now, in order to cancel their plans to drop a nuclear bomb on Israel. In the merit of that gathering, even if they actually try to drop their bomb on Israel, it will all just turn into candies [i.e., be 'sweetened,' spiritually.]*

"Everyone should come to the prayer gathering at the Kotel, to cancel the terrible decrees that are being passed on the yeshiva students. They want to put every yeshiva student in the army! They want to try to extinguish the fire of Torah and teshuva! But it's only going to continue to grow from moment to moment. They're promoting the lowest types of people and behavior, and they want the lowest people to rule the Jewish

people… Instead of building more yeshivas, they want to build more prisons, so that there'll be more work for the policemen, the judges, the lawyer, and the prison guards.

"But instead of spending a billion dollars on building more prisons, better to spend a million dollars building a new yeshiva [so that people's characters will be refined, and they won't be sent to prison in the first place]. The prayer gathering will nullify all the decrees hanging over the whole of Israel."

As the day for the prayer gathering rolled around, on March 13, 2014, Israel was hit with a fierce rainstorm. One of the organizers recalls: "Despite the fact that there were a lot of students with the Rav in Zimbabwe for Purim and the weather was so awful, when I got down to the Kotel I was amazed to see it was still packed with people. People had come from the City of Eilat, from Nahariya, and from all over the country to sing and dance together and to hear some words of Torah from the Rav."

All told, between 300 to 500 people showed up, despite the very inclement weather, to pray, sing and dance together. The organizers were a little disappointed by the turnout, but when they contacted the Rav later on to tell him how it had gone, he reassured them that every single person who's come had been equivalent to 10,000 people, because of the amount of self-sacrifice that had been required to brave the terrible weather.

"Afterwards, the Rav told us that the gathering had helped matters a great deal, and that if we would continue to do something similar every week, he believed he could be back with us in Israel before Passover 2014," recalls the organizer.

While that didn't happen, some of the prayer rally's effects were felt much sooner. That same night, terrorists in Gaza fired four rockets at Israel — and every single one of them miraculously landed in an open area, where they detonated harmlessly.

★   ★   ★

Rabbi Berland and his followers spent the Jewish holiday of Purim in the city of Bulawayo, one of only two cities in Zimbabwe that still has anything resembling a fixed Jewish community. In the whole of Zimbabwe, there is now less than 150 people officially registered as belonging to the Jewish community, and less than half of them live in Bulawayo.

Which is why it was so strange that when the Rav's followers got to the city of Bulawayo, they discovered an enormous new synagogue and events hall that was filled with Jewish books, but virtually empty of Jews.

When he saw Bulawayo's magnificent synagogue, Rabbi Berland said: "This place has been waiting for Shuvu Banim to come and spend Purim here since the sixth day of creation!" And it really did seem that way, as the Rav's followers found themselves staying in the synagogue hall connected to the enormous new synagogue that had recently been built by the remnants of Bulawayo's tiny Jewish community.

The head of the Bulawayo community invited Rabbi Berland to come and stay with him at his house, which was less than a 10-minute walk from the synagogue, while the men bedded down in the adjacent hall on mattresses, and the women and children found rooms to rent in a hotel that was close by.

In one of his lesson given during Purim 5774, (March 16th, 2014), the Rav said the following:

"Why have we still not managed to rebuild the Temple? Because if we built it now, it would just immediately burn down again. At the very moment that a person came to the Temple thinking bad thoughts, it would burn down. People

don't know that their bad thoughts are like the fire of purgatory. Every time you look at things that you shouldn't — that's the fire of purgatory. A person can burn down the Temple literally every second.

... In another month, they [the Iranians] want to drop a nuclear bomb on us. We'll have exactly five minutes [from the time they press the button] because it will have to travel 1,500 kilometers to get to us, and their rockets cover a distance of five kilometers every second. Three hundred seconds is five minutes. So assuming the warning siren goes off immediately, there'll be just enough time to say the Tikkun HaKlali, or at least some of it.

Just reciting a single Tikkun HaKlali has the power to explode every nuclear bomb in the world, and to change everything into candies. [Meaning, to 'sweeten' everything.]

At every moment, we are facing terrible decrees, like the decree to forcibly enlist yeshiva students. Every day, we hear of more problems, and all this is only happening because of evil thoughts and evil fantasies. That's the reason it's happening! Rebbe Nachman taught that the first priority has to be rectifying the covenant, and that's the main focus of Breslov and the main focus of Shuvu Banim — to have holy, pure thoughts."

As more of Rabbi Berland's followers flocked to Bulaweyo, to share their milestones and marriages with them, one of the leaders of the Zimbabwe Jewish community in Bulawayo told him there had probably never been such a big gathering of Jews in a Zimbabwe synagogue. "Now that you've come here with your *chassidim*, you've really livened the place up," he said.

The Jews of Bulawayo weren't the only locals who celebrated Purim with the Rav. Two Jews from Harare, the capital city of Zimbabwe, drove seven hours to visit Rabbi Berland, once they heard he was in their country. One of the Harare Jews brought his small, black-skinned child to greet the Rav. The Rav paid this child particular attention and bent down to speak to him. He told the father a few times that the child had the eyes of a Torah genius. This father and son were with the Rav for four days.

After Purim, these two Jews returned to their homes, taking along with them two students from the *yeshiva*, as they had a return flight to catch from the airport in Harare at 9:15 p.m.

By 7 p.m., they were still three hours from the airport, so the students called the airport officials and asked if they could hold the flight for them. They were told no, and that check-in was going to close at 8 p.m. The driver told them that there was no way they could make their flight, and then, just to cap things off, it also started to rain really, really hard.

But the two students reassured their driver that in the power of the Tzaddik, they would see miracles. They started to sing a Jewish melody and to say the *Tikkun HaKlali*, and they reassured the driver that in the merit of the Rav, they'd have a miracle.

While the driver was very impressed with the students' optimism and faith, he still didn't think they had any chance of making the flight. In fact, he told them that if they managed to make their flight, he'd start keeping kosher. As the words left the driver's mouth, the rain cleared up, and somehow they managed to reach the airport in Harare at 9 p.m., a quarter of an hour before the plane took off.

The staff at check-in initially told them they'd have to leave their bags behind and just run to catch the plane, but in the end they were allowed to take their bags with them, too. As they were running through the gate, they heard the Jewish driver who'd brought them muttering to himself, "Why did I promise to keep kosher? You can't even find any kosher food in Zimbabwe!"

The plane took off as soon as they boarded.

★ ★ ★

After Purim, Rabbi Berland spent many hours talking to and meeting with his followers. Anyone could come in and talk to the Rav for as long as they needed. One of the Rav's followers asked him, "What can I do to help the Rav?" and the Rav replied, "Pray for me each day that I'll come back to Israel!"

The Rav also said that anyone who took it upon himself to recite the *Tikkun HaKlali* three times a day for the Rav's success, the Rav would be indebted to him.

In the meantime, Yaron Yamin announced that anyone who wanted to stay in Africa for Passover was invited to remain in Zimbabwe, instead of having to fly back to Israel. Sixty people, including a few families, decided to stay with the Rav. Rabbi Berland told the students that they could only stay if they sat and learned Torah full-time.

A couple of days later, Rabbi Berland returned to Yamin's home, close to his diamond mine, while all the students stayed in Bulawayo. There, they opened their own synagogue and *kollel*, in fulfillment of the Rav's prediction that Shuvu Banim would open a *yeshiva* in Southern Africa.

As word of the *"Garden of Eden"* in Africa filtered back to Israel, more and more of the Rav's students and followers - including people who'd never met him before - started to make the trip out to Zimbabwe. But good as things were, the big question on everyone's mind in Zimbabwe was still: "When is Rabbi Berland returning to Israel?" One of his followers actually came out and asked the Rav himself this question. The Rav responded, "In the merit of the prayer gatherings that you're holding for me by the Kotel, God willing, I'll be back by Passover." But no-one knew which Passover the Rav was really referring to.

★   ★   ★

In the meantime, the signs that the redemption of the Jewish people appeared to be imminent continued to multiply during 2014. One such clue was the recent statement made by Rabbi Moshe Sternbuch when he said, "When you hear that the Russians are subduing the city of Krim [the Crimea], then you'll know that the redemption has begun. And here we see that last week, the Russians subdued the Crimea, and the whole world is now in an uproar over this. But according to the tradition that we have from the Vilna Gaon, this is a sign of the time of Moshiach."

Rabbi Sternbuch was referring to the conflict between Russia and the Ukraine, which had begun on February 20, 2014, when pro-Russian separatists sparked a wave of violence in the Ukrainian capital, Kiev, leading to the deaths of about 90 people.

The separatists were demanding autonomy for the eastern region of the Ukraine known as the Crimea, which they wanted to see returned to Russian rule. Russian President Vladimir Putin quickly threw thousands of Russian troops into the conflict, invaded the Ukraine, and caused tensions in the area to shoot through the roof.

Also around this time, the neighboring country of Turkey warned Russia that unless it scaled back its military activity in the region, Turkey would close the Bosphorus Strait to Russian ships and commercial activities, severely limiting Russia's access to Middle Eastern oil, and the Middle East in general. The Ukrainian conflict finally petered out toward the end of 2015, temporarily easing tensions in the area[i].

Another "clue" occurred on March 2, 2014, when more than 600,000 Jews gathered just at the outskirts of the city

---

[i] As of November 2016, the situation in the Crimea was very unstable, and tensions in that region are rising once again.

in a place called Sha'arei Yerushalayim, or the "Gates of Jerusalem," to pray for the Torah world in Israel, and to protest the government's plans to force *yeshiva* students to serve in the IDF.

A few months before this gathering took place, students of Rabbi Dov Kook of Tiberius had put together a booklet that contained more of what the Vilna Gaon wrote about the coming of Moshiach in a book called the *Kol HaTor.*

"Rabbi Binyamin of Shklov asked our master the Vilna Gaon what he could do to try to hasten the coming of Moshiach ben David and the redemption of the Jewish people. The Vilna Gaon answered his student: "If you can gather together 600,000 Jews in a place called the 'Gates of Jerusalem,' whenever you're able to do that, a gathering of 600,000 Jews can completely cancel out the power of the dark side that rules at the Gates of Jerusalem — and then, you'll merit the complete redemption."

When the Vilna Gaon first wrote those words more than 200 years ago, no such place called the "Gates of Jerusalem" even existed, and barely a handful of Jews lived in the holy city, as economic conditions in the Holy Land were very difficult under the Ottoman Turks.

Similarly, when the students of Rabbi Kook wrote this information in their booklet, before Rosh Hashanah 2013, no plans for a huge gathering had even been considered. It seemed to be another clear-cut sign that the redemption was imminent.

THE ZIMBABWEAN IDYLL ENDS

"Fanning every piece of graffiti or vulgarity by who-knows-who, in who-knows-what venue, into a "fundamentalist, haredi bonfire" that will soon consume us all has long been the bread and butter of Reform fundraising.

Eric Simon describes a 1996 address by Uri Regev, the newly appointed head of the worldwide Reform movement, to American Reform lay leaders: "[Regev] convinced me that the Chief Rabbi of Israel had called for the murder of Reform Jews, and that there were daily death threats and violence by Orthodox yeshiva students against Reform institutions in Israel. . . . [The speech] left me -- a peace-loving, liberal-minded child of the '60s -- ready to attack the first Orthodox Jew I met."

– Jonathan Rosenbloom writing in
the Jerusalem Post, June 2002[i]

Shortly before Passover, 2014, hundreds of Rabbi Berland's followers started arriving in Zimbabwe en masse, to start getting ready for the holiday. Once again, the Rav's enemies saw that their tremendous efforts to tear the Rav away from his followers hadn't worked, so

---

[i] *Reforms Deafening Silence*, by Jonathan Rosenblum Jerusalem Post June 14, 2002 - http://www.jewishmediaresources.com/481/reforms-deafening-silence

they decided to change tack, and to bribe some corrupt bureaucrats to do their dirty work for them.

On April 7, 2014 – the same day that the world's leaders were meeting in Vienna again, to try to come to some agreement about Iran - the Zimbabwean police came to arrest the Rav in Bulawayo. They told the Rav that he was being placed under arrest because his visa had expired (even though it hadn't). They then forced the Rav to wear a prisoner's uniform, and publicly handcuffed him.

When Rabbi Berland heard that the police had come to arrest him, he recited a blessing, thanking God for bringing him to this new situation. From the moment the Rav was arrested, he continuously held a bottle of water in his hands, even while wearing handcuffs. As the Rav never asks for something to eat or drink, and usually eats only a little, and takes very few sips of liquid, this struck many of those who knew him personally as strange.

So why was the Rav going to such great trouble to take a bottle of water with him? Afterwards, it became known that the Rav had been concerned about not being able to ritually wash his hands before every prayer, as is required by Jewish law. The Rav didn't know where he would be taken after his arrest, or for how long he would be there, so he wanted to make sure that he would have enough water available to wash his hands.

The Rav spent many hours being interrogated in prison, and then went to court on April 8, where he was given the choice of paying a fine and being expelled from the country, or going to prison.

Rabbi Berland's persecutors had left no stone unturned to maximize his public humiliation. They arranged in advance that the Rav would be forced to dress in prisoner's clothing for 10 minutes, and that someone would remove the *kippah* from his head. The photographer would be on-site, ready to take the picture as soon as they'd stage-managed the 'special' image they were after.

In the past, many people had returned to religious observance just from seeing Rabbi Berland's picture, so his persecutors figured they'd give the world an image of the Rav they'd never forget. But instead of turning people off, the picture of the Rav being so profoundly humiliated actually had a boomerang effect. Suddenly, it became clear to many people what sort of people had been chasing the Rav all over the world, ceaselessly harassing and maligning him, while the Rav accepted everything that happened to him with love.

More and more people starting to question why Rabbi Berland was being treated in such an unnecessarily extreme and disgraceful way.

As the press went all out to make the Rav a household name, both in Israel and abroad, for all the wrong reasons, a lot of people who'd never even heard of him before started trying to find out more about him. Who was this Rabbi Berland, who was at the heart of so much controversy? What was he doing in Africa in the first place? Why had he been arrested in such a public, shameful way, if the only complaint the Zimbabweans could come up with was that his visa had expired?

At this time, one of the Rav's students, Rabbi Chaim Ness, was spending a lot of time in Tel Aviv working with more secular people, trying to bring them closer to Jewish observance. He recounts that people started approaching him and asking for more details about what was happening with Rabbi Berland. To keep up with the demand, Rabbi Ness started organizing gatherings in Tel Aviv that attracted hundreds of participants.

As a result of these gatherings, many formerly secular Jews began keeping more Jewish observances — and the people who get the credit for that are, ironically, the Rav's persecutors.

One man wrote into the Shuvu Banim *Yeshiva* to say: "I'm not a Breslover *Chassid*, and until today I didn't even have an opinion about everything surrounding Rabbi Berland. But after I saw that picture [of the Rav handcuffed in Zimbabwe], I began to understand that the Rav really is suffering for us. 'He takes our sickness upon himself'[i]."

At the same time, many of the Rabbis who had been staying silent about the matter started to comment on what was going on, and to publicly come out in support of the Rav. A number of religious leaders who'd been sitting on the fence, or who were even considered to be against Rabbi Berland, completely changed track after they saw that picture. Some even went as far as to call the Rav up directly to offer their support, and to ask forgiveness for the earlier doubts they'd harbored against him.

★ ★ ★

On April 9, the Rav left Zimbabwe to fly to South Africa. When he landed at the airport in Johannesburg, the South African police detained him for a couple of long hours while they checked his legal status in Israel.

While all this was going on, another mass prayer rally for the Rav's success was being held at the Kotel. Throughout the prayer rally, the Rav's followers were in close contact with some of the people who were traveling with the Rav, and miraculously, the moment they finished saying the last words of the prayer service at the Kotel, the Rav was given permission to stay in Johannesburg.

At exactly the same time that all this was going on, the meeting between the world leaders in Vienna ended without any agreement being reached about the Iranians.

Throughout his ordeal at the hands of the Zimbabwean

[i] A quote from *Isaiah 53:4*.

authorities, Rabbi Berland maintained his composure and *emunah*, and the people who were accompanying him even reported that he seemed to almost be in a state of rapture, as though he was engaged in the biggest *mitzvah* of his life. His happiness was contagious, and when he was released from prison in Zimbabwe and allowed to fly out to South Africa, the Rav left the country like a king, wearing his prayer shawl and phylacteries.

The picture of the Rav in handcuffs appeared on news sites around the world on April 10, 2014, exactly 30 days after he'd first spoken about the Iranians' plan to drop a nuclear bomb on Israel the next month. Everyone with a Jewish heart was completely shocked when they saw that terrible picture. Some people literally tore their clothes, (a traditional custom of Jewish mourners), while others sat on the floor and just cried their eyes out. That image landed like a bombshell in the heart of the orthodox Jewish world — but the humiliating media blitz seemed to have taken the place of the Iranians' nuclear bomb.

One of the students who'd been with the Rav in Johannesburg related what the Rav had said to his daughter just after that picture was publicized. Rabbi Berland had said to her, "When I was handcuffed and dressed in the prison clothes, I felt as though I was holding the nuclear bomb in my hands."

The Rav himself later commented about his two-day incarceration in Zimbabwe: "How good it was for me over there [in Zimbabwe]! I sat on the floor with the local criminals, and the whole time I sang and thanked God and I reached [spiritual] levels that I otherwise would never have reached in a million years!"

At around the same time that the shameful picture of Rabbi Berland in Zimbabwe hit the news, many Rabbis in Israel were sent a fake newsletter that had been deliberately designed as an exact copy of Shuvu Banim's own Knishta Chada newsletter, with the exact same name, logo and design. This phony newsletter was filled with lies and slanderous stories about the Rav, and also included entirely falsified quotes from a number of leading Rabbis.

As the outrage mounted, more and more people who saw this forged newsletter began to seriously question the integrity of the people who had been persecuting the Rav within the Breslov community itself. Many of the Rabbis who'd been falsely quoted contacted Shuvu Banim to set the record straight, and once again, the trap these Breslov zealots had set for Rabbi Berland rebounded on themselves. A number of the rabbis who contacted Shuvu Banim explained that now, they were starting to understand the moral caliber of some of the people who'd been persecuting the Rav — and also the greatness of the Rav, who'd borne all the abuse and affliction in silence, for decades.

When Rav Eliyahu Ifargan, the founder of Mosdot Keter Shalom, was told that the Rav had been arrested, publicly handcuffed, put in prison and then expelled from Zimbabwe, he sat down on the floor in middle of his Torah class.

Rav Ifargan then told his students: "Rabbi Eliezer Berland took upon himself exile and humiliation before Passover, just like Rebbe Eliezer HaGadol[i]"

Rabbi Ifargan continued that according to the esoteric sources, when a Tzaddik takes such harsh judgments upon himself, it's only because of the sins of the Jewish people, and that not every *tzaddik* could stand up to such a harsh test.

"This big *tzaddik*, who is the soul of Rebbe Eliezer HaGadol and a spark of Moshiach himself, is rolling around in the dirt because he chose to do this."

---

[i] Rebbe Eliezer HaGadol was the most senior Rabbi of his generation, and lived around 2,000 years ago.

Rabbi Ifargan concluded that he had a tradition passed down from his forefathers that "in these days" [i.e., the period of time before Moshiach], the evil side would continue to grow stronger, and would appear to get more powerful from one day to the next. "Therefore," he said, "anyone who shares… in the sorrow of the Tzaddik in this very hard time, will help to ease the Tzaddik's sorrow, and give him more power to bring the redemption."

While the Zimbabwe authorities' main target was Rabbi Berland himself, they also revoked the visas of the students who'd been staying with him in Zimbabwe since Purim. While his followers had been prepared for the Passover holiday in Zimbabwe, they were singularly unprepared for a last-minute forced exile to a different country, literally a day or two before the festival was due to begin.

Although a few of the Rav's students and his main attendants flew out with him to Johannesburg by plane, many of the other students, together with their families, were forced to arrange buses to take them across the border into South Africa. The authorities in Zimbabwe threw them out of the country so quickly, they didn't even give them time to collect the 600 kilograms of matzos they'd arranged for the holiday, plus their other Passover provisions.

In a scene reminiscent of the original Exodus, Rabbi Berland's students hurriedly rented four buses and left for the long journey to South Africa. One of the buses got stuck on the way, and its passengers were delayed in the hot African weather for around 24 hours, with almost no food or drinks to sustain them because they'd been given no time to prepare food or other provisions.

The whole time the bus was stalled by the side of the road in Zimbabwe, the Rav was also "stalled" at the airport in Johannesburg as the South African authorities interrogated him, deciding whether to send him back to Israel or let him into the country.

Some of the students on the bus managed to get through to the Rav on the phone and explained the severity of their situation, that they were stuck in the middle of nowhere, with no food or drink, and with women and small children on board. Rabbi Berland reassured his students and told them to dance for an hour, and then everything would turn out okay. After the students had danced for a few minutes, some locals arrived bearing bananas and drinks, and an hour later, a replacement bus turned up to take them on the last leg of their journey.

Meanwhile, back in the Johannesburg airport, the Rav sat there serenely. As was his custom wherever his wanderings took him and whatever difficulties he encountered, he continued his routine of praying, learning Torah, dancing and singing while the South African officials checked and double-checked his legal status.

A short while later, Rabbi Berland was granted permission to enter South Africa.

When the Zimbabwe authorities came to arrest Rabbi Berland at Yaron Yamin's home in Bulawayo, the wealthy businessman had told them, "Beware of this holy man! If he gets deported from here all the rain will stop! Just look at the months he was here, what tremendous blessing the country received. Nearly every day, you had strong rainstorms which are much needed for the economy. Tell Mugabe[i] that if the Rabbi gets deported there will be no more rain!"

The Zimbabweans ignored the warning and proceeded to publicly dress Rabbi Berland in prison clothes and handcuff him, before arranging for him to be photographed, and then carted off to the local prison for two days. Then, they deported him and his followers to Johannesburg three days before the Passover festival began.

Very soon after that, the rain in Zimbabwe stopped. By the beginning of 2016, the *New York Times* was calling the El Nino drought in Zimbabwe "the worst drought in more than a generation." As the rain dried up, so too did the crops and the exports which supported the entire Zimbabwean economy. The U.N. World Food Program announced that 1.5 million Zimbabweans needed urgent food aid, as a result of the famine.

Shortly after this on the 28th of January, 2016, the niece of Zimbabwe President Robert Mugabe traveled to South Africa to meet Rabbi Berland and ask his forgiveness, in the name of her uncle and all the Zimbabwean people.

---

[i] The president of Zimbabwe.

South Africa: Part I

"In a most unaccustomed manner, the Jo'burg Shtetl area of Glenhazel became a tourist hotspot as Jews and gentiles alike poured in to photograph... tourists! The 2,000-plus colourful tourists who seemed to have descended out of nowhere were easy to spot – they all dressed the same. They were Breslov Hareidim."
– South African Jewish Report, April 24th, 2014[i]

"We wish to notify Rabbanim to be aware of the situation so that our community not be involved with sheltering or supporting Berland and his followers. Please notify any members of your congregation who you feel may be drawn into supporting or sheltering Berland and his followers."
– Letter sent out by South African Jewish Communal leaders, April 11, 2014

★ ★ ★

The Israeli authorities never issued an arrest warrant, or even officially opened a case against Rabbi Berland until shortly before he returned to the country, on July 18, 2016. While the story being spun by the Rav's persecutors — and eagerly embellished by the unethical media — was

---

[i] https://www.sajr.co.za/news-and-articles/2014/04/23/confusion-silence-reign-over-rabbi-flock

that Rabbi Berland was "escaping from justice," the truth is that Rabbi Berland left Israel a free man, came to Morocco as a free man, and entered Zimbabwe, and then South Africa as a free man, traveling on his own Israeli passport.

If any of the journalists who were covering the story had taken a moment to dig even just a little bit deeper into the "facts" of the story they were telling about Rabbi Berland, they'd have noticed a number of things that simply didn't add up.

Firstly, people "on the run" don't tell hundreds of students where they can come and visit them within a few days of arriving in a new location. They don't travel around with hundreds of people, including men, women and children. They don't try to start yeshivas, houses of learning and even kindergartens in their international "hideouts." Wherever the Rav went, there too went his followers — hundreds and sometimes even thousands of them.

While the media rushed to portray Rabbi Berland as a "fugitive from justice," the truth is that the Israeli government never had a case against him, or any evidence other than the claims of some very suspect individuals.

As Yaron Yamin said in one of the interviews he gave to the media: *There is no warrant for his arrest, nothing on Interpol, no reason to detain him at any border. I myself crossed four borders with the Rav, and as a successful businessman I wouldn't dream of helping a criminal or fugitive from justice. Everything they are saying against the Rav, all the people involved in this, it's a group, a handful of people who are working against the Rav. There is absolutely no evidence.*

Yet despite this, from the moment Rabbi Berland set foot in South Africa, the persecution against him intensified, and even spilled over into physical violence.

Who were the people chasing Rabbi Berland in South Africa, if the country's authorities were willing to let him in not just once, but twice? In this chapter, we'll try to answer that question, and we'll also reveal a little more of how the Rav's persecutors worked hand in hand with the media to portray an image of him that was completely disconnected from the truth.

Long before he arrived there, the Rav's persecutors back in Israel had a strong suspicion that Rabbi Berland would cross the border into South Africa after being deported from Zimbabwe.

They decided to get a head start on making the Rav's life in South Africa as difficult as possible by unleashing the "character assassination by media" that had already worked so well in Israel and Morocco. Before he even set foot in the country, the persecutors had "primed" the Johannesburg Jewish community that Rabbi Berland was a "fugitive" and a "wanted criminal" — claims that were patently untrue, as no case had ever been filed against the Rav in Israel.

The Rav's persecutors also went to great pains to try to influence the local Rabbis to shun the Rav and his community, going as far as writing each Rabbi in the community a personal letter, and taking out advertisements in the local paper which contained a number of the false accusations they were making against the Rav. They encouraged the Jewish community to shun this "dangerous fugitive" and his followers, and not to even give them the time of day.

All this was taking place just a day or two before the Passover holiday was due to begin on April 14, 2014.

Before any of Rabbi Berland's followers even arrived in South Africa, one of the country's leading Rabbis issued a letter on April 11, 2014 to all the local Rabbis, which they asked should be distributed among all the Jewish communities in South Africa.

In that letter, this Rabbi warned the Jews of South Africa that a group of *chassidim* were about to arrive in the country, and that it was forbidden to shelter them or help them in any way. The text read as followed:

"We wish to notify Rabbanim to be aware of the situation so that our community not be involved with sheltering or supporting Berland and his followers. Please notify any members of your congregation who you feel may be drawn into supporting or sheltering Berland and his followers."

Most of South African Jewry obediently followed the dictates of this letter, and brought enormous pressure to bear on anyone who opened their doors to the Rav's students. Even those students who had made arrangements to stay with friends and even family members in South Africa discovered that their invitations had been withdrawn, as a result of the communal pressure that had been brought to bear on their hosts.

Things got so intense, that protesters against the Rav and his community even took to the streets in South Africa - and all this occurred long before the Rav or his students had even entered the country.

But sadly, the pressure to boycott anyone from Shuvu Banim worked. When the buses bringing the Rav's followers from Zimbabwe arrived, they had no idea where to take the hundreds of men, women and children they were transporting, because all of the arrangements and plans that had been so carefully made had now been scuttled. So, the bus drivers decided to dump their passengers in one of Johannesburg's local parks.

The situation looked dire. These families were in the middle of a strange country, with Passover just a couple of days away, and prominent figures in the South African Jewish community were warning everyone not to lift a finger to help them.

Most of the Jewish community in South Africa had no idea what was really going on. If Rabbi Berland was innocent, why were the Israeli authorities going all out to blacken his name and cause him so much suffering? But if the Rav was guilty, then why had no arrest warrant been issued in Israel, and why were so many of the most highly-respected religious leaders back in Israel publicly supporting him?

And when it came to the Rav's followers, it was even harder to figure out what to do. Even if the Rav was guilty of all he'd been accused of, God forbid, surely that didn't preclude the community from helping their fellow Jews to celebrate Passover?! As the debate within the Johannesburg Jewish community raged on, Rabbi Isaac Vaknin, the Sephardi Chief Rabbi of Johannesburg, contacted Rabbi Yitzchak Yosef, the current Chief Sephardi Rabbi of Israel and son of the late Rabbi Ovadia Yosef, to ask him whether the Jewish community in Johannesburg should be helping out the newcomers who'd arrived, despite the harsh decree that had been issued by this other senior Rabbi.

Rabbi Yosef replied that it was a *mitzvah* to help Rabbi Berland's followers with all of their needs. Next, the Rabbi asked Rav Yosef for his opinion of Rabbi Eliezer Berland, to which he replied, "If my father respected him, I trust my father's opinion[i]." But, Rabbi Vaknin persisted; Rabbi Berland leads his community according to strange customs... To which Rabbi Yosef replied: "Every *tzaddik* has strange customs."

---

[i] Shortly before he passed away in October 2013, a few months after the accusations against Rabbi Berland had begun, Rabbi Ovadia Yosef's grandson came to ask about the rumors he'd heard about Rabbi Berland. Before he could speak, Rabbi Ovadia told him, to hold his tongue. "You are about to speak ill of an angelic man!" said Rabbi Ovadia. "Beware! Anyone who speaks ill of him is playing with fire!"

Important letter

By The Tzadik Rav Shalom Arush shlit"a

אדר ב' תשעו

Dear Friends and Brothers, citizens of Johannesburg and all South Africa,

Please hear the plea that ushers forth from the depths of my being. My blood churns within my heart over the persecution of my teacher and Rebbe, the Rav and Tsaddik, **Rav Eliezer Berland, Shlit"a**. For a number of years now my rav has been pursued and persecuted for having done no wrong, as the tsaddik accepts on himself the heavenly decree to go into exile for the sake of the entire Am Yisrael.

And now you have merited that my teacher and rav is with you. Fortunate is anyone who honors him, as befits honoring a tsaddik whose entire life is devoted to the holy Torah and service of Hashem. The level of my rav's mesiras nefesh, his devotion and self sacrifice, would have been considered outstanding even in previous generations, and is way, way beyond anything we would expect of a person today. Anyone who takes part in aiding and hosting my teacher and Rebbe, **may he live and be will, will Biezrat Hashem merit long life, health, and financial blessing for himself and his family.**

I would also like to use this chance to warn in the name of the our holy Torah, that no one dare insult or pain this tsaddik in any way, chas vishalom, either directly or indirectly. **This matter causes him and the members of his family great suffering, with no relief for their pain**, as we have unfortunately heard has happened, may Hashem have mercy.

I wish to end with a blessing that any person who metis to aid the tsaddik in any way will see nachat from his entire family.

May we all merit seeing the consolation of Zion, Amen.

Shalom Arush

Once the Sephardi Rabbi in Johannesburg got this clear ruling from the Sephardi Chief Rabbi of Israel, he tried to persuade his Ashkenazi peers to open their doors to the Rav's students, and to listen to Rabbi Isaac Yosef - but sadly, his words fell on mostly deaf ears.

This Sephardi Rabbi decided to do whatever he could to alleviate the suffering of the Rav's followers, so he put out his own message to the South African Jewish community, urging them to help in very strong tones.

Unfortunately, even after the intervention of Israel's Sephardi Chief Rabbi, and the letters that were sent to the

South African Jewish community signed by some of the biggest rabbis in the Jewish world, some of the local people continued to believe the lies being spread by the media, and they started picketing the Rav's lodgings. These local vigilantes held big signs saying: "We don't want criminals and their followers here!"

Yet amidst all the chaos, rumors and deceit, the small Sephardi Jewish community in Johannesburg, which accounts for just 5% of South African Jewry, together with some big-hearted members of the Ashkenazi community, decided to open up their homes to the Rav and his 150-plus followers. While some of Rabbi Berland's followers found themselves sleeping in living rooms and garages of these kindly Jews in Johannesburg, others weren't so lucky, and ended up sleeping on benches outside, or inside the main Sephardi synagogue, Keter Eliyahu, until the Sephardi community could figure out what to do with them.

In a true act of charity, the Sephardi Jewish community in Johannesburg arranged for a huge tent to be erected to accommodate all of the visitors, and organized hundreds of meals to be cooked for them over the Passover holiday.

Later on, one of the Johannesburg Jews found Rabbi Berland's followers a permanent place where they could stay, eat, sleep and learn Torah. The Rav gave his blessing to start a fundraising drive in Israel to help pay the rent on the premises, and from that point on the situation started to improve a little. But South Africa was not an easy place to be, and relations with the local Ashkenazi Jewish community continued to be difficult.

Rabbi Berland said that the self-sacrifice of his students was sweetening many of the decrees hanging over the Jewish people, but in the meantime, it had been a very chaotic, difficult introduction to South Africa for everyone involved.

★ ★ ★

Forty years ago, Rabbi Avihu Levy moved from ISrael to Johannesburg to take up the position of Sephardi Chief Rabbi and establish a religious framework for the city's Sephardi Jews. When Rabbi Levy first arrived in South Africa, there were barely enough Sephardi Jews to make a *minyan*. Some four decades later, there are now three large Sephardi synagogues in the city of Johannesburg.

Rabbi Levy knew Rabbi Berland from the time they spent together in the Volozhin *Yeshiva* as young men. He recalled: *"The last time the Rav came to the community, he was drawing people to come and hear him speak like a magnet,"* he recalls. *"I could see how people were literally drawn to him like a magnet from the moment he arrived, and they were trying to spend as much time as they could with him, praying and so on.*

"People were also giving him notes and requests — one after another — until you could really see how he'd drawn them all closer... Everyone was looking at the Rav, and just waiting for the Rav. There was the feeling like we'd been visited by Moses or something, because people just couldn't stop gazing at him."

Rabbi Berland also occasionally prayed in the 'Keter Eliyahu' Sephardi synagogue, as he did on the Passover holiday. *"After the services, the South African special forces showed up looking for the Rav, and started asking everyone if they'd seen him,"* continues Rabbi Levy. *"So I went over to them and asked them what they wanted. They told me, 'This fellow is an illegal immigrant from Zimbabwe.'*

"So I told them, 'So what? What's the problem? You let him into the country with no problems, so now what do you want with this Rav?' I also told them, 'You better be very careful, because he's a tzaddik! If you manage to get even one small blessing from him, your life would completely change!"

Rabbi Berland and his followers also received a great deal

of support and help from the smaller of the two local Chabad houses in Johannesburg, and especially from Rabbi Shlomie Kinn, originally from London.

When Rabbi Berland's followers started to unexpectedly appear in Johannesburg just before Passover, Rabbi Kinn moved heaven and earth to try to help them settle in, and to make sure they had everything they needed to properly celebrate the holiday. On the Shabbos after Passover, he turned up in person with two huge containers of *cholent*, plus two huge platters of kugel, and started handing the food out to any of the Rav's followers who wanted it.

One of the Rav's students noticed how much unusual effort and self-sacrifice Rabbi Kinn was displaying to help the community, and was very impressed. After Shabbos, this student happened to meet Rabbi Kinn again and he asked him why he was making such an effort to provide so much help and support to a group of strangers who weren't even from the same *Chassidic* group.

Rabbi Kinn told him: *"At the beginning of this year, on the second night of Rosh Hashanah, I had a dream that subsequently returned many, many times. I dreamed exactly the same dream over and over again, and it only stopped a little while before Chanukah.*

"In that dream, I saw that a group of chassidim, including men, women and children, suddenly landed in Johannesburg. In the dream, I didn't know which group of chassidim they belonged to, I just knew they weren't Chabad, because the men all had very long side-curls and were wearing the striped Jerusalem kaftans and shtreimels. In the dream, I saw that people weren't treating them nicely, and that they were surrounded by a lot of negativity and objections, particularly from the immigration officials in the government and the Rabbinic courts and so on, and there was a lot of confusion.

"But I saw that out of the middle of all this confusion, Moshiach would come!

"And I also saw that all these problems and issues had to happen as part of the birth pangs of Moshiach, and that these chassidim would have to come to Johannesburg, and all the other things would have to happen, before Moshiach came.

"Although all these things were only happening in a dream, each time I dreamt about what these strange chassidim would have to endure, it bothered me a lot, to the point that I didn't want to have the dream anymore, and I didn't want to think about it anymore. But the dream just kept on repeating itself, over and over again, until one day I promised that whenever those chassidim showed up, I would do everything in my power to help them, and also encourage other people to help them, too. From the day I said that, the dream didn't return."

★　★　★

Despite the very rocky start that Rabbi Berland experienced in South Africa, over time things appeared to quiet down, at least in some ways, as many of the Jewish residents of South Africa started to develop some appreciation and respect for the sage who'd temporarily joined their community. During this leg of his stay in South Africa, the Rav spent quite a bit of time with the Sephardi community, teaching Torah and praying with them.

Many people started to come to him for advice and to receive a blessing, including some non-Jews who were enamored with the Rav and wanted him to oversee their conversion to Judaism.

One of the Rav's hosts in South Africa happened to have all of the halachic works of the late Rabbi Ovadia Yosef, and while the Rav was at his home, many members of the Sephardi community in Johannesburg started dropping in to ask the Rav questions on Jewish law. Often, they were amazed when the Rav would start quoting whole sections of the *Yabia Omer* — the multi-volumed halachic work penned by Rav Ovadia — and also Rav Ovadia's rulings, by heart.

The host recalled that on one occasion his son asked Rabbi Berland a halachic question, and just on that one topic alone the Rav gave his questioner 165 sources to refer to. The Rav's host remarked, "I have an angel staying with me, and I'm not worthy of discussing him."

On another occasion, the Rav started to explain more of the spiritual reasons as to why he was in South Africa. In the city of Johannesburg, it was possible to cancel all of the judgments hanging over the whole world. The Rav stated that he wouldn't leave Johannesburg until the Iranians had been forced to give up their nuclear bomb. He told the local Chabad Rabbi there: "I promise you, the first place that Moshiach will come to is Johannesburg!"

Perhaps this explains why Rabbi Berland returned to South Africa again later on, despite the enormous dangers, difficulty and immense suffering he knew would be waiting for him there upon his return. Because while many people in Johannesburg were starting to appreciate the holiness and greatness of Rabbi Berland, others in Johannesburg continued to view him and his followers as a problem that needed to be "eliminated."

★   ★   ★

South Africa suffers from an alarming amount of violent crime, corruption is rife at all levels of public life and bribery is endemic. In order to try to maintain some semblance of order in an increasingly violent and lawless country, the South African Police Service created a special division officially called the Directorate for Priority Crime Investigation, but commonly referred to as "the Hawks."

The Hawks in South Africa operate above the law and answer to no one but themselves. Sadly, the organization is also rife with corruption, with the Hawks happy to sell themselves out as "hired guns" to whoever is willing to pay the price of their services.

Rabbi Berland's enemies were very unhappy that despite their best efforts, the Rav would still be spending Passover together with his students in Johannesburg. So, despite the fact that Rabbi Berland had been cleared to enter South Africa and that there was no arrest warrant against him, they decided to hire the Hawks to "take care" of the Rav in a different way.

The Rav arrived in South Africa on April 9, 2014, less than a week before Passover began. A few days later, as the holiday of Passover was in full swing, the Hawks started combing Johannesburg, searching for the Rav and generally harassing his students and followers.

The Rav himself was keenly aware of the danger the Hawks posed to him, and shortly after arriving in South Africa, he contacted a few of his more senior followers in Israel to tell them that he was being chased from place to place, and that the spiritual stakes were getting higher every day.

The Rav requested that his community should increase the number of *Tikkun Haklalis* they were saying on his behalf from seven repetitions a day, to 10 a day, to reflect the seriousness of the danger that both the Rav and the Jewish people were facing.

In the meantime, the Rav, together with two of his closest students, took a room in a local hotel and tried to keep a very low profile. They didn't tell anyone else where they were staying, to try to stay under the Hawks' radar.

Rabbi Nachman Isaac was one of the people who stayed with the Rav in Johannesburg, and he takes up the story:

"The Rav's stay in the hotel was kept very secret, but somehow, on the first day of the intermediate days of Passover, the secret was revealed, and the hotel was soon full of the Rav's chassidim who wanted to come and pray the morning prayers with him," begins Rabbi Isaac.

As is the Rav's way, he just went with the flow and accepted whatever God wanted for him, even though logically it didn't look like it was so good for him. He went out to the crowd and enthusiastically prayed all the prayers with them.

The prayers continued unhurriedly until around 2 p.m. But before the Rav began the concluding prayers, he abruptly left the building together with me and one of the other attendants. We started walking in the direction of the fields and villages. Exactly 10 minutes after the Rav left the hotel, the Hawks arrived — but didn't find him. Where they were until 2 p.m. in the afternoon — I have no idea! Throughout all the years they were chasing the Rav, they seemed to coordinate things perfectly with him — they'd always show up a few minutes after the Rav had already left."

When one of the Shuvu Banim students started making preparations to go join the Rav, his host insisted that his guest take his Jaguar to drive over to the Rav, instead of hiring a taxi.

He told the student, "I want my car to have the merit of taking you to be with the Rav, and who knows? Maybe I'll also have the merit that the Rav himself will travel in my car." But driving an expensive Jaguar around an unfamiliar country like South Africa was the sort of big responsibility that the student just didn't want.

He told his host that he wasn't familiar with the roads or the city (they drive on the opposite side of the road in South Africa, the same as in the United Kingdom), and that he preferred to take a taxi — but his host insisted that he take the Jaguar, and wouldn't take no for an answer. Just as the student was approaching the hotel, he discovered that the Rav was apparently waiting for him. The Rav came straight out of the foyer, got into the car, and told the student to start driving.

There are many famous stories about Rabbi Berland's trips, but one thing that's commonly known about the Rav is that he always seems to know the roads, wherever he happens to be in the world. On many occasions, he's told his driver to take a left or right, or given him other directions, often without even raising his eyes from the *sefer* he happens to be reading from. So it was on this occasion too, as the Rav told his student exactly where to go.

After the Rav and his student had been driving for some time, the Rav suddenly told him to pull over. A second car appeared and the Rav got into it and drove off in it, again without any prior warning or planning. The whole time the Rav was tremendously happy and lively, telling jokes and singing joyous songs, as he switched from one car to the next.

In the meantime, once his followers realized that Rabbi Berland had left the hotel, word spread that he must have gone on to one of the local synagogues, where he'd been scheduled to give a Torah class after the morning services. So his followers hailed a number of taxis to take them to the synagogue where they thought he'd be. When they arrived, however, one of the members of the local Jewish community came out to warn them that the Hawks were already there, searching for the Rav.

The students responded that they were also searching for the Rav, so they went inside and were immediately accosted by a group of Hawks who were waiting for them.

The Hawks had a booklet with them that contained a

number of different pictures of Rabbi Berland at different stages of his life, which they'd been given by the Rav's persecutors. Many of the Rav's more senior followers also have white hair, a beard and long side curls, so the Hawks checked each student against the book of pictures. When they saw Rabbi Eliyahu Succot, one of the senior Rabbis from the Shuvu Banim community, they thought he might be Rabbi Berland, and asked him for his passport.

Rabbi Succot wasn't carrying his passport with him, so the Hawks whisked him away and escorted him back to his lodgings to get it. While all this was going on, unbeknownst to the Hawks or anyone else in the hotel, the real Rabbi Berland was already far away.

Rabbi Isaac continues the story: *"We came to some village, and we managed to rent a room there, probably the shabbiest place the Rav stayed in, in all the years [of exile],"* he says. *"The room didn't even have a chair or a table; it just had two beds and that was it. Yet the Rav was full of spiritual illumination!*

We hadn't eaten since the morning. The Rav said we should first pray the afternoon prayers— and he prayed with so much vitality! Then he asked us if we had a Jewish book. All we had was Likutei Moharan, which the Rav opened up and started learning with us so nicely — he'd translate and explain things to me, and I don't remember having any other study session quite like it with the Rav.

Suddenly, the Rav remembered that we hadn't eaten since the morning, and he said to me, 'You're probably feeling weak.'...The Rav was enormously happy, and was so pleasant to be with; it's hard to even explain.

"A little later, the Rav went out to look for a pool, or something he could use as a mikveh, but he couldn't find anything. In the meantime, we decided to go for a walk in the fields, and the Rav started singing songs of praise and gratitude to God — even though we hadn't eaten since the morning!

When you're with the Rav, you feel so satisfied and pleasant that you don't need anything, you're just praying that the experience will continue for as long as possible.

We prayed the evening prayers, and because we were feeling a little stressed, my father-in-law, Rabbi Shlomo Chaim Reicher, started to dance, while I did a headstand and the Rav did a somersault (!). To cut a long story short, it was a very joyful atmosphere. Later on, we found something to eat, but I saw that the Rav himself still didn't eat. I realized he was fasting on purpose, to try and sweeten the judgments.

I could see that the Rav understood the seriousness of the situation, and he mentioned a couple of times that he was in exile. You could see he was greatly tormented by the situation — but that was still no excuse for sadness! Even if you're being tormented and tortured in exile in order to sweeten the judgments [over the Jewish people], that doesn't mean you can't still be happy.

This is exactly the opposite of how regular people react. When we get hit by some difficulty, our mood immediately becomes very black, but by the Rav we saw the opposite. Even when he hit a difficult patch and was going through hell, he stayed happy throughout his ordeal. In the morning, I saw that the Rav was weak from fasting, but we were still unable to get him to agree to eat something," concludes Rabbi Isaac.

After this first attempt to capture the Rav failed, despite the huge amount of effort and manpower they'd put into the job, the Hawks gave an interview to a local journalist in South Africa where they were quoted as saying: "We're not sleeping at night, because all the time we're trying to work out how to catch Rabbi Berland."

★   ★   ★

Despite the fact that this was one of the most difficult

times of his exile, with the Rav having to move around every two days or so to avoid being captured by the Hawks, he didn't let it disrupt his learning schedule and other religious devotions.

One of Rabbi Berland's grandsons, Rabbi David Rubinstein, recalls: *"When the Rav was in Johannesburg, most of the time he used the swimming pool that was next to the house as a mikveh. In the winter, the pools there are very cold, even a little frozen. The temperature of the water could be -3 degrees, even in the daytime, and at night even colder.*

Some of us grandchildren used to try to go into the pool in the middle of the day, while there was some sun to warm us up, but we didn't manage it. One of the grandsons went in once, but being in the frozen water weakened him for the rest of the week. But the Rav dipped in that pool regularly, as per his regular schedule — and not just once a day! He'd dip again and again.

And that's not to say that the Rav didn't feel the cold. Each time he came out of the mikveh he'd immediately get dressed to try to stop the cold from completely penetrating his bones. Sometimes, we'd have to wrap him in a couple of extra blankets to help him warm up again.

What we young people couldn't manage to do in the middle of the day, the Rav was doing at his advanced age, even in the middle of the night."

On another occasion while the Rav was staying in South Africa, his host once spotted him leaving the house in the middle of the night, so he rushed after him to ask him where he was going. The Rav pointed to the forest that was close to where he was staying and indicated that he was going there to do some *hisbodedus*.

The host explained to the Rav that even in the daytime, people were scared to go to that forest, because it was full of poisonous snakes. The Rav reassured his host that nothing would happen, and that he didn't need to be afraid. He then invited his host to come with him.

The two of them entered the thick of the forest — and came face to face with an enormous, aggressive-looking elephant. Again, the Rav turned to his host and told him not to be afraid, because nothing would happen — and that's how it was.

Rebbe Nachman teaches that when a person is doing talking to God, he doesn't have to be scared of anything, because he's engaged in a *mitzvah*, and it's known that no harm comes to someone who is busy with a *mitzvah*.

Another time, one of the huge thunderstorms that are common in South Africa erupted and enormous bolts of lightning started striking the ground all over the city. Usually when this happens, the locals huddle together in their homes and don't go out to any open areas while an electrical storm is raging.

As the lightning continued to strike, the Rav's host was shocked to see him getting ready to go outside to the local grove, where he'd speak to God for hours at a time. "The lightning in South Africa is dangerous," he told the Rav. "It can strike people who are walking around outside and kill them."

"Who made the lightning?" the Rav replied and told his host that the lightning and the spiritual work of the *tzaddikim* were directly connected to each other. He also explained that Rebbe Nachman had written about thunder and lightning that they were sent to straighten out man's heart, which had become crooked from all of his sins. But if someone already had a straight, pure heart, they had nothing to fear from the lightning.

★　★　★

While his students and followers back in Israel were celebrating the festival of Lag B'Omer, Rabbi Berland was still trying to avoid being arrested by corrupt authorities in South Africa.

During this time, only very few of the Rav's followers succeeded in meeting with him. One of them recounts how the Rav arranged to meet with him in a parking lot, he got very upset and pained to see the Rav going through such difficulties and tribulations. Rabbi Berland could see how upset his student was, so he reminded him of the discussion in the *Gemara Shabbos* that recounted the story of when Rabbi Shimon Bar Yochai left the cave where he'd been hiding out for 13 years to escape the Romans.

Rabbi Shimon was covered in terrible sores, as a result of sitting up to his neck in earth for 13 years. When one of his colleagues saw the Torah sage in such a sorry state, he cried out: "Woe to me, that I should see you like this!" Rabbi Shimon replied, "I'm fortunate that you see me like this, because if you hadn't seen me like this, then I wouldn't be like 'this'" – i.e. with a much higher level of spiritual insight.

The first time the Rav went into hiding in South Africa, he spent a period of time in a place called Pecanwood, and even his closest followers didn't know where he'd gone. While he was spending this time in Pecanwood, the Rav willingly didn't eat or sleep for many days in a row, against fasting as a sort of atonement.

The house where he was staying was filled with holy books from floor to ceiling. The Rav would dip in the *mikveh* at midnight, in water that was freezing cold, and then go out to the most isolated places and fields to do hours upon hours of *hisbodedus*, in a sort of mini exile-within-exile. During this time, no one knew where he was.

But although the Rav was now out of touch and out of reach of his students, many of the men, women and children who'd traveled out to be with the Rav weren't about to give up so easily and simply return home. They decided to wait for him to return. One night, he turned up unexpectedly at the Chabad House in Johannesburg, where many of his followers were staying.

From that time on, Rabbi Berland started praying with his followers again, learning with them, singing with them, and giving over a number of brilliant Torah lectures. At this time, many of the local Jewish residents of Johannesburg started to draw closer to this holy man from Israel who'd suddenly appeared in their community. Even the non-Jews in Johannesburg got wind of the fact that a "miracle-maker" from Israel was now staying locally, and before long they were lining up in large numbers to see the Rav. Many of them expressed an interested in converting to Judaism.

One of the people who'd accompanied the Rav in his exile was Rabbi Yosef Shor, an expert *mohel* from Jerusalem, who'd already performed tens of circumcisions over the past few months in all the different countries where the Rav had found himself. As well as performing circumcisions for the residents of the different countries where the Rav stayed, many members of the Breslov community back in Israel would fly out specifically with their newborn babies, in order to have them circumcised by this *mohel* with the Rav acting as the *sandek*, or Godfather.

Unfortunately, not everyone was thrilled with the Rabbi Berland's increasing local influence and some members of the Johannesburg community eyed these developments with growing concern. When word started getting around that a Rav from Israel was starting to perform circumcisions and weddings and prayer services outside the existing communal Jewish framework in Johannesburg, many people were disturbed by what was going on.

Panic set in that Rabbi Berland was going to somehow

take over the Johannesburg Jewish community, and worse yet, turn everyone into *hareidim*. Once again, the Hawks were asked to intervene to remove the "problem" of Rabbi Berland and his followers.

The Hawks' second attempt at capturing Rabbi Berland occurred when one of the members of Shuvu Banim became engaged to the daughter of one of the more important families in South Africa. The couple booked a hall, hired the caterers, and asked Rabbi Berland if he would officiate at their wedding ceremony.

As the big day arrived, on August 11, 2014, friends and family of the couple arrived from all four corners of the globe to come and celebrate the happy occasion with them. But then they hit a snag, Rabbi Berland had agreed to officiate, but on the very day of the wedding, he requested that the celebration be pushed off for a week. The groom and his family were more than happy to comply, as they had a lot of prior experience with the Rav, and they knew that he would never request such a thing without a good reason.

But the bride's family, understandably, were very distressed about this turn of events. They'd invited friends and family from around the world to join them, and it was going to be very awkward for everyone, to say the least, should the ceremony be postponed for a week. The bride's family conveyed their feelings to the Rav's attendant, who told the Rav about the family's concerns.

Rabbi Berland immediately nullified his request to postpone the ceremony, in view of the great distress it was causing the bride's family. His attendant called the groom's family and asked them to be ready at the wedding hall in half an hour's time, because the Rav was on his way to officiate.

The hall quickly filled up with men, women and children from every corner of the world, representing every type of Jew imaginable. A few minutes later, the Rav's attendant called back and requested that all the guests at the wedding should sing a particular Hebrew melody, *'and all mouths shall praise You'*, until the Rav actually arrived.

The first time the Hawks had tried to catch the Rav had been during the Passover holiday. On that occasion, the groom happened to be in the car that drove the Rav to safety out of Johannesburg, and the Rav had sung this same song at that time, too.

The Rav appeared, and after being joyfully greeted by the families of the bride and groom, the wedding guests started praying the evening prayers before the ceremony would take place.

From the moment the Rav arrived, a distinguished-looking man stood right next to him. Everyone assumed that he must be one of the guests, even though no one actually knew who he was. Midway through the evening prayer service, this man suddenly grabbed the Rav's arms. At exactly the same moment 50 armed Hawks burst into the wedding hall, while an officer with a rifle took up a position on the roof.

The South African police were carrying assault rifles with lasers, all of which were pointed at the Rav and the other wedding guests. The police were pointing their guns and flashing their lasers across the whole hall as a feeling of mounting confusion and panic took hold of the wedding party.

People started shouting, women and children started crying hysterically, and some of the guests even fainted on the spot from the sheer terror of being dramatically confronted by 50 armed and aggressive men. Still others were so scared, they ran straight out of the hall and didn't return.

The groom recounted afterwards: *"The whole place looked like a war zone, or something. I'd just returned from Israel, where the rockets were still falling [this story occurred*

*during Operation Protective Edge], so I was still living with
that reality. The first thing that I thought when I saw all these
people with their drawn weapons was that Hamas was staging
some sort of terrorist attack, God forbid. Without missing a
beat, the Rav stared at the intruders, and it looked like they all
just somehow froze in place."*

What happened next sounds like the script of an action
movie, but this is how the situation actually played out.
The yeshiva students and guests were sure that they were
witnessing a terror attack, and that people were trying
to harm or kill Rabbi Berland. Instinctively, they started
fighting for their lives.

An eyewitness takes up the story:

*"One of the Rav's students was standing near the infiltrator,
and grabbed the man's hands so that he'd release Rabbi Berland.
While this was happening, a commando officer came up from
behind the Rav and grabbed him again. This time another
student jumped on the commando's back, and miraculously
pulled him to the floor.*

*A second commando then grabbed the Rav, so yet another
student pushed his hand away. When the commando grabbed
on to the Rav again, this student turned around and hit
him so hard the commando flew backwards onto two other
commandos, knocking all three men to the ground.*

*Then another student came running towards the
commandos, yelling at them and holding a boulder in his hand.
The commandos pointed their guns at him, so another student
kicked one of the commandos who again flew backwards,
knocking down the two other commandments and some of the
wedding guests.*

*Another commando put his gun against the head of a
teenage student, so someone kicked the commando behind the
knee, so he collapsed on to the floor. Another student also had
a gun against his head, but he managed to kick the commando*

*to the ground by himself. The head commando then yelled at
the others to shoot, but for some reason no bullet was fired."*

One of Rabbi Berland's senior students was standing
behind the Rav when the first commando was knocked to
the ground, and he describes what happened next:

*"I turned around to see what was happening, and I saw
a group of armed commandos. One of the younger students
came up to me and told me, 'You are the Rav, ok?' I said 'ok',
and he grabbed me and we started running towards the exit.
Immediately, one of the officers started pointing at me and
yelled out, 'that's him! That's him!'*

*Then a large number of officers jumped on me, two of them
held on to me very tightly, and they dragged me to their car. All
the women and children were yelling and crying hysterically,
people were fainting and having panic attacks. They took me
and left the hall, convinced that they had the Rav in their
hands."*

The Hawks only realized they had the wrong man much
later, when they asked the student to bring them his passport.
He was released, and a relative was called to pick him up from
the police station and drive him back to the wedding.

Meanwhile, the Rav continued on with his evening
prayers as though nothing was happening, still singing the
same beautiful tune. One of his followers had been holding
the Rav's hand for comfort, and afterwards he reported that
when the Hawks had suddenly burst into the room, the
Rav's pulse didn't change in the slightest, despite the very
dramatic, panic-stricken events that were unfolding around
him. The Rav just took everything in stride and didn't waver
for a second.

Once things had calmed down a little, Rabbi Berland was
escorted out through a back door to a waiting car, but he told
the wedding party to continue dancing and singing, and that
this evening would be considered as the formal engagement

ceremony, while the wedding proper would take place on a different day.

As the reality sank in, the families began to realize the scope of the miracle they'd just been witness to.

As soon as Rabbi Berland got to his home, he was greeted by one of his followers, Y.N., who'd flown out from Miami to see him and request a blessing. This man asked the Rav if he'd be willing to give an impromptu *Torah class* that he'd live-stream and record for the Miami Breslov Center.[i]

On the spot, despite the drama he'd just experienced, the Rav gave a beautiful Torah class in English[ii], about the importance of loving our fellow Jew.

★   ★   ★

While the Rav was teaching his Torah, the Hawks back at the wedding hall were extremely irritated about their failed attempt at arresting the Rav, and started harassing the wedding guests to tell them where the Rav had disappeared to. One of them told Yaron Yamin: "Tell us where the Rav is staying, because in the end we are going to catch up with him, but next time we're just going to shoot him and send him back to Israel in a coffin!"

After this traumatic event, most of Rabbi Berland's followers were sure that he would have to go into hiding again, while his attendants were trying to persuade the Rav that maybe South Africa had gotten too dangerous for him to stay any longer, and that he should move to a different country. But the Rav told them that they had nothing to be scared about, and that he was going to continue to carry on as usual.

---

[i] The Rav founded the Miami Breslov Center at the beginning of his exile, in 2013.

[ii] The *Torah class* can be seen here: https://youtu.be/VWVC1TPQRRw

He told them: "There are still some judgments here that need to be sweetened, and with God's help, we need to sweeten them."

In the meantime, the wedding actually took place the following week in a private home in Johannesburg, exactly as the Rav had stated at the beginning of the story. The Hawks were badly stung by their second failed attempt to apprehend the Rav, so they resorted to fabricating some more stories and lies for the local press about how the "dangerous" criminal they were after had escaped "justice" once again, and circulated the Rav's picture together with a false story of how there was an international arrest warrant out for the Rav.

They asked the local Jewish community to call them with any details of Rabbi Berland's whereabouts, and also instructed all the hotels in the area to be on the lookout for a Jewish man with a white beard, who they described as being 'armed and dangerous'. One hotel actually contacted them shortly afterwards, to report a suspicious character who appeared to fit the bill. The Hawks arrived soon afterwards, to find Moshe Levinson, another of the Rav's senior students. But this time, they realized it was a case of mistaken identity, so they left him alone.

The Rav's next brush with the Hawks came on September 9th, 2014. Another member of the Johannesburg Jewish community who had drawn close to Rabbi Berland was getting married and the couple asked the Rav to officiate at their wedding on that date. The wedding itself was being held in one of the big homes in Johannesburg.

One of the Rav's followers who attended the wedding explains what happened next: *"I got to the wedding a little beforehand, and from the moment the Rav stepped out of his car, he told me that I would be his chief bodyguard, because in a few more minutes some commandos were going to show up and were going to try to arrest him,"* he explains. *"To be honest, I didn't really pay a lot of attention to what the Rav was saying because I thought he was telling me a joke, as is his way. I put the conversation completely out of my mind.*

Everyone went inside and the Rav officiated at the wedding, and then one of the locals asked the Rav to lead the congregation in saying the Tikkun HaKlali. After that, we said the blessing on the new moon, and the Rav began to sing wedding songs, and to dance. He also began singing some Uman songs, and the atmosphere was very joyous and happy.

The dancing continued for around half an hour, until the Rav suddenly stopped what he was doing and decided to leave. The Rav's car was parked on the sidewalk on the road outside, and he entered the car and waved good-bye to us. Just as the Rav's driver pulled away, a huge van arrived and pulled up, effectively blocking the Rav's car, with another small car behind it. Together, these two vehicles tried to block in the Rav's car, and then, all of a sudden, they switched on their sirens."

"I really felt like I was in a dream," continues the wedding guest. *"I ran over to where the police vehicles were parked and stood in their way, to try to stop them from moving. Meanwhile, the Rav's driver was trying to reverse away from the roadblock. A soldier suddenly got out of the van and pointed a gun at me, while the small car bypassed the van and started chasing after the Rav's car. All the vehicles were still driving in reverse, because that particular road was very narrow.*

Then the van also bypassed me and started reversing after the Rav. Somehow, the Rav's driver managed to turn the car around by driving up on the pavement, and he escaped. The Hawks still tried to chase after him, but eventually they gave up. That's when it hit me what the Rav had said earlier, that I would end up being his chief bodyguard."

The chase didn't end there. The Hawks tried to track down the Rav using a helicopter, plus tens of vehicles, but in the end the Rav experienced a number of miracles that enabled him to return safely to where he was staying.

When one of the bystanders at the wedding heard the chief commando ask one of his junior commandos why he hadn't just shot Rabbi Berland in cold blood and finish things that way, he realized that the Rav's life was in serious danger as long as he stayed in South Africa.

It's worth remembering that all of this was going on despite the fact that the Hawks had no arrest warrant and no legal justification for detaining the Rav in the first place. So to cover their tracks, the Hawks started giving more interviews to South African journalists describing this elderly *tzaddik* as a very dangerous criminal who was endangering lives by driving on the sidewalk and so forth, and asking the public to help them catch this "menace to society."

The Rav's followers started to fear that the situation was becoming too dangerous, and that there was a serious risk that the Rav may not make it through in one piece. Yet the Rav himself continued to act with his characteristic self-composure, emuna, and unshakeable trust in God.

One morning shortly after the Hawks' third failed attempt to capture the Rav, a few of Rabbi Berland's followers were in the central *mikveh* in Johannesburg when a Satmar *chassid* entered the building. He asked the other men there if Rabbi Berland came to this *mikveh*.

The Satmar *chassid* explained that he'd come to Johannesburg on business, and that he'd heard about the Rav and was interested in seeing him and asking him for a blessing. The Rav's followers explained that Rabbi Berland never came to that *mikveh*, and that even when he'd been going out regularly he'd been using a *mikveh* in a private house that was an hour's drive away.

As they were leaving the *mikveh*, they were shocked to see Rabbi Berland standing outside the building, about to enter it. One of the Rav's followers happened to have a *shofar* in his *tefillin* bag, as it was Elul, and the Rav motioned to him and asked him to blow his *shofar*.

The follower was a little confused by the request and didn't really know what to do. After all, the whole country was currently looking for the Rav, and if he blew the *shofar* in such a central place, and at such a busy time of the morning when everyone was out and about, it would certainly draw the attention of a lot of people.

The Rav said to him, "Don't be afraid! Don't be afraid!"

So the follower took out his *shofar* and blew it loudly a few times, as he'd been asked to do. The Rav's attendants told the followers that after he went to the *mikveh*, the Rav was going to pray in the nearby Sephardi synagogue, Keter Eliyahu. His followers found this incredible, as Keter Eliyahu was the central shul of Johannesburg, and a very public place for the Rav to be praying in.

The Rav's followers went on ahead to the Keter Eliyahu synagogue, and as they feared would be the case, they saw a number of the Hawks' police vehicles waiting outside. However, once the *Shacharis* service actually began, the Hawks left.

Suddenly, Rabbi Berland entered the shul wrapped in his customary *tallis* and *tefillin*, sitting down as though he was a regular participant in the service. When the synagogue's Rabbi saw Rabbi Berland come in, he was pretty shocked. He immediately got up and asked Rabbi Berland to sit in his place at the front of the *shul*, as a sign of respect.

At the reading of the Torah, word quickly spread that the Rav was in the shul, and before long many of the Rav's students arrived to come and see him. After the *praying*, the Rav told his students before he left that he would be coming again tomorrow.

It was a miracle that the Rav had come and gone from

the shul without any problems with the Hawks, and that the Hawks had left literally seconds before the Rav arrived. But how could the Rav come tomorrow, when the Hawks would certainly know that he'd been in the synagogue today, and would be sure to be waiting for him?

But the following day, God made another miracle and the Rav again arrived for the morning prayers undisturbed by the Hawks.

At the same time that the Rav's persecutors were continuing their "war" against Rabbi Berland in South Africa, back in Israel the war against the Torah world and the yeshivas was also heating up, as the government started to implement its plans to forcibly draft *yeshiva* boys into the IDF.

But in the middle of all this, God interrupted the persecution of the Torah scholars inside and outside of Israel with a war of a different kind.

THE GENERATION THAT MOSHIACH COMES IN

The *Gemara* in *Sanhedrin* 97 describes the way the generation will look at the time that Moshiach comes in the following words: "In the generation when ben David [Moshiach] will come, Torah scholars will be few in number, and the rest — their eyes will be weak with worry and groaning. And much suffering and harsh decrees will be renewed [upon the generation]. Before the first [problem] has ended, the second one will be hurrying to come."

A Jewish commentator by the name of the Maharsha explains that when it says that the Torah scholars will be few in number, it means that men of truth will go and hide in the wilderness, on account of the evil generation. He also explains that the *tzaddik* will be regarded as a fool and a wild man in the eyes of the people. The Maharsha explains that the reference to their eyes being weak with worry and groaning is referring to the people who are left behind, without a *tzaddik* and without a leader.

THE THREE MARTYRS AND WAR: SUMMER 2014

"Everything that we're doing here is only to sweeten the judgments hanging over the Jewish people."
- Rabbi Eliezer Berland speaking to his students in Johannesburg, 2014

★ ★ ★

On the evening of June 12, 2014, three Jewish young men, Naftali Frankel, 16; Gilad Sha'ar, 16; and Eyal Yifrach, 19, were picked up and kidnapped by Arab terrorists from the hitchhiking post in the Gush Etzion region, just south of Jerusalem.

For weeks, Israel was gripped with a mounting sense of dread over the fate of these three young men — but also with a stronger sense of unity than had been evident for many long years. All the arguments over religion and politics took a back seat as Israel's citizens buried their differences and prayed together that the three young men would be found, alive, and returned to their families.

Different communities all over the country organized events in the merit of finding these three boys alive— so many books of *Psalms* were recited, so many challahs were baked, so many special services were arranged in local synagogues, and many other things besides. But after weeks of searching, the teenagers' bodies were finally tracked down to a shallow grave in the Arab town of Chalchul, close to Hebron, on June 30, 2014.

They'd been brutally murdered very shortly after being picked up from the side of the road in Gush Etzion. Less than 48 hours after they were found, on July 2, 2014, Israel found itself back at war, as Arab riots in Jerusalem and other locations were joined by hundreds of rockets which started to rain down on the country from the Gaza Strip.

Thousands of miles away in South Africa, Rabbi Berland appeared to have known the fate of the three missing teens long before their remains were discovered by the army. On Thursday, June 19, 2014, ten days before the boys' bodies were discovered and officially identified, he made a statement that sounded eerily like an eulogy, about the three missing teens:

"The three kidnapped boys were[i] sparks of Abraham, Yitzchak and Jacob...They came to save the Jewish people, and to cancel the terrible decrees. The Jewish people was deteriorating spiritually from moment to moment, and from second to second, and nobody could stop this from occurring.

These three young men took it upon themselves to be the Nation of Israel's representatives, in front of God's Heavenly throne, and to cancel all of the terrible decrees that had been made against us, and particularly the spiritual holocaust that has been unleashed against us, particularly in Israel.

All they are asking from us now is to wake up. To wake up and go to the mikveh every day; to wake up and start keeping Shabbos; and to stop speaking evil words; and to uproot all the baseless hatred. The next Temple is only going to be built with baseless love... with unity. Now is the moment for all of the

---

[i] By using the past tense "were", Rabbi Berland made it clear that they were no longer with us.

Jewish people to return to being like 'a single man with a single heart,' like it was at the giving of the Torah... [I]f there's even just one, single Jew at the end of the world who's suffering, then we all feel it. This people is one 'body,' with one heart."

Rabbi Berland then requested that everyone without exception should fast the following day, Friday, June 20, 2014, between 4:20 a.m. and 6:50 p.m., the hour before halachic sunset, and requested that everyone should take an additional *mitzvah* upon themselves, too, and in this merit the [bodies of the] boys would be found.

Despite the short notice and the difficult timing of fasting on the eve Shabbos, more than 8,000 people all over the world registered to fast with Shuvu Banim, including whole families who until that moment hadn't been keeping Torah and *mitzvos*.

The day of the fast, the Rav was sitting with one of his students when he asked him to bring him one of the holy books that had been written by the Arizal. He remarked that in the merit of the Arizal, he would be able to reveal where the three boys were. He then asked the student to bring him a map of the area of Hebron, so that the Rav could show him exactly where they were — but in South Africa, they didn't have such a map on hand. But the Rav was still able to show them that they were somewhere close to Hebron.

All this occurred around 10 days before the remains of the boys were ultimately found in the village of Chalchul, near Hebron.

From the moment the news of the kidnapping broke, the Rav had taken it upon himself to fast from sunrise to sunset — and sometimes even whole nights and days. He spent the whole time hidden away in his home in South Africa, devoting himself to learning Torah and performing his other *avodas* God. He also encouraged any of his students who could manage it to fast with him, from sunrise to sunset, every day. And so it continued for 18 long, painful days.

The sister of one of the three boys contacted the Rav on Sunday June 23, 2014, a week before the army finally found the bodies, and asked for a *blessing* that they should find the boys. The Rav told her that she should arrange for 1,000 people to fast for an entire week, until the following Monday, and then they would see miracles. Many people fasted, as requested, and as a result of their fasting and all the other prayers that were said, the bodies were indeed discovered on the following Monday, June 30, 2014. The boys were brought home to be given a Jewish burial, and to be properly mourned by their families.

Throughout this period of time, the Israeli army was out in full force, looking for clues as to where the boys were. The Rav remarked to a student that the boys would be found soon — but not because of all the army's efforts. This is what actually happened. The boys were ultimately found by a couple of Palestinian locals who'd volunteered to help with the search effort.

After the bodies were recovered, the Rav said that the three kidnapped martyrs had been very high souls, of a type that hadn't been seen for many generations already, and that they'd only come down to the world in order to die to sanctify God's Name. They were *tzaddikim* who had fulfilled the whole Torah, except for the commandment to die sanctifying God's Name. Hence, they returned to the world just to complete this *mitzvah*.

The Rav told his followers that just before his bar mitzvah three years earlier, one of the boys, Gilad Sha'ar, had told his parents that he'd like to get a *blessing* from Rabbi Yitzchak David Grossman, the Rav of Migdal Ha'Emek, as his bar mitzvah present. His parents took him to see the Rav, and young Gilad asked the Rav to bless him that he should fulfill the commandment of sanctifying God's Name. Even then, on some level he knew what was to come.

After the funeral, Rabbi Berland told his students:

"There haven't been souls like this in the world since the beginning of time… It would take many hours to explain who these souls really were, who came down to protect us. On exactly the same day that these three boys were kidnapped, [our enemies] wanted to fire a nuclear bomb at us, and who knows how many people they would have killed? … If not for those three boys, everyone would have been erased, turned into dust. See how God was arranging everything! … We're here for a reason. We need to wake up."

★ ★ ★

The kidnappings led to the start of an all-out war with Gaza, as the Palestinians started bombarding the country with rockets. The Israeli government initially didn't respond militarily, but on July 2, 2014, Operation Protective Edge began, to try to stop the rocket attacks.

Four days before the start of Operation Protective Edge, Rabbi Berland insisted on dipping in a natural *mikveh* outside, despite the fact that the outside temperature was -4 Celsius and the water was freezing cold. After reciting his customary midnight prayers the Rav then spent four hours singing the same melody *"Avinu Malkeinu - Our Father and King have mercy and us and save us for we have no good deeds."* When one of his followers asked him why he was deviating from his usual schedule, the Rav replied that there were many judgments hanging over the people of Israel, so he'd been busy asking God to have mercy on the nation of Israel.

Then, he told his follower: **"Publicize the following**

statement in my name: Any soldier who's killed now, I guarantee that he'll go straight to the Garden of *Eden.*"

At the time, there'd been a debate raging in Israel over the spiritual fate of soldiers killed in combat. A film had recently come out in Israel called 'A Place in Heaven', which had tackled the subject, and a number of high-profile news stories were being written about a fallen soldier who had reportedly been contacted during a séance (which is completely forbidden according to Jewish law). The journalists reported that the spirit of this fallen soldier had stated that there were no guarantees that IDF soldiers who fell in combat would automatically get to Heaven.

At this crucial time, four days before thousands of Israeli soldiers would be risking their lives fighting in Gaza, Rabbi Berland made it crystal clear that he would stand as a guarantor that any soldier killed in combat would indeed go straight to Heaven. But in the meantime, there was still no public sign that the Israeli Government was going to move against the terrorists in Gaza.

Two days before Operation Protective Edge finally began, the Rav spoke out against the Israeli government and its weak leadership in the face of Israel's enemies. "Every day, a hundred rockets are being fired at every part of the country, and Prime Minister Binyamin Netanyahu isn't doing anything about it," he said[i]. "He should resign!"

Rabbi Berland continued:

"Israel's leaders have lost the plot. People are being killed, people are being murdered and no one is shocked. The kidnapped boys called the police, and no one took any notice at all. If they would have sent a few police cars there immediately, they would have apprehended the terrorists with their hostages

---

[i] http://www.bhol.co.il/news/759136

that night. What kind of a police force is this? What kind of an army is this?!

Why isn't it possible to liquidate all the head terrorists in Gaza, and to capture all their stockpiles of weapons and rocket arsenals? Netanyahu chose to form a government with Ya'ir Lapid[i], whose only real concern is that another hareidi baby with side crus will be born, and who might get a subsidized cup of milk to drink. And the whole country is being thrown into an uproar solely because a hareidi baby might get a cup of milk. At the same time, they're still paying social security payments to Arab terrorists, and paying compensation to the families of Arab terrorists who killed themselves in suicide bombing attacks[ii].

They want to recruit the hareidim to the army! Which army?! This army abandons its soldiers! That's not how the IDF [is meant to behave.] This army is protecting the terrorists!"

The Rav continued that it was now common knowledge that the Hamas had used all the trucks and concrete mixers that they'd been given by Israel to develop the infrastructure in Gaza to build terrorist tunnels into Israel instead, and called for a change in Israel's leadership. A few days after the Rav publicly said this, a poll showed that 70 percent of Israelis agreed and were also disappointed with the

---

[i] As Finance Minister, Yair Lapid was responsible for punitively cutting funding to the Torah-observant world and its institutions that same year.

[ii] Israeli law states that the family of anyone dying in a terrorist attack gets compensated with a monthly stipend. The law does not differentiate between the families of victims and the families of the terrorists themselves. Terrorists take advantage of this law, and it's become another incentive for suicide bombers to kill themselves, as they know that their families will be taken care of for the rest of their lives.

Government's lack of leadership, when it came to dealing with the terrorists.

Shortly after the Rav's statement, even members of Netanyahu's own party started publicly heckling him in the Knesset and calling for him to resign, which promptly lead to the start of Operation Protective Edge, as Netanyahu scrambled to keep his job. Rabbi Berland's statement was widely covered in the Israeli press and met with a lot of public approval.

As Operation Protective Edge raged on with no end in sight, on July 14, 2014, the Rav spoke on the phone with the kabbalist Rav Yitzchak Meir Morgenstern, back in Israel.

Rabbi Berland told Rabbi Morgenstern: *"Now, we will see big miracles, and no Jew will be killed anymore... [T]he tzaddikim have the power to ensure that no Jew will be killed anymore, and that people will do teshuva because of the war.*

That's how it was in 1973, in the Yom Kippur War, that the Jews did teshuva, and all the Jewish religious returnees came from 1973. Now, in this war, all the Jews will also do real teshuva. Once, wars meant that we would just kill some terrorists. Now, they are firing rockets at us, and they have mountains of rockets without number, and they are building tunnels underneath Israel.

Now it's time to go pray at the Kotel and Hebron and at Rabbi Shimon Bar Yochai's grave in Meron, and to storm the heavens with our prayers, that no Jew will get killed. No Jew! No Jew! No Jew!

The most important thing is to stop the war, and the rockets that are falling every day. We have to stop it. More than 20 Jews were killed in this war... They sacrificed themselves for the nation of ISrael, and even though they weren't mitzvah-observant, and they didn't keep Shabbos, and they eat on Yom Kippur and don't fast, the secular world really doesn't know any better.

The Jews that are walking into the fire now, they're sacrificing themselves for God, they're walking into the fire. And we don't have any idea who is sacrificing themselves for the Jewish nation.

They could have dropped out of the army and done other things, but they are going with all of their enthusiasm, simply in order to save Jewish lives. And now we need to pray to stop the war."

About a month after rockets started raining down on Israel, one of his followers contacted Rabbi Berland to ask him if he had any words of wisdom, or *chizuk*, to share about the rocket attacks.

The Rav said the following: "Tell everyone not to be afraid, and not to start running away from one city to the next. As soon as the siren sounds, take your *Tikkun HaKlali* out of your pocket and start to read it slowly, word by word, and if you do this, you have nothing more to worry about, and there will be miracles, with God's help, and the rocket won't fall anywhere near you."

Whatever type of violence the terrorists were engaged in, the Rav's message was always the same: "*Terrorists are created from our sins! God is simply dressing up our sins in the guise of a terrorist. The terrorists don't have permission to harm anyone who is doing teshuva. It's only if we're not doing teshuva that the terrorists are given permission to harm us. And when we recite the Tikkun HaKlali that neutralizes the sins that created the terrorist.*"

In the past, Rabbi Berland had said that the nation of Israel was engaged in so many terrible sins, and that if things continued this way, the sins would transform into terrible fire and pillars of smoke — which exactly described the situation in Israel during the rocket attacks.

But the Rav reassured his students that the sins — and the terror they were dressed up in — could be destroyed at their roots by the Jewish people wholeheartedly returning to God. During Operation Protective Edge, the Rav told his students to publicize the *segulah* of reciting the *Tikkun HaKlali* to as many people as possible and revealed that if 10,000 people would start to regularly recite the *Tikkun HaKlali* every day, no more Jews would be killed in the current war.

★ ★ ★

As the rockets from Gaza continued to rain down on Israel, reaching further and further into the central, heavily populated parts of the country, the Rav wrote a prayer where he made it clear that the only option left was to rely on God. With the rocket fire continuing unabated, and the international community firmly against the Israeli government's attempts to subdue the Hamas terrorists in Gaza militarily, it was becoming clearer and clearer that there was no way the State of Israel could really "win."

Many years before this latest conflict with the Arabs, the Rav had stated that it was impossible to rely on the IDF to protect Israel from its enemies, because even when they started military operations, they were no longer capable of carrying them through to the end.

By the end of June 2014, the Rav's words, uttered many decades before, appeared to ring more true by the day: "There is no one to rely on, except God! The government can't help anyone; even the army can't protect us anymore!" The only thing the politicians had managed to do, with their misguided attempts to achieve "peace" with the Palestinians, was to make things a whole lot worse for the Jewish citizens of Israel.

Who armed the Palestinians in the first place and gave them weapons? Who gave them Gush Katif, which they quickly turned into a launch pad for the most sophisticated missiles and rockets, all aimed at Israel's largest cities? Who looked like they were scared to go into Gaza, and tackle the terrorists head on?

Without wisdom of Torah, to guide their military and political decisions, Israel's politicians were bumbling from one security disaster to another.

As more and more rockets were fired into the heart of Israel, reaching cities that hadn't heard a siren for decades, a new dilemma arose in many yeshivos. Should the students be encouraged to run to the security room when the siren went off, or should they stay where they were and continuing learn Torah? Some *Roshei Yeshiva* decided that learning Torah was truly the best defense against the rockets and told their students to stay put and learn hard when the sirens went off.

Some concerned parents sought the advice of Rav Chaim Kanievsky about whether that was truly the best course of action, and Rav Kanievsky told them, "The Torah protects and leads to success. It's not the rocket that kills people, it's the sin that kills people.[i]"

On a separate occasion, Rav Kanievsky was asked how it was possible that dangerous debris from the rockets was falling into Bnei Brak, when the Chazon Ish had guaranteed that Bnei Brak would be safe and protected, because of the amount of Torah being learned there. Rabbi Kanievsky replied, "He wasn't talking about a Bnei Brak where people have iPhones and internet access."

The *tzaddikim* were telling the Jews in Israel at this time that if they started doing what God wanted from them, God Himself would take care of our enemies. Thousands

---

[i] A play on words from a famous saying from the *Gemara* that it's not the bite of a snake that kills, but the sin that kills.

of rockets had fallen on Israel, yet there had been so many miracles that the number of people who had been killed and wounded was negligible. In contrast, one rocket from Gaza that was directed at Israel had fallen on Egypt by mistake — and it had killed seven people and wounded roughly a hundred more. By contrast, the rockets fired at Israel either seemed to disappear in mid-air or landed on an empty patch of ground.

Speaking in South Africa, Rabbi Berland said, "Israel is protected! Everything is protected! Even though we see rockets and so forth, it's all just sparks of the Third Temple, starting to come down from Heaven." He also told his student Rabbi Tzanani in a phone call on Friday, August 1, 2014) that Israel is the safest place in the world, and that Rebbe Nachman was fighting on behalf of the soldiers in Gaza.

On August 25, 2014, the Hamas terrorists and the Israeli government finally agreed to a cease-fire that would last for 30 days. In its terms of acceptance, Hamas stated that if the Israeli government didn't reopen the borders of the Gaza Strip in the interim, the war would resume in another 30 days, on September 25th.

In the meantime, the world rushed to help the Palestinians by pouring many millions of dollars into the terrorists' bank accounts. Official diplomatic accounts stated that the money was to ward off the Palestinians' humanitarian crisis, but it seemed more likely that the funds would be used to re-stock the rockets and re-arm the terrorists for the next round of fighting.

The 30-day truce would end precisely on Rosh Hashanah 5775 — the seventh year the *Gemara* had singled out for "war."

★　★　★

One direct miracle that came about as a result of the terrible kidnapping of the three boys was the discovery of a new network of underground tunnels that the Hamas terrorists had built, encroaching well past the boundaries of Israel.

As a result of the kidnapping and the subsequent "mini-war" that followed, Hamas's secret plans to use the tunnels to launch a number of surprise, murderous raids on Jewish towns around the Gaza periphery and to channel a large number of Arab terrorists into the Israeli heartland was discovered and foiled.

The Hamas leadership had planned to launch their murderous attacks on the first day of the Jewish new year, Rosh Hashanah 5775 - September 25, 2014 — the seventh year. Ancient Jewish texts explain that: "In the seventh [year] there will be wars." But the almost unprecedented unity, *teshuva* and prayers that had been sparked by the boys' kidnapping turned everything around. As a result, the war with Palestinians in Gaza started earlier than they'd planned, and the tunnels were discovered before they could be used.

But the miracles didn't stop there. It's recorded that more than 4,000 rockets fell on Israel throughout the duration of Operation Protective Edge, yet just eight Israelis were directly killed by the rocket fire, and just another 60 injured over the entire two-month course of the war.

While the government and military were quick to pat themselves on the back for deploying the Iron Dome missile defense system, the Hamas terrorists were much more realistic in their assessment of why so few of their rockets were hitting their targets in Israel, and landing in open fields. One senior Hamas operative complained in a newspaper interview entitled: 'Their God changes the path of our rockets in mid-air'[i] that the terrorists were extremely careful to program the rockets correctly, and were using the latest technology, but that God was saving the Jews.

There's an ancient Jewish text written about the final wars that will take place before Moshiach comes, where it says that even the non-Jews will start to acknowledge that the reason they were unable to destroy the Jewish nation throughout history was only because God was protecting us. This text continues that once the enemies of Israel realize this, they will turn their attention to trying to fight God Himself — and as soon as they do that, God will deal with them personally.

Rabbi Berland gave an additional explanation for the miracles occurring with the rockets during Operation Protective Edge. He said, "*The strength of a simple Jew is such that when he lays tefillin, and he winds the strap around his hand, in that same second a miracle is performed and a rocket winds around in a different direction and ends up landing in an open space. The 'strap' of the tefillin is protecting us from the 'Strip' of Gaza.*"

---

[i] https://www.wnd.com/2014/07/their-god-changes-path-of-rockets-in-mid-air/

IN THE SIXTH YEAR, VOICES;
IN THE SEVENTH YEAR, WAR

In the Gemara (Sanhedrin 97a) it describes the pre-Messianic era as follows:

"Rabbi Yehuda says, 'In the generation when ben David [i.e., the Moshiach] comes, the meeting place will be used for debauchery; the Galilee will be laid to waste; and the Gavlan will be desolate. The border people will wander from city to city and not be shown favor. The wisdom of the scribes will become putrid, and those who fear sin will be despised. The generation will have the face of a dog, and the truth will be absent.

As it's stated, 'Truth will be missing, and the person who flees from evil will seem like a crazy person.'⁵

There will be eating, drinking and rejoicing and the knowledge of Torah will return to those who study it. In the sixth year there will be voices. In the seventh year there will be wars. And in the year after the seventh, year] ben David will come."

★   ★   ★

The Jewish Talmud discusses what the world is going to look like, shortly before the Jewish redeemer comes. In that passage, it states: "Rabbi Elazar says, 'There is also no clearer indication of the End than this… "Even Torah scholars…[6] will have no peace from the adversary."

At the time when Rabbi Berland went into exile, many Torah scholars and religious leaders were being persecuted in a number of different ways: Some were being falsely accused and put into prison, some were being physically attacked and abused, a large number of the Hebrew-speaking study houses and yeshivas (that didn't have wealthy backers from outside of Israel supporting them) effectively closed their doors as a result of the government's swinging budget cuts which meant they had no money to pay their students' stipends and some *yeshiva* students were also being forcibly taken from their holy books and conscripted into the IDF, or jailed for failing to enlist.

As has happened so many times before, what ultimately stopped this "war on Torah" was a war of a different kind — Operation Protective Edge, which was begun in response to hundreds of rockets being fired at Israel by Hamas and other terrorist organizations in the Gaza Strip.

While Israel has been through many wars since its inception, Operation Protective Edge was in a different category right from the start. There was a spiritual battle for the nations' soul raging as the rockets continued to fall, and even people who were very far away from observance and religion started to feel that the Jewish people were on the cusp of a monumental change.

Within the observant world, barely a day went by without another message or statement stating that Moshiach and the redemption were imminent. At this time, Rabbi Yehuda Bracha, *Rosh Kollel* of Yechaveh Daas, told his students that all the signs stated in the *Gemara* regarding the coming of Moshiach had now been met, aside from the "voices in the sixth year, and the war in the seventh."

Rabbi Bracha explained that Rashi had two comments on

"voices in the sixth year." Rashi explained that it meant "a voice would ring out that Moshiach ben David was coming," or alternatively, it was referring to the sound of the *shofar*, calling the Jews to repent.

The "sound of the *shofar*" had been ringing out in Israel's cities and homes all summer, as the silence was repeatedly pierced by the wailing of the siren warning that another barrage of missiles was on its way from Gaza. At the same time, throughout 2014 there had also been a number of reports in the international press of people in all parts of the world hearing the strange sounds of a *shofar* playing a single, long note coming from the heavens[i].

The whole world was extremely puzzled about this strange "*shofar* noise" that they'd been hearing all year, and that they couldn't locate the source of.

Rabbi Bracha told his students that he believed the temporary cease-fire between Hamas and the State of Israel was solely in order for the war to return in the seventh year, as the *Gemara* said, "In the seventh year, wars." Rabbi Bracha explained that according to the Arizal, the year 5775 would be the main process of clarification and selection, in preparation for the Moshiach's arrival.

Towards the end of 2014, Rabbi Chaim Kanievsky also went on record to say: *"The Moshiach is no longer waiting at the entrance, he's already been given permission to open the door!"* And when he was asked specifically what he meant, he replied, *"It's possible that we've reached the end of the exile."*

When Operation Protective Edge began in July 2014, another leading kabbalist in Israel known as "the Milkman", Rabbi Chaim Perachia Cohen, made the following statement: *"They informed me from Heaven that the redemption process started today. The Jewish people is going to be redeemed. No*

---

[i] Other accounts stated that the noise was coming from the ground.

one knows how long it will take, dear brothers, but know that the complete redemption process has begun, and because of this, the troubles are not going to cease in coming."

Meanwhile, the kabbalist Rav David Chaim Stern from Bnei Brak told his students in the autumn of 2014 that the situation was only going to get worse from day to day, and that only Moshiach could solve the problem.

There were many, many other statements and predictions from many different sources all saying the same thing: If "voices" had indeed been heard in the sixth year, then that meant that in the seventh year, 5775, "war" was looming on the horizon, with the promise of Moshiach coming in the eighth.

While the leaders of the Jewish people were calling for more unity and love, the Iranians were also calling for more unity among Israel's sworn enemies. In 2014, a senior Iranian Ayatollah, Mohammed Ali Movahedi-Kermani, said, "The issue of Palestine is an Islamic issue. The Islamic world must come together to destroy the false Israeli regime... If this happens, nothing will be left of Israel." This, and other similar statements, was the standard rhetoric coming out of Iran.

Many of the weapons being fired at Israel from the Gaza Strip were made in Iran, and it was no secret that the Iranian regime was also pulling the strings of the Hezbollah terrorist organization up in Lebanon too. At this time, the Israeli government was falling over itself, trying to prevent Hezbollah from re-opening the Lebanese front when the country was barely coping with the thousands of rockets raining down from Gaza.

Rabbi Berland once wrote: "From America to Russia, and from Europe to Africa, they all want to destroy us. There is no concept of unity between the nations of the world. It's only their hatred of Israel that unifies them."

And 'Israel-bashing' wasn't just a problem for Israelis living in the holy land. As the fighting continued in the Gaza Strip, the world's media happily whipped up as much anti-Semitism and anti-Jewish feeling as they could, particularly within Europe. Everywhere you looked, there was growing anti-Semitism, and growing 'anti-Israel' feeling on display.

And who knew what this hatred could lead to? As the Jewish year 5774 turned into 5775, it felt as though the spiritual stakes being played for had never been higher. On the table, there was the redemption of the Jewish people, or its destruction, or maybe — both.

Rabbi Berland commented at this time that every day that something terrible wasn't happening to the Jews, it was a miracle.

Even as the cease-fire with Hamas took hold, the papers continued to be full of headlines about the Iranian nuclear bomb, and the very fragile "peace" on Israel's borders. Was a full-fledged war about to break out again, or was God planning something else for the seventh year?

HOLLAND

"The relationship between the State of Israel and its haredi population is of concern to the entire Jewish world. From the economic and social instability of an exponentially growing community of non-productive citizens, to the unsavory headlines about extreme and violent behavior, it is clear that a policy of laissez-faire can no longer be tolerated."

– From the Makom website, the self-styled 'Israel Education Lab' of the Jewish Agency for Israel[i]

"A day after being arrested by Dutch police at the request of the Israeli police, Rabbi Eliezer Berland was released from arrest in Amsterdam. Talks are ongoing between Israel and the Netherlands to bring an extradition hearing, which Berland's lawyers say could take as long as a year. His passport was retained but he has freedom of movement in Holland and the entire EU.... The Court denied the Israeli application as they were unable to produce an arrest warrant from Israel."

- South African Jewish Report,
September 15, 2014[ii]

★   ★   ★

[i] http://makomisrael.org/blog/haredialiyah/
[ii] "They have nothing!" says Rabbi Berland - https://www.sajr.co.za/news-and-articles/2014/09/15/they-have-nothing!-says-rabbi-berland

After the last incident with the South African Hawks in August 2014, Rabbi Berland's attendants were becoming increasingly worried that the lawless Hawks of South Africa would stop at nothing to put an end to the Rav's activities in Johannesburg, even if it meant physically harming him.

The plan had always been for the Rav to leave South Africa to travel to Uman for Rosh Hashana 5775, (October 3rd, 2014) but his attendants asked the Rav if he would be willing to move forward his departure for Uman, and if so, if he'd be willing to leave South Africa that day, September 11, 2014, if they could arrange a ticket. The Rav agreed and told his attendants that they should arrange for him to fly to Uman via Holland, with a stopover in Israel[i].

When the Rav, his wife and his attendants got to the ORT airport in Johannesburg that Wednesday night, they saw that the newsstands were piled high with papers featuring a picture of the Rav on the front page. Thanks to the Hawks, he'd apparently now become the most wanted man in South Africa. But that didn't stop the Rav and his Rebbetzin from sailing through all the passport controls, as his name didn't appear on any Interpol checks. Rabbi Berland boarded the KLM flight to Holland in exactly the same way as the other regular passengers.

The news that Rabbi Berland had left South Africa and was on his way to Uman for Rosh Hashanah spread like wildfire among the Breslov communities around the world. Unfortunately, the news also reached the ears of some of the Rav's persecutors back in Israel, who immediately began notifying the South African authorities, including the

---

[i] Remember that Rabbi Berland left Israel of his own accord, and not because there was any police record on file, or any criminal charges against him at this time, so there was no apparent problem with stopping in Israel.

Hawks, as well as the Dutch police, that a "very dangerous individual who'd been on the run from the police in Israel for two years" was about to land in Holland.

The Rav's persecutors advised the Hawks to contact the Dutch police, too, in order to lend credence to their story and to ensure that the Dutch officials would take it seriously. As soon as Rabbi Berland's plane landed in Amsterdam's Schiphol airport, two Dutch policemen boarded the flight to tell the Rav that he was under arrest, because he was wanted for crimes in Israel.

When the Rav heard this, he replied, "Great! Take me to Israel!" but the Dutch policemen told him that wasn't the way things worked, and that he'd first have to have a hearing in Holland, to decide what to do with him. They escorted the Rav off the plane and held him in custody in the airport for five hours.

As usual, the Rav didn't let the crazy circumstances pull him away from his spiritual devotions. He prayed his customary lengthy evening prayers there in the airport, while the Dutch officials ran around trying to get a straight answer out of the Israeli police about whether the Rav truly was a wanted man, and if so, what crimes he was meant to have committed.

The Dutch officials were confused, because the Rav's name wasn't on any Interpol lists and hadn't been circulated anywhere among the international law enforcement agencies. The reason for this was simple. There was no arrest warrant out for the Rav in Israel, and there was no case to answer. Rabbi Berland was being persecuted by the Israeli government for political and religious reasons, but that was hardly something they wanted publicized in a Dutch court.

While the Dutch authorities were trying to clarify Rabbi Berland's legal situation, they freed him. However, they forbade him from leaving the country, which meant that, once again, the Rav would not be able to reach Uman for Rosh Hashanah 5775.

At this time, even casual observers began to marvel at the "war" that the Israeli government seemed to be waging against this elderly *tzaddik*, Rabbi Eliezer Berland. It was common knowledge within the international community that the State of Israel had never spent so much time, money and energy tracking anyone down before, not even the biggest war criminals from the Holocaust — so what was going on here?

But even while he was being persecuted, falsely accused and slandered on all fronts, the Rav evinced nothing but forgiveness and kindness toward his persecutors, to the point of regularly praying for them and forbidding his followers to take any steps to try to defend him or publicly clear his name.

By contrast, the people who were persecuting the Rav resorted to just about every dirty trick in the book to try to convince the Dutch officials to bypass the official extradition procedures and put the Rav on the next flight out to Israel.

But things don't work that way in Europe. The Dutch police informed their Israeli counterparts that if they wanted the Rav released into their custody, they'd first have to travel out to Holland to formally present their case to a Dutch court. In the meantime, the Dutch arranged for the Rav to have two lawyers of his own to represent him in court — Sharon Nahari, from Israel, and Louis de Leon, of Dutch origin. De Leon told Yaron Yamin that there was no chance the Rav would be released in time to make it to Uman for Rosh Hashanah.

De Leon explained that there had almost never been an occasion where Holland had refused an extradition request from a country that it had an extradition treaty with. If, by some small chance, the Dutch judges would refuse to extradite the Rav back to Israel, that certainly wouldn't occur during his first appearance in a Dutch court. Whatever happened next, it looked as though the Rav was going to be staying in Holland for quite some time. The best outcome they could hope for would be if the judge agreed that the Rav should just stay under house arrest, instead of sending him to prison...

The first court hearing was arranged for the following Friday morning, September 12, 2014, with the representatives of the Israeli police force appearing in full force. Rabbi Berland appeared in court wrapped in his customary *tallis*, and spent the whole time engrossed in his holy books, as though what was happening around him didn't interest him in the slightest.

Yaron Yamin accompanied the Rav to court, and later described how the Rav told him during the proceedings: "We've reached the time of redemption."

RABBI BERLAND IN TORAH CODES

Rabbi Matisyahu Glazerson is an expert in Bible codes, the author of many books on the subject — and also an old friend of Rabbi Berland's, from when they studied together 60 years ago at Kfar Chassidim.

Rabbi Glazerson has written about Rabbi Berland appearing in Torah codes on many different occasions. The first time was when the Rav came to Johannesburg; the second time was when the Rav moved to Holland; and the third time was when Rabbi Glazerson traveled to Holland to meet with Rabbi Berland.

On that occasion, they sat together for two hours, and after the meeting, Rabbi Glazerson published some additional hints that he'd found in the Torah codes connected to Rabbi Berland. Rabbi Glazerson also released a film clip during his trip to Holland called, 'The appearance of Rav Eliezer Berland in Torah codes."

In the film clip, Rabbi Glazerson showed how the words "Eliezer Berland Tzaddik" appeared together with the words, "The arising of the *Erev Rav* against Judaism." Rav Glazerson also pointed out that this same Torah code revealed the words "Breslov" and "*HaTikkun HaKlali*."

In a separate film clip put out by Rabbi Glazerson in December 2018, there were even more clues that everything Rabbi Berland was going through was closely related to the redemption, and the coming of the Moshiach. (See picture)

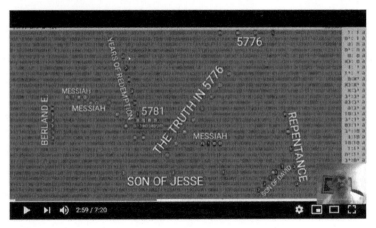

YEARS OF REDEMPTION MESSIAH RABBI BERLAND code Glazerson

The Dutch judge spent eight hours pouring through all of the 'evidence' that the Israeli police had cobbled together as part of their false allegations against the Rav, and then concluded: "There is nothing here!"

The Dutch judge stated clearly that there was no evidence that could justify bringing Rabbi Berland before an Israeli court. The judge then went on to tell the Rav: "I'm really sorry that this is how people in Israel act toward holy people like you." The Dutch judge then freed Rabbi Berland completely, without any restrictive conditions whatsoever.

One of the lawyers commented afterwards that this was "an historical event which will be taught in law schools" — the first time ever that a European country with an extradition treaty with Israel turned down an extradition request after just one court hearing.

But the Israeli police weren't done yet, and immediately requested appeal proceedings to try to get the judge's decision overturned, which caused the Dutch judge to rebuke them sharply. "You should be ashamed of yourselves!" he told the Israeli officials.

At this time, the Rav's followers undertook a "thank you" prayer service at the Kotel and sang and danced until daybreak. Rabbi Berland also spoke in a live broadcast to the students at the Shuvu Banim *Yeshiva* to strengthen them and encourage them to still make the trip to Uman, even though he once again wouldn't be with them, as until the court proceedings in Holland were concluded, he couldn't leave the country.

Around this time, a TV crew from Israel's Channel 2, one of the station's that had broadcast the allegations about the Rav two years earlier, came to interview him in Holland.

The Rav told them: *"I'm disappointed that there are only very few claims being made against me, because the first thing the Torah says is that you should always be someone who is being pursued and harassed, if you want to succeed in life. You should say 'welcome' to every bit of criticism and every allegation[i].*

I've spent two years in Purim already, where everything and everyone is wearing a costume. Channel 2 says that an

---

[i] A clip of this interview would later be used as the basis of one of the forged video 'confessions'.

Israeli Rav is suspected of these types of things, so I understand that there is a war against the Torah, and against religious people. They're going against me, in order to stop people from doing teshuva, and in order that people will say that even Rabbis are doing the same sort of filthy things that they themselves are doing.

But this is not appropriate at all! This one is as far from the other as the east is from the west. It's as far [from the truth] as Saturn, Uranus, Neptune and Pluto [are from the earth],... more than 10 billion kilometers away!"

When they asked the Rav why he'd left the country, the Rav answered:

"I have a mission in the world, to stop Jewish assimilation. Jewish men are marrying non-Jewish women, and intermarriage is up to 70 percent in Scandinavia, and 50 percent here in Holland."

Channel 2 then asked Rabbi Berland if he was aware that the Israeli police were looking for him. The Rav responded, "Of course I know. Thirty armed men with their guns pointing everywhere showed up to two weddings I officiated at, so of course I knew they were looking for me! And I say 'welcome' to them, that they're looking for me. Here I arrived in Holland, let the Israeli police come to Holland now.

Let them send 10 police representatives here, together with the police chief. Let him tell the justice minister that he wants to extradite this man from Holland. I'll pay for his ticket! I'm prepared to pay for your television station to come here, and we'll sit at this table and I'll pay for this conference room here at the Sheraton. Bring the plaintiff and all the people that you say are complaining against me. Let them sit here and tell me what they have against me. I'll pay for their tickets, you will be here with your TV sets and let these people step forward and say to me what they have against me."

When Rabbi Berland's persecutors saw how many of the

Rav's followers were flying out to Holland to be with him, and how many more were expected to come out to celebrate Yom Kippur, Sukkos and the rest of the High Holidays with him, they hit on a new plan. They lodged a formal protest with the Dutch court, and requested that even though the Rav had been freed unconditionally until the next hearing, he should still be prevented from celebrating the Jewish holidays with his followers.

They argued that as the Rav had been "on the run," as they termed it, for two years already, he could very easily escape the country before the next hearing. They asked for a new hearing, this time with three judges, and requested that the previous judge — who had gone through all the evidence and rebuked the Israeli police for wasting everyone's time — should be disqualified from participating.

The Dutch acceded to the Israelis' request, and the new hearing was scheduled just two days before Yom Kippur. Once again, Rabbi Berland came to court wrapped in his *tallis*, and carrying a stack of holy books with him, which he proceeded to study the whole time he was in court. Every time the judges asked him for his opinion or view on what was happening, he replied, "If you want to arrest me, then please, go ahead and arrest me. It's a shame to be wasting everyone's time like this."

The Israeli prosecutors falsely alleged that Rabbi Berland had been running away from Israeli justice for two years. They also falsely asserted that the Rav had deliberately been staying in countries that didn't have an extradition treaty with Israel, in order to escape "justice."

The Rav's lawyers showed that both claims were patently untrue. They informed the Dutch court that the Rav had left Israel voluntarily on his own Israeli passport as a completely free man. No case was being prosecuted against him, and no arrest warrant had been issued. They also showed how the

US, Switzerland and South Africa — and many of the other countries the Rav had passed through on his travels — did, indeed, have extradition treaties with Israel.

When the Dutch judges questioned the Rav about why he'd been traveling to all these different places the last two years, he replied that he was on a mission to try to end all the Jewish assimilation that had been occurring in these places, and explained to the court what the rate of assimilation was in each of these places.

(Of course, the deeper reason that the Rav had left Israel was the deal he'd made with Heaven to endure many years of exile and public humiliation in order to save the Jewish people from a harsh fate, but that wasn't a discussion the Dutch judges could hear, much less comprehend.)

Ultimately, the Dutch court completely rejected the Israeli government's request to imprison the Rav until the next hearing, which meant that he was free to celebrate the High Holidays with his followers.

★ ★ ★

After this second hearing, the Rav made the following comments to some of his followers: "*The terrorists in Gaza are getting help from the Israeli government. The next prime minister of Israel will already be from Hamas, maybe [Ismaiel] Haniya himself. It's impossible to know exactly who. Because today, all the wars they make [referring to the Israeli government] are only against rabbinic scholars, and against people like Rabbi Berland. Instead of waging war against Hamas, they're just waging war against Rabbi Berland. It's a sign that in the next election, Haniya himself will be the next prime minister of Israel, or maybe it'll be Arafat's nephew?*

The only focus of the [Israeli] government seems to be to unite with the terrorists, and to persecute Rabbis, so there'll be less Jewish continuity. So that's why they're fighting their 'war' [against the Torah world], and all the world is laughing at this, and saying, 'We have no idea what's going on here, or why [the Israeli government is chasing after this Rabbi] so very much!' They have no idea what's going on, after six million Jews got killed, and yet they still see the Israeli government supporting the terrorists [financially], and even giving them more weapons.

I explained in the court how the only 'gangsters' the Israeli government is interested in these days are Rabbis and Roshei Yeshiva, and that's why the Israeli police are going out of their minds, asking themselves, 'How are we going to blacken his name?' [In Johannesburg,] they sent 50 armed men after me… I officiated at four weddings in Johannesburg, and at the last one the police arrived with their patrol cars and sent armed commandos after me.

We're really seeing God face-to-face in all of this, and everything is going to be transformed into beautiful things. Every second, we're seeing miracles and wonders. Now, this is really a big sanctification of God's name, and everyone is going to do teshuva, because they're all seeing on television how [the Israeli government] is chasing after the Rav day and night. It's simply showing everyone that this is just a war against Shuvu Banim, and a war against Rabbi Berland, because we're bringing people back to teshuva.

Today, there are nearly a million religious returnees [in Israel], and they just can't stand the idea that people who were once gangsters are today Rabbis with side curls and beards."

★   ★   ★

The Dutch judges had told the Israeli police that unless they had an arrest warrant prepared against the Rav in Israel, there were simply no legal grounds for them to extradite him back to Israel. Instead of admitting the truth — that there was no case against Rabbi Berland, and there never had been — the Israeli authorities asked for a few more weeks to allow them to "arrange" the evidence required to extradite the Rav. The Dutch court fixed the date of the next hearing for November 17, 2014 and informed the Rav that according to Dutch law he needed to stay in Holland until then.

In contrast to the relatively low cost of living in South Africa, Holland was very expensive, and the problem of where the Rav's followers should stay loomed large, as hundreds of people began arriving in anticipation of the Jewish holidays. A holiday village on the Dutch Island of Texel, located close to Amsterdam, was suggested as a possible solution to the problem.

The holiday village owned by a righteous convert named Abraham ben Abraham. When the Rav's followers came to see the location, Abraham ben Abraham welcomed them warmly and showed them the guesthouses that he owned, which included a number of different holiday cottages and even a shul.

He told the Rav's followers that he'd been waiting for a group of Jews to come and pray in his shul for 10 years. His parents, before they died, left instructions in their will saying that they knew that the God of the Jews was the true God and had requested from their son that all of their money and property should be used to help the Jews in some way.

Abraham told the followers of the Rav that almost no Jews had ever come to the island before, despite the fact that he'd built a beautiful shul full of holy books that was currently standing unused — something that upset Abraham greatly.

So it was that Rabbi Berland spent his first Rosh Hashanah in Holland on the Island of Texel, together with those of his followers who hadn't traveled out to Uman.

Before the holiday began, he told his community, "My heart is broken for all of us, that we won't merit being together in Uman. But if the heart is broken, then it's possible to bring down all the light of Uman, even to Amsterdam. Uman is here, and we are in Uman. The holy Rebbe is with us. We can't be separated from the gathering in Uman! We're all together still, like one man."

On Yom Kippur 5775 (October 4, 2014), 400 of the Rav's followers flew out from Israel to Amsterdam to spend Yom Kippur with him there. Some more students had flown in from Uman or Israel, while a third group of around 100 people had traveled on two buses overland from Uman to Amsterdam — a journey of some 54 hours — demonstrating extreme self-sacrifice in order to be with their Rav.

When the first bus arrived in Amsterdam it drove up outside the Rav's lodgings. The Rav immediately came out of his home, boarded the bus, and gave his followers a rousing *Torah class* for half an hour, discussing the greatness of the Tzaddik, Rebbe Nachman, and about Rosh Hashanah and Yom Kippur.

He continued that he wanted to build a *yeshiva* for his followers in Amsterdam, but only on condition that his followers would commit to learning Torah in Holland 24 hours a day. The Rav concluded: "*Next week, we'll already start reading Genesis... Whatever curses a person has to deal with, ultimately they are all just blessings. The more curses and problems he has, the more he'll ultimately merit to have blessings. There is no such thing as a curse that can't become a blessing. All the curses in the world are going to be transformed into blessings... There's no such thing as a curse! End of story!*"

After the Rav's talk, the coach continued its journey to the Island of Texel — where it was discovered that the first "blessing" had occurred, as more of the Rav's followers had arrived in Holland than could be accommodated in Texel.

While the women and children in the group were given the cottages, many of the men found themselves literally sleeping on the sidewalk until the last minute, when someone managed to rent a couple of big halls where they could stay in the meantime.

This anonymous helper also arranged for the delivery of a number of mattresses for the Rav's followers to sleep on and organized a pre-fast meal for the Rav's followers, many of whom hadn't eaten the whole day, with the eve of Yom Kippur fast approaching.

It was one of the largest gatherings of the Rav's followers since he'd begun his exile from Israel two years earlier. The number of Breslovers in Texel surpassed even the numbers of Breslovers in the main Breslov shul in Meah Shearim. The more the Rav was being chased and persecuted, the more followers he seemed to be attracting.

One of the people praying with the Rav and his community happened to be an important member of the Belgian Jewish community who was a follower of Rabbi Dov Kook of Tiberius. This man had heard that Rabbi Berland was going to be leading the prayers at Texel on Yom Kippur, and he decided to join the service to come and see Rabbi Berland for himself. This was the first time that this Belgian Jew had ever laid eyes on the Rav, and as he described it afterwards: "The Rav is the Holy of Holies. There are no words to describe him!"

When this Jew returned to Belgium, he told the members of the Belgian Jewish community who the Rav and his followers really were and told them to stop listening to all the lies being spread by the media in Holland and elsewhere. As the situation continued to develop in Holland, this Belgian Jew was instrumental in ensuring that many of the Rav's followers who later ended up coming to Belgium were received with great respect and hospitality by the Jewish community there.

*   *   *

When it became obvious that things weren't going their way in Dutch courts, the Rav's persecutors fell back on their tried-and-tested strategy of slandering the Rav to the local media, with the aim of turning public opinion against him and his followers.

This reprehensible strategy had been very successful in Morocco and South Africa, so now the Rav's persecutors started stirring things up against him in the Dutch press, too. The European media generally doesn't need a lot of encouragement to write disparaging, negative lies about Jews, especially Israeli Jews who happen to be big Rabbis. But where the story gets even more repugnant than usual is that the Rav's persecutors decided to stir things up on Yom Kippur, the holiest day of the year.

While Rabbi Berland and his followers were fervently engaged in getting ready for the Yom Kippur prayers, the Rav's persecutors in Israel called up as many news agencies, newspapers and journalists as they could, warning them about the "dangerous, wanted criminal" who was hiding out on the Island of Texel.

So it was that on the holiest day of the year, tens of journalists and photographers suddenly descended on the otherwise peaceful Island of Texel and began harassing all the Jews they could find, in the middle of the Yom Kippur services. The journalists asked the Rav's followers all sorts of loaded questions in the hopes that they'd say something explosive that they could then take out of context or twist into another headline-grabbing false story.

ANTI-SEMITIC JOURNALISM?

While the Jewish communities in Europe were coming under increasing threat from radical Islam, the whereabouts of Rabbi Berland and his followers was continually and openly publicized by the Dutch media, which encouraged its readers to view Shuvu Banim as a type of "lethal sect" or the "Jewish ISIS."

The Rav and his followers tried to keep a low profile wherever they went in Holland, but they were constantly tracked down by the Dutch media, who made it a *holy duty* to force the community out of whichever holiday village or premises they'd managed to rent.

Remember, Rabbi Berland was being forcibly detained in Holland only at the request of the Israeli government, yet he and his community were never granted any security protection by the Dutch authorities, while the Dutch press continued to write about them in a manner reminiscent of the worst Nazi propaganda.

One article, written in the *Dutch Telegraph* on November 15, 2014, was headlined "The Lethal Sect", and was illustrated with a big picture of Rabbi Berland superimposed over the Al Aqsa Mosque. This article included the following quotes, guaranteed to get European anti-Semites a little hot under the collar:

"Someone from that group [Shuvu Banim] may just blow up the Al-Aqsa Mosque."

"His supporters are a mix of outcasts, criminals and fanatics."

Quoting an 18-year-old named Mohammed, discussing his opinion of the Shuvu Banim *Yeshiva* in Jerusalem: "They're just a bunch of weirdos."

Discussing the "many women" who apparently didn't come forward with complaints against Rabbi Berland because they were 'scared for their lives': "[These women] don't want to bring down on themselves the wrath of the fanatical members of Shuvu Banim. The supporters, who have links with Zionist leaders and the Israeli underworld, stop at nothing."

So there you have it: The Dutch media was portraying Rabbi Berland and his followers as a bunch of weirdos, criminals and fanatics with links to the Israeli underworld, murderous tendencies, and a secret plot to blow up the Temple Mount... And if it appeared in the media, then of course it *must* be true.

★ ★ ★

As the media circus outside the holiday village of Texel continued to grow, the residents urged the mayor of Texel to do something about the strange visitors who were causing such a commotion on the quiet island and bringing all the press out on the streets. The mayor came to Abraham ben Abraham, the owner of the holiday village, and told him that he had to take down the huge tents that had been erected to temporarily house the Rav's followers. The mayor then told him that he needed to evict the whole congregation from his holiday village — effective immediately!

The mayor explained that Texel was a peaceful, quiet place, and that his Jewish guests were causing far too much commotion with the press to be able to stay. Abraham ben Abraham tried to explain to the mayor, and to the other officials who'd accompanied her, that it was currently Yom Kippur, the holiest day of the Jewish calendar, and it was completely impossible to accede to their request and throw everybody out onto the street. According to Dutch law, the government is obliged to respect other people's religious traditions, so the island officials reluctantly gave the Rav and his community a day's respite.

As soon as Yom Kippur ended, a fleet of buses drove up to the holiday village, under orders from the mayor and her colleagues, to get everyone — all the Jewish men, women and children — out of Texel ASAP. All this took place under the beady eyes of the Dutch media, who had television crews set up everywhere to publicize the "invasion" of Texel by a bunch of *chassidic* Jews from Israel.

Before long, the Dutch police also appeared on the scene, to enforce the evacuation order from Texel. Some of the police officers started acting in a very aggressive manner toward the visiting Jews, particularly the many mothers who were trying to get their belongings together, pack their things and gather their children, under very short notice and very stressful circumstances.

The Dutch police started yelling at the women and children who weren't moving fast enough for them, and literally started to push them onto the waiting buses, in a scene that was all-too-reminiscent of the horrors visited on European Jewry during World War II.

Abraham ben Abraham, the kind Dutch host, was moved to tears by what he was witnessing. For days afterwards, he was seen wandering around Texel looking disturbed and upset. While all the Jews in the holiday village were evicted immediately after Yom Kippur, another 40 followers who had rented apartments on the island were given permission to stay on in Texel for a little while longer.

Back on the buses, the Rav's followers had no idea where they were headed, or what they could expect when they got there. A small number of them decided to get off the buses in Amsterdam and try to make their own arrangements, but the majority decided to stay on the buses, which were now heading for Belgium, at Rabbi Berland's suggestion. They had no idea what was waiting for them in Belgium, but they were certain that if Rabbi Berland told them to go there, something or someone would surely turn up to assist them.

And that's exactly what happened. The Belgian Jew

who'd spent Yom Kippur with the Rav on Texel came back to Belgium with such glowing reports of the Rav and his community, that the Belgian Jews welcomed the refugees from Texel with open arms. They rented a big vacation village for them with big, beautiful vacation cottages in the Belgium countryside where they could spend the entire Sukkos, and also arranged 5-star kosher catering for them for the duration of the festival.

Most of these people had already spent Rosh Hashanah in Uman and Yom Kippur in Texel, and now, God had arranged for them to spend Sukkos in the beautiful Belgian countryside, replete with lakes and rivers. Wherever their devotion to Rabbi Berland took them, in each place they clearly saw how God's Divine providence was smoothing the path.

In the meantime, another 300 of Rabbi Berland's followers managed to spend the holidays with the Rav himself, back in Amsterdam. The mayor of Amsterdam had given permission for a local Jewish school to be opened to accommodate them, and mattresses were brought over to the school hall, so people could sleep and eat there.

During the time in Holland, one of Rabbi Berland's followers went outside to get some air and somehow stepped on a broken tile that caused him to fall flat on his face. He found that he couldn't move, and he just lay on the floor until other people came out and discovered him.

The people who found him didn't know what to do, and whether they should call an ambulance for him or not, as he didn't have health insurance. The man's son-in-law immediately ran over to the Rav, gave over his name, and explained that his father-in-law was immobilized. He asked Rabbi Berland whether they should call an ambulance for him.

The Rav replied that they should, because it was really

a matter of saving a life. He began to explain to the son-in-law about all the bones in the pelvis, and how they all fit together. The Rav continued that there was one bone located between the pelvis and the leg, and if it was broken, it would require an emergency operation to prevent it from becoming a potentially life-threatening issue.

He explained all the different medical issues connected to the situation, including what medical examinations were required, what the results would show, and what treatment they needed. The Rav concluded that the father-in-law would have to stay a full week in the hospital after the operation, and that he'd then have to rest at home for a further three months until his pelvic bone was completely healed.

In the meantime, no one even knew what had actually happened to the man, or whether he'd even broken something, let alone what he might have broken. But they called the ambulance, as the Rav had told them. However, the man's daughter refused to let him travel in the ambulance until the Rav came to give her father a blessing, and to guarantee him that everything would be okay.

As soon as Rabbi Berland heard this, he immediately came out to the scene of the accident and began to explain to the paramedics in English what had happened, what was broken, and how to fix it — and that it was an emergency situation that needed to be dealt with immediately, as the danger was growing with every passing moment.

The Dutch paramedics were very surprised that the Rav appeared to have the medical knowledge of a doctor, and that he seemed to know exactly what the problem was. The man was taken to the nearest emergency room where the doctor took a number of X-rays and then started explaining to the son-in-law what the problem was: The man had broken a specific bone between his pelvis and leg, and it was actually a very dangerous break and needed urgent treatment to prevent the fracture from widening...

Word for word, the doctor gave over exactly the same information that the son-in-law had heard previously from Rabbi Berland. Afterwards, the son-in-law asked the doctor how long his father-in-law would have to stay in hospital and then recuperate post-op — but really, he already knew the answer.

The doctor told him: "One week in the hospital, and three months resting at home."

After *Simchas Torah*, it became clear that there weren't enough places for the Rav's followers to stay in Holland, so most of them returned to Israel. Some followers stayed in Amsterdam, while a full busload of people traveled to Uman.

Before the bus departed for Uman, the Rav told the travelers: "No one will remain at the border." He then repeated this unusual phrase a number of times, but his followers had no idea why he was saying it, or what it all meant. When the bus finally pulled up to the Ukrainian border, they discovered that one of the passengers had lost his passport, and it looked like he was going to be forced to stay at the border, unable to travel on.

Then they remembered what the Rav had said, so they stubbornly refused to continue their journey without him. In the end, the Russian border guards allowed him to continue on with the group, and "no one remained at the border" — just as the Rav had predicted.

★ ★ ★

On November 17, 2014, Rabbi Berland was back in court in Holland, as the Israeli authorities continued to twist the arm of the Dutch authorities to try to get him extradited back to Israel, despite their lack of evidence.

The Dutch announced that they would hand down their decision on the case on December 1, 2014.

While the Dutch courts were deliberating over whether to accede to the Israeli government's request to extradite the Rav, Israel was rocked by another awful, shocking act of terrorism.

On November 18, 2014, two Palestinian terrorists — cousins living in an East Jerusalem suburb — drove over to the Har Nof neighborhood in Jerusalem, entered the Kehillas Bnei Torah synagogue, and started shooting and stabbing the worshippers, who were in the middle of the morning prayers.

Four men died of their wounds immediately, while a fifth person finally succumbed to his injuries almost a year later, after having spent 11 months in a coma. One of the policemen who engaged the terrorists in a gun battle, a young Druze policeman from northern Israel, was also killed in the attack, which left another seven people injured. It was the deadliest attack in Jerusalem since the Mercaz HaRav atrocity in March 2008, when a Palestinian terrorist entered the Mercaz HaRav *Yeshiva* and gunned down a number of teenage boys in cold blood.

It's a tenet of Jewish faith, however uncomfortable, that the death of *tzaddikim* atones for the sins of the generation. As the Jews of Israel were mourning the Har Nof massacre, the Shuvu Banim community in Amsterdam sadly also had their own tragedy to deal with.

Two of the Rav's younger followers, Shmuel Meir Langlavan and Natan Druck were killed in a horrific accident on the Dutch highway as they were returning from spending a Shabbos with Rabbi Berland in Amsterdam at the beginning of December 2014.

They were flown back to Israel for burial, and during the service, the Rav eulogized them from Holland. He said:
"These two tzaddikim also could also have brought the

redemption, if they hadn't been taken from us. This year, the year 5775, is the 'etia HaMoshiach'[i]. The Chasam Sofer explains that 'in every generation, you can find the soul of Moshiach ben Yosef'. But if the generation isn't worthy, God removes that person from the world before the age of 20. If these two had remained in the world, and had reached the age of 20, they could have brought the redemption and Moshiach ben David.

But the generation wasn't ready, and lacked the vessels [to receive] such holy, pure souls...

And now, these two tzaddikim have canceled all the decrees hanging over Am Yisrael... If they had reached the age of 20, the redemption would have happened immediately, and they would have brought Moshiach ben David and rebuilt the Temple... Now, we are at the most sublime, transcendent moments for the Jewish people. We've reached the moment of redemption, truly. Now, God wants to bring the redemption. God wants to bring the biggest light of all."

With all these harsh judgments manifesting themselves in the "war against the Torah," the days continued to tick down to December 1, 2014, the day when the Dutch court was to hand down their decision about what to do with Rabbi Berland.

That same Monday, two students from Shuvu Banim visited the synagogue of one of the generation's biggest *tzaddikim* and kabbalists, the late Chacham Abraham Chai. The students told Chacham Abraham that the State of Israel had taken Rabbi Berland to court in Holland, and the Chacham immediately replied: "Lies! It's all lies!"

The students explained that the Dutch court was due to give their judgment at 2 p.m. that day, and the Chacham

---

[i] 5775 has the same *gematria* as this Aramaic phrase which means "the time of Moshiach."

then said to them, "There is still no judgment that has been made, because judgment has a smell." The Chacham then lifted his hands up to Heaven, and he began to cry and pray on the Rav's behalf.

Sure enough, later that day the judges in Holland announced that the decision on whether to extradite the Rav to Israel had been postponed once again.

BACK FROM THE BRINK

"We are past red alert at this stage, it's all hands on deck because, sadly, the question is not whether the French Jewish community will be targeted, but when," Chlomik Zenouda, vice-president of the National Bureau for Vigilance against anti-Semitism, told JTA before the assault on the Hypercacher supermarket."
– Time Magazine, January 9ᵗʰ, 2015[i]

★ ★ ★

Although Rabbi Berland has always defied the normal way of the world when it comes to matters of health — barely eating, barely sleeping, dipping in freezing cold *mikvahs*, standing on his feet and dancing for 18 hours a day, even in his later years — and even though the Rav happily accepted even his most difficult circumstances as being God's will for him, the spiritual "war" against him still took an enormous toll on his physical health.

While the non-Jewish world was ushering in their new year of 2015, news reached Israel on January 1, 2015 that the Rav had fainted twice, gone into sudden cardiac arrest, and had been admitted to the hospital in Amsterdam in an unconscious state. His situation was extremely precarious,

---

[i] Kosher Grocery Assault Confirms Worst Fears of French Jews - http://time.com/3661697/paris-terror-attack-kosher-grocery-jewish/

and the call went out to his followers back in Israel to immediately drop everything they were doing and run to the Kotel to pour their hearts out in prayer that the Rav should pull through and recover fully.

The night before he was admitted to the hospital, the Rav gave a class over the phone where he had told over a story about Rav Hersh Leib Lippel, one of the leading Breslover *chassidim* from the previous generation. The Rav said that after two of Rav Lippel's friends had died, he himself fell sick and was brought to the hospital, where it appeared that he, too, had passed away.

The Jewish burial society was called to come and attend to the dead Rav Lippel — which is when Rav Lippel shocked everyone by waking up. He told them that he'd just seen the Angel of Death, who'd come for him with a sharp, drawn sword and taken him to Heaven. There, Rav Lippel had seen his two friends waiting for him at the entrance to the Garden of Eden, because they didn't want to go in until Rav Hersh Leib had arrived.

But Rav Hersh Leib didn't want to go to the Garden of Eden just yet! So he'd fought with the Angel of Death and had beaten him, and then he'd been returned back to this world.

On the day that he'd gone into sudden cardiac arrest and had been admitted to the hospital, the Rav told one of his followers: "Just as I said it in the class yesterday, so it was with me today. I was already in Heaven, and I fought with and succeeded against the Angel of Death."

At the time the Rav fainted, at 1:45 p.m. on Thursday, January 1, 2015, he was in a room on the fourth floor of the hotel in Amsterdam where he was staying. The ambulance that was dispatched to bring him to the hospital used a crane from the Fire Department to lower him down through the fourth-floor window of the hotel, as they needed to ensure that the Rav remained in a horizontal position and the stretcher was too long to fit into the hotel elevator.

From the eyewitness reports from the scene, it seems that at the same time that the Rav's body was being lowered to the ground, the Rav's soul was returning back down to this lowly world.

One of the students who was with the Rav at the time he was taken down through the fourth-floor window later described how the Rav had been covered with a *tallis*, and said that it was a fearful sight to see, just like when the Satan had showed the Jewish people a mirage in the sky that Moshe had died in the desert.

Two weeks earlier, on December 15, 2014), the Rav had given his followers a number of instructions. He'd told them to start reciting the *Tikkun HaKlali* seven times a day, in order that he should live. He'd also announced that everyone should come to him on Shabbos Chanukah (December 19-20, 2014) and that no one should be missing.

On Sunday, December 28, 2014, the Rav had arrived at

the morning prayer service with the Breslov community, and unusually, recited the *Avinu Malkeinu* prayer— even though it is usually only recited on fast days and during the Ten Days of Repentance between Rosh Hashanah and Yom Kippur. The prayer is a supplication for Divine mercy.

The Rav recited this prayer with great emotion, and afterwards told the congregation that everyone should fast for three days from dawn until nightfall — the men, women and even the children. The community had no idea what was going on, or why they'd been asked to fast in this way, but it was obvious that something very serious lay behind the Rav's request, so no one asked any questions and everyone accepted upon themselves to fast.

On the second day of the fast, the Rav again came to the morning prayers, and told the congregation that they could eat that day, because part of the decrees had already been canceled via the subsequent death of two other *tzaddikim*, Rav Ephraim Baruch Rackman and Rav Mordechai Reuven Rokeach. But the Rav concluded that on the following day, everyone needed to fast again. Shortly before this happened the Rav had also asked his followers in Israel to gather together every day at the Kotel to pray for him.

Once the news reached Israel that Rabbi Berland had been hospitalized due to a sudden cardiac arrest and was in serious condition, all the pieces started to fall into place that the Rav had foreseen what was about to happen. It later transpired that the Rav had been unconscious for a full hour. The people who were attending to the Rav in Holland at this time truly believed the worst was happening, and frantically called the community back in Israel to run to the Kotel to start praying. Rabbi Berland's life was on the line.

The Rav's attendant, Reb Natan Becanson, was by his side the whole time. Afterwards, he recounted exactly what had happened: *"On Thursday, January 1, 2015, after the Rav prayed the morning prayers, which lasted for quite a number of hours, with the kehillah in the village, the Rav returned home, and on the way he eulogized Rabbi Rackman on the telephone for around 20 minutes.*

When he arrived back at his lodgings, the Rav fainted, and he had to go and rest on his bed for half an hour. We already realized that the situation was not looking so good, so we called an ambulance. In the meantime, before the ambulance arrived, the Rav returned to his Torah learning as though nothing untoward had happened. The whole time we'd been with the Rav, we'd never once seen him with any weakness or sickness.

In the middle of his studies, the Rav fainted for a second time, and this time he fell unconscious on the floor. The ambulance arrived two minutes later, and the paramedics figured out that the Rav had suffered a cardiac arrest, and that it would be dangerous to move the Rav and that he needed to be taken to the hospital on a stretcher."

Reb Besanson continues: *"At some point while the Rav was lying on the floor, he regained consciousness long enough to tell me, 'Bring the Ketzos HaChoshen[i], Part A.' The next thing I knew, the paramedics had arranged for a crane to come from the fire department, and that's how they brought the Rav down to the ambulance. In the hospital, they connected him to an external pacemaker, and I was by his side the whole night.*

During the night, I saw a white line [on the monitor] a number of times, showing that the heart's rate was very low and required external intervention in order to keep the heart beating. But at no time did I see any change in the Rav. The Rav simply continued to learn the Ketzos HaChoshen. The Rav didn't appear changed at all by his experiences. He was the same Rav, doing the same learning, with the same determination, and displaying the same self-sacrifice.

---

[i] An in-depth halachic commentary on Choshen Mishpat.

In the middle of the night, the doctors decided that there was no choice other than to operate on the Rav the next day and implant a pacemaker. In the morning, the Rav told me that everything that the Jewish people was going through, and everything that was happening in Israel, had affected him greatly. The Rav had taken it all very much to heart — all of the stabbings that had happened during the 'Knife Intifada', the various tragedies that had been occurring, all the people who weren't keeping Torah and mitzvos — he'd been affected by it all.

The Tzaddik is the heart of the world, and he feels all the sorrows of Israel."

Once it had been determined that Rabbi Berland had suffered a cardiac arrest, his heart was hooked up to an external pacemaker, while the doctors informed the Rav's family and attendants that the Rav urgently needed surgery to fit him with an internal pacemaker. The Rav's attendant double-checked this recommendation with other specialists to ensure it was correct, but then subsequent events decided the matter. On Friday, the Rav's heart stopped responding, and was completely dependent on the external pacemaker.

Once that happened, the surgery was scheduled as quickly as possible. The surgery was carried out and the Rav was already back home by erev Shabbos, January 2, 2015. However, the doctors told him to stay in bed and not to go out for up to three months.

Rabbi Besanson continues: "*The doctors told the Rav that he should rest for a minimum of four days after the operation, but that same day the Rav left the hospital, because he'd arranged to officiate at a wedding for a couple who'd flown out to Amsterdam especially to have him attend. On the following day, the Rav recited the blessing on the moon with a minyan outside. The Rav immediately returned to his way of studying in a very methodical way, without any deviations or weakness."*

Another of the Rav's students, Rav Raphael Gwirtz, kept a diary of all the events that occurred to the Shuvu Banim community in Holland. Under the entry for January 3, 2015, he wrote the following:

"After Shabbos the Rav officiated at a wedding for a family that came from Israel. The Rav was very weak and looked pale. During the next few days we were constantly praying for the Rav. In Israel there were daily prayer rallies and round-the-clock recitations of Tikkun HaKlali. They asked that for now, no more people should come from Israel to visit the Rav. On the next Sunday, visitors started coming again. On Monday, the Rav was back to immersing in the river.

The Rav requested that we pray for him, because he's still very weak."

The Rav's attendant later found a note that the Rav had written at the beginning of the year (5775), but he didn't understand what was written there until after the shocking episode with the Rav's near-death experience.

That note said the following: "Tishrei = *Chesed* (kindness), Cheshvan = *Gevurah* (judgment), Kislev = *Tiferes* (splendor), Teves = *Netzach yivaleh hamaves hanetzach* (may death be abolished forever)."

When the attendant asked the Rav about this note when he was in the hospital, the Rav said, "That was the decree. And with God's help, it has been completely canceled."

After the operation to implant the pacemaker, when the Rav left the hospital, he asked everyone back in Israel to go to Rachel's tomb, and to the Tomb of the Patriarchs in Hebron, and to say the *Tikkun HaKlali* for him seven times, with the intention that "May death be abolished forever."

After the Rav was hospitalized, many members of the Shuvu Banim community did some serious introspection about how much they were really listening to the Rav's requests. The day before Chanukah, back in Kislev, senior representatives from Shuvu Banim had spoken with the Rav over the phone, and they had asked him whether they should continue holding the weekly prayer gatherings at the Kotel for the Rav's success. The Rav had previously said to stop them for a couple of weeks, when a number of serious terrorist attacks were rocking the country.

Things had quietened down a little, so his followers wanted to know whether the weekly prayer gatherings should be restarted. The Rav told them: "Yes! And you should gather there every day now!" The representatives were a little shocked and replied, "Isn't it going to be too hard for people to come to the Kotel every day?" But the Rav simply repeated what he'd said, and again confirmed, "Every day! Every day!"

It was Chanukah, and many people in the community felt it was too difficult to organize a prayer gathering every day, so the matter was quietly dropped. Less than a month later, when the terrible news hit Shuvu Banim that the Rav's holy soul had already gone up to the World of Truth, and that he'd had to fight with the Angel of Death to return to this world, many of his followers were filled with enormous regret that they hadn't done as the Rav had requested a month earlier.

As an atonement, the students at the Shuvu Banim *Yeshiva* arranged a daily gathering to be held at the Kotel, where they would say seven *Tikkun HaKlalis* for the Rav's success and good health, in addition to the weekly gathering being held for the Rav at the Kotel on Wednesday evening, which also continued.

★   ★   ★

On the January 7, 2015, less than a week after the Rav was

hospitalized and fitted with a pacemaker, Muslim terrorism hit the French capital, Paris, in a dramatic way. First, armed Muslim gunmen forced their way into the offices of a French satirical periodical called *Charlie Hebdo* and started firing. They killed 12 people and injured another 11, before being tracked down by French police and killed in a gun battle.

At the same time the *Charlie Hebdo* massacre was occurring, another armed Muslim terrorist broke into a kosher supermarket called Hypercacher in the Île-de-France region, where five Jews were murdered in cold blood and another 11 were wounded.

The twin terror attacks on the French capital shocked the world, and signaled the beginning of a new, and increasingly violent, chapter in Islamic terrorism. A couple of weeks later, on January 21, 2015), the Rav delivered the following rousing call to his followers, and to the nation of Israel:

"Now, we're in a war. This is a new intifada. In Paris, they murdered five Jews. In Holland, they also tried to kill a couple of Jews. They closed all the schools, and they closed all the offices. The children are scared to go to school now, because of what happened in Toulouse[i]. Am Yisrael, we're in more danger now than ever before. This is a terrible intifada that is spreading throughout the whole globe, the whole world."

"Yesterday, they stabbed 12 innocent, sinless Jews on a bus[ii], and no one even paid any attention; no one was even shocked by it. No one is talking about this, but we need to publicize this. The whole world is applauding each Jew that is murdered and killed.

It's impossible to sweeten the harsh judgments over the

---

[i] On March 19, 2012, four Jews, including a father and his three small children, were shot to death by a gunman at the Otzer HaTorah Jewish school in the French city of Toulouse.

[ii] On January 21, 2015, 12 Israelis were stabbed by a Palestinian terrorist on a Tel Aviv commuter bus.

people of Israel, except by jumping into the fire [i.e. acting with self-sacrifice]. Only if we jump into the fire will we be able to sweeten all the judgments, so that there won't be any more judgments against the nation of Israel.

Every man is obligated to guard his eyes! This is true self-sacrifice! If people would guard their eyes, it would sweeten all of the harsh decrees. All the bad decrees are due to a lack of guarding the eyes. Each time an eye is opened [to see forbidden things], a Jew is killed. Each time an eye is opened, a Jew is stabbed.

If someone would see how many demons and spirits [there are in every square meter of the world], even a little, then immediately his soul would leave him. Therefore, God gave us the ability not to see. And now is the time when all of the demons and spirits are coming out of the bottle and are bursting forth. All of the terrorists are demons and spirits. All of Hamas and all of Al-Qaida and all of ISIS, they are demons and spirits.

[When a person is praying,] he needs to have the proper intention, he needs to have proper attention when saying God Aechad [God is one]. AecHaD also stand for: Al-Qaida, Hamas and Da-ash (the Arabic name for ISIS). A person needs to have the correct intention that God Aechad, God is One. If a person has the intention that God is One, then he will excise all of Al-Qaida, all of Hamas, and all of Da-ash (ISIS), [those] who decapitate others, and kill children and babies.

"This whole intifada is being encouraged by the nations of the world. The whole world is egging on this intifada, all of the nations, and all of them are sorry that Hitler (may his name be erased) didn't finish the job.

Now, they're relying on the terrorist [to finish the job]... All the nations of the world long for Jewish blood... Now, there's an intifada like there hasn't been since the beginning of the world. Twelve innocent people got stabbed on a bus, and

*the [nations of the world] don't flinch. The world didn't shake,
and the world didn't even pay it any attention. They only pay
attention if a shot is fired in Gaza [in self defense], then the
whole world is shaken up. 'They fired a bullet in Gaza!? How
could they do such a terrible thing!? Who did this terrible
crime?! Judge him in The Hague, judge him in Brussels!'*

*So, we have arrived at the end of days. This is the prophecy
of the end of days. This is why Jacob was scared to reveal the
prophecy of what would happen at the end of days."*

The attacks in Paris and elsewhere created a sense of
fear and panic among the non-Jews that quickly spread to
every Western country with a Muslim population. Islam's
war against the Jews had always been complacently viewed as
the State of Israel's problem. But in 2015, the *Charlie Hebdo*
and Hypercacher massacres made it clear that the winds of
war had now blown over to Europe too.

★ ★ ★

Chaim Biton is a student of Rabbi Berland and a relative
of Zarie Sibony, one of the girls who was trapped in the
Hypercacher supermarket in Paris when a terrorist went on a
murderous rampage there. He told us about an open miracle
that happened to his relative, in the merit of the Rav:

Zarie Sibony was working as a cashier in her brother's
supermarket, Hypercacher. On that Friday, shortly before
Shabbos, a terrorist broke into the store and immediately
started firing at anyone who was standing near the entrance
or near the checkout, before taking the rest of the people in
the store as hostages.

Zarie was standing closest to the entrance, but
miraculously didn't get hurt by the initial burst of gunfire.
She fell to the floor and thought she was going to die like the

others who'd already been shot and killed, while the terrorist forced his way into the store.

When Chaim heard that his cousin was working at that time in the supermarket, he immediately called the Rav's hotline, to request a *blessing* from the Rav. The message was passed on to the Rav and he said, "Tell them that they don't have anything to worry about. She will come out on Shabbos, and by Motzei Shabbos you will hear that she has been freed and that nothing happened to her."

In the meantime, the family didn't know what had happened to Zarie, and the news was already reporting that several people had been killed in the store. Despite the Rav's *blessing* they were still very nervous, so they contacted the Rav again, this time through his driver. At this point, the terrorist was herding all the hostages together in the supermarket and the world was fearfully following the developments in Paris. The Rav again said, "Tell them that they have nothing to worry about, and that they can calm down. She will come out on Shabbos, and on Motzei Shabbos they'll hear that she came out healthy and whole."

In the meantime, the terrorist was scanning the shop and saw Zarie's foot moving. At that moment, he shot directly at her leg — and again a miracle happened, because the bullet didn't hit her. The terrorist came over and shouted at her, "What's going on?! It looks like you don't want to die!" It seemed as though he understood that she was being protected from Above.

He told her to stand up and said, "Good, if you don't want to die then you can help me. You'll do what I tell you to do." Then he told her to close the shop's shutters before the police arrived. She began to close the shutters, and when she came to the last section an older man of around 60 peeped under the shutter and asked if he could come in. She told him, "No, no, no, we're closing, don't come in!"

He pleaded with her that he just wanted to buy challos for Shabbos, and that he didn't have any challos for Shabbos. He bent down and tried to get in under the shutter — and the terrorist immediately shot him dead. Meanwhile, Zarie's family still didn't have any information about what was happening, as there was no communication with anyone inside the supermarket.

Despite the Rav's double blessing, the family still couldn't relax. Rav Jacob Biton, Chaim's father, contacted another of the Rav's attendants to ask the Rav, "What will be?" The Rav responded, "Tell them that they have nothing to worry about, they can calm down. She will leave on Shabbos and on Motzei Shabbos they will know that she came out healthy and whole."

After they heard the Rav's *blessing* the third time, with exactly the same words, they were confident that the promise of the Tzaddik would be fulfilled, and that nothing bad would happen to their relative. They continued saying *Psalms* with *emunah* and hope as they went into Shabbos.

As the saga unfolded, the terrorist ordered Zarie to bring all the hostages who had fled downstairs to the shop's basement up to him. Zarie went downstairs, and then came up with only one man, who claimed to be the only one down there[i]. The truth was that there were another 20 people hiding in the store's freezer.

The terrorist didn't believe him and started to get angry. He told Zarie to go down again and call to the other people down there and tell them to come up, and that if she didn't do it, he'd kill her. Immediately, some more people came up, including a three-year-old boy, whom the terrorist wanted to kill on the spot.

---

[i] This one man volunteered to sacrifice his life in order to save the others who were in hiding.

At that moment, one of the hostages jumped on the terrorist and took his weapon away. Unfortunately, though, the terrorist had another weapon, and he shot the person who'd tried to disarm him in the head and killed him. He also tried to shoot Zarie in the head, too, and she felt the bullet graze her cheek — but miracle of miracles, again nothing happened to her. This was the third bullet that miraculously missed her.

At the same time, another hostage tried to escape from the store and the terrorist shot him in the face. The wounded man struggled for another three hours, until he eventually succumbed to his wounds and died. God should avenge their blood.

One of the people who was hiding in the freezer downstairs sent an SMS message to journalists and told them where they were. The journalists didn't realize that the terrorist was checking the news channels on the TV screens in the supermarket the whole time throughout the siege, so they wrote a headline that people were hiding in the freezer downstairs at Hypercacher. That piece of information flashed up on the screen at precisely the same moment that the terrorist got distracted and turned away from the screen.

Zarie's brother was one of the shop's managers. Although he wasn't actually there, he still managed to access the shop's closed circuit cameras to show the police what was going on inside the store. At that point, the police believed that they were dealing with two terrorists, a man and a woman, but he told them that the woman "terrorist" was actually his sister, and that the terrorist was forcing her to help him against her will.

The terrorist said to Zarie, "If you don't do what I tell you one more time, I'm going to kill everyone." She pleaded with him, "I'll do whatever you want, but please, just don't kill the boy." He listened to her and didn't kill the three-year-old.

Then the terrorist went downstairs with her and told her that he was going to kill anyone he found down there on the spot, including her. Another open miracle happened. There were still a number of people hiding downstairs, who went and crouched in a corner when they heard the terrorist coming. Miraculously, the terrorist simply didn't see them. He went back upstairs and told Zarie that she could live, after all.

A moment after this, the terrorist decided he needed to pray, and when he bowed down, the police saw what he was doing via the CCTV. They immediately burst into the shop and killed him. It was already Shabbos, and all the hostages left the store, including Zarie Sibony, who will never forget the miracles that God did for her.

As Rabbi Berland repeatedly said, Zarie herself left the store on Shabbos, but the family only heard about her release on motzei Shabbos. The three separate blessings she'd received from the Rav had apparently saved her from the three bullets that the terrorist had aimed directly at her, but which all miraculously missed their target.

Shortly after the attack in Paris, the secret service in Belgium busted a large terrorist cell that was planning to launch a wave of attacks against the Jews living in Europe. Once the news become public, some of the leaders of the Jewish community in Belgium publicly thanked God and said that they believed they'd been rescued from the terrible decree of destruction in the merit of hosting so many of Rabbi Berland's students after Yom Kippur, as 'charity saves from death'.

★ ★ ★

Meanwhile, harsh judgments of every type continued to follow hard on the heels of each other. Barely a month after the Rav had suffered his near-fatal cardiac arrest, news came that another leading Rabbi in Israel by the name of Eliezer, Rabbi Eliezer Shlomo Schick, had passed away at the age of 75. Rav Schick was a giant in the Breslov community, building thriving communities of followers both in Boro Park, New York and also in the northern Israeli town of Yavniel.

Rabbi Schick passed away in New York on February 6, 2015, after a stay in the hospital where he was being treated for complications related to leukemia. After his passing, Rabbi Daniel Stavsky, head of the Beit Baal Shem Tov outreach organization, commented that Heaven had taken "an Eliezer for an Eliezer." Rabbi Eliezer Berland had recently had a very close call with the Angel of Death and had fought mightily to return to this lowly world and continue his holy work. But once the Heavenly decree had been issued to return the soul of a "Rabbi Eliezer" to its Maker, it appears that Rabbi Schick took the decree upon himself, and went in Rabbi Berland's place.

Within weeks of Rabbi Schick's passing, Rabbi Berland was back in court dealing with more judgments of a different kind. After their last failed attempt back in December 2015, the Israeli authorities had been redoubling their efforts to pressure the Dutch to agree to extradite Rabbi Berland back to Israel. Their efforts had been repeatedly hampered in the Dutch courts as they had no arrest warrant or credible evidence to present to the judges, so the Israeli government decided 'to go to the top' and turn the extradition of Rabbi Berland into a diplomatic affair.

On February 12, 2015, the Dutch Secretary for Justice, Klaas Dijkhoff, ordered the Dutch courts to agree to the extradition of Rabbi Berland, the lack of evidence against him notwithstanding.

While the Rav's legal team in Holland immediately lodged

an appeal against this decision, the Rav continued on with his regular schedule of learning Torah, praying and doing acts of kindness for the community, completely unfazed by all the commotion surrounding him in the Dutch courts.

The next casualty in that terrible year was the kabbalist Rav David Chaim Stern. Rav Stern collapsed during a visit to the U.S.A. around February 2015, and was also found to have suffered a serious heart attack. One of the students who was traveling with Rav Stern happened to be a first responder for Magen David Adom, and he immediately started to administer CPR to the Rav. For 40 minutes, this student fought for the Rav's life, even though the Rav had stopped breathing and no longer had a pulse.

Eventually, his pulse returned and the Rav was taken to the intensive care unit in Maimonides Medical Center in New York. When he was admitted, the hospital staff considered his condition to be somewhere between critical and non-recoverable. The doctors didn't really hold out any hope that the Rav would recover, and the word went out to his students and followers around the world to start urgently praying for Rabbi Stern's welfare and recovery.

On the advice of Rabbi Shmuel Wosner, Rav Stern was also given the additional name Alter. An information hotline was set up to inform the public about the Rav's condition, and to enable people to participate in round-the-clock prayers for Rav Stern's recovery. Yet despite all these efforts, Rabbi Stern's condition only continued to deteriorate.

After he was admitted to the hospital, he suffered a further two heart attacks, and a short while later it was discovered that both of his lungs had also completely collapsed, which meant he was now 100 percent dependent on life-support to breathe. If that wasn't bad enough, on the following day his kidneys also collapsed, and the attending physician told the Rav's son to call his other children to come to the hospital immediately, so they could be there when their father passed away.

One of Rav Stern's sons knew how much his father respected Rabbi Berland, whom he'd known for more than 45 years, ever since Rabbi Berland had been the Steipler Gaon's learning partner back in Bnei Brak. In fact, he was still regularly in touch with him. He decided to phone Rabbi Berland, who was then in Holland, and tell him the whole situation.

Rabbi Berland's attendant, Natan Salamon, passed on the message to Rav Stern's son that Rabbi Berland recommended to immediately do a *pidyon nefesh*, or 'soul redemption' and that if he did that, his father would get up and live.

Natan Salamon related that ten minutes after the *pidyon* had been arranged, a great miracle happened, and Rav Stern woke up. Even more miraculously, Rav Stern then proceeded to shock the doctors at Maimonides by very quickly regaining his health and strength.

A little while later, Rav Stern was healthy enough to fly back to Israel, to his home in Bnei Brak, and he marked the occasion by holding a gathering where he could properly express his gratitude to God for the enormous miracles that had occurred. This gathering was the first time that Rav Stern publicly explained what had happened to him and he revealed how many open miracles had taken place.

One of Rav Stern's sons spoke at the gathering and said the following: "Anyone who wants to know and understand what the subject of the revival of the dead, is all about, only needs to see what God, in His tremendous mercy and kindness, did in front of our eyes [referring to his father's miraculous return from the dead]. Even the doctors admitted wholeheartedly that what had happened here was nothing less than the revival of the dead."

It was also told over at the gathering that during the

time when Rav Stern was clinically dead, his soul had been in Heaven and he was being judged in the Heavenly Court. Suddenly, the proceedings were interrupted by a Heavenly voice that was heard throughout all the spiritual worlds, saying that Rabbi Stern had to be returned to life.

At the gathering, they also read a letter from the senior doctor at Maimonides who'd been responsible for arranging the medical aspects of Rabbi Stern's flight home, who wrote the following: "I'm here to set down in writing the size and magnitude of the miracle that we witnessed with our own eyes. What occurred here was truly a case of the revival of the dead. The Rav suffered a heart attack and spent 40 minutes without breathing and without a pulse. In the emergency room, he suffered another heart attack and had to be resuscitated again. The first three days he was in the hospital, he really wasn't 'there' at all, physically.

According to the attending physicians, his chances of coming back to life and regaining consciousness, and especially of regaining his mental faculties, were zero. But it appears that God healed [the Rav] by Himself. Even in our generation, I have had the merit of seeing miracles as big as those done at the time of the Exodus from Egypt." The letter was signed by Dr Kerstein, the head of the intensive care unit in Maimonides Hospital, New York.

★　★　★

Rabbi Berland and his followers continued to learn Torah, pray and participate in their regular religious devotions in Holland, although circumstances were frequently very trying. Yet despite all the court hearings, the near-death experiences, the terrible tragedies engulfing the Jewish community in all parts of the world and the more basic daily difficulties involved in trying to accommodate hundreds of the Rav's followers in Holland, by the time Purim 5775 rolled around, more than 700 visitors made the trip to come and celebrate the festival with the Rav.

In an effort to avoid problems with the local authorities and to properly accommodate everyone who had arrived, the Rav's attendants managed to rent another holiday village on the Dutch-Belgian border, a half-hour journey away from the city of Antwerp. Despite the unusual circumstances, Purim 2015 by Rabbi Berland was a very joyful, holy affair.

Many of the people who gathered in Holland for Purim were seeing the Rav for the first time in their lives, and they had such a spiritually uplifting experience that they were already planning their next trip.

Indeed, so many visitors were expected for Passover that the Rav's attendants sent out a message informing prospective guests that they had to tell them in advance if they were planning to be in Holland for Passover, in order to avoid any problems with finding suitable accommodations that could provide the local media with more ammunition to use against the Rav and his followers.

Back in Israel, a few of Rabbi Berland's students spent Purim at the home of Rabbi Dov Kook of Tiberius and told him about all the things that had been happening to the Rav in Holland. For example, they mentioned how the Rav had been moving around the country from one holiday village to another together with his students, and how some of the troublemakers in Holland kept stirring things up so the community had to keep moving from place to place.

Each time, the Rav and his students would find a new location, but after a few days, the trouble would start again, and everything would be heavily publicized in the Dutch papers, to the point that it almost seemed as though they were being paid to print negative stories about the Rav and his community. But each time the Rav and his community got kicked out of their latest location, God would send someone new to help them.

In Holland, an increasing number of Dutch non-Jews heard about Rabbi Berland — ironically, thanks to all the negative press coverage — and, impressed by his obvious holiness, they started donating money and resources to help keep him and his community together and afloat, financially. Some of these non-Jewish Dutch supporters were even talking about converting, just as had happened previously in Zimbabwe and South Africa, where many non-Jews had also been very strong supporters of the Rav, and keen to convert to Judaism.

When he heard all this, Rav Kook smiled and commented, "There's some profound Divine Providence going on. He's going to come and redeem us, and when he comes, Moshiach will come too."

The longer the Rav stayed in Holland, the more miracles stories started to circulate about him. Rabbi Chaim Elazar Bransdorfer (son of the late Rabbi Meir Bransdorfer) was visiting Rabbi Berland in Holland when someone delivered a note thanking the Rav for a *pidyon* he'd made for his terminally ill daughter, who was now coming back to life again.

Rabbi Bransdorfer remarked that he was no longer surprised to hear all of the miracle stories concerning the Rav, as he'd already heard about thousands of such wonders, and he knew that doing wonders came very easily to Rabbi Berland.

Rabbi Bransdorfer continued that what *had* astounded him was the way Rabbi Berland had managed to reach so many Jews who were so distant from Torah and bring them back to being true returnees to religious observant. He recounted that he'd heard from one such returnee, who'd been extremely distant from Judaism, how the Rav had brought him back to Judaism without even saying a word to him, and Rabbi Bransdorfer commented that he had no idea how that could be possible — until that week in Holland.

That Shabbos in Holland, he'd seen it with his own eyes, when he'd been eating the Friday night meal at the Rav's home, expecting the Rav to give over some wondrous words of Torah. Instead, the Rav didn't say a word, and just sang Shabbos songs for many hours on end.

Rabbi Bransdorfer continued, *"I truly saw with my own eyes how so many of the people who'd come to spend Shabbos with the Rav just sat there, gazing at the tremendous light that the Rav was generating simply by doing what he was doing, particularly when he was singing the Shabbos songs. I saw with my own eyes the huge changes that were occurring [as a result], and that they were being brought closer to God much more [that way] than anyone could possibly do with words."*

★ ★ ★

As 2015 continued, the feeling of impending doom that had enveloped the Jewish people (and the world more generally) continued to deepen. Many of the leading Rabbis put out messages at this time, including the following one from Rabbi Chaim Kanievsky, which was publicized around Passover 5775 (April 2015) by Rabbi Chizkiyahu Mishkovsky.

Rav Mishkovsky made the following comments while he was speaking at a conference organized by the Jewish outreach organisation Lev L'Achim:

"Today, we find ourselves at one of the most critical moments for the Jewish people," Rav Mishkovsky announced. "One of the close relatives of our teacher and Torah giant, Rav Chaim Kanievsky, recently came to visit him, and the 'prince of Torah' [i.e. Rav Chaim Kanievsky] told him: 'Go and announce to the nation of Israel that we are at the time of 'the footsteps of Moshiach,' and that Moshiach is at the threshold, and the only possibility of surviving this period is through Torah and acts of kindness.'"

The grandson of Rabbi Kanievsky was also present, and wrote down the message as follows:

"To the children of Abraham, Yitzchak and Jacob, including those who are called 'secular': I was requested by my teacher and Rabbi, the Rabbi of Israel, shlit"a, to inform you that the only way to survive this generation is by following the path of Torah and doing good deeds, and that there is no other way."

Rabbi Kanievsky then confirmed the wording of this message.

The grandson asked Rav Kanievsky, "How should I publicize this? Should I announce it with a loudspeaker?" Rabbi Kanievsky replied, "Yes! Take a loudspeaker and go all over the country!"

As the tension was mounting across the world[i], Rabbi Berland had his final court hearing at the Dutch Supreme

---

[i] The headlines at this time were full of stories about ISIS decapitating hundreds of people in Iraq and Syria, and threatening to do the same to Westerners, too.

Court on June 30, 2015. After months of being pressured by the Israeli government, the Supreme Court in Holland finally ruled that the Rav could be extradited to Israel.

Less than a week later, the Rav failed to appear for his regular 6 p.m. appointment at the local police station in Amsterdam, despite being under close observation by the Dutch authorities, who had also confiscated his passport. Nevertheless, by July 6, 2015, the unbelievable news filtered out that Rabbi Berland had apparently left Holland for good, and no one had any idea where he'd gone.

While the Dutch Prosecutors Office were scratching their heads, wondering how on earth the Rav could have left the country undetected, his Dutch lawyer, Louis de Leon, said what many other people were thinking, namely, that if the Rav had really managed to leave Europe without a passport, this clearly showed that he was a holy person, with supernatural powers.

Following the news of his miraculous disappearance from Holland, the international media started publishing all sorts of wild rumors about where the Rav had gone, and how he'd gotten there. Some journalists told their audience that the Rav had gone to Guatemala; others claimed that he was hiding out on a Caribbean island. But the truth was that no one knew where Rabbi Berland really was.

On August 6th, 2015 precisely 40 days after Rabbi Berland miraculously disappeared from Holland, he finally made contact and told his students that he wanted them to prepare for "good tidings" in the coming month of Elul.

In that recorded *Torah class*, the Rav spoke a great deal about the Prophet Elijah, Moses, and about the forthcoming year of redemption, 5776 — but he still didn't tell them where he was. It was only on Rosh Hashanah that the news leaked out that the Rav had returned to South Africa.

On Rosh Chodesh Elul 5775, the Rav announced that

Moshiach would come that year, 5776 (2015-2016). He said: *"On the evening after the first day of Sukkos, the King Moshiach will already be standing and reading from the Torah. We're already waiting for Jerusalem to be rebuilt, and to see the King Moshiach read from the Torah. This is now the 40 days that we're preparing ourselves beforehand for the birth. The King Moshiach will already be born before Yom Kippur... Forty days before Yom Kippur, the King Moshiach will already be born!"*

The Rav also gave his students a sign that would help them know that Moshiach's coming was imminent: "If you see that the whole world is warring, that is the moment that the Moshiach will be revealed," he said. The Rav repeated the by-now familiar refrain: on the evening after the *seventh* year, wars. The moment that Moshiach comes, all the world would be aroused to war.

But what sort of "wars" was the Rav really referring to?

★ ★ ★

A few days after the Rav spoke on the 25th of Elul and explained that the whole world would be sending their warships to Israel, Russia surprised the international community by sending warships and aircraft carriers to the Middle East, and also a number of soldiers to Syria. The ships were anchored in the Eastern Mediterranean Sea, practically on the border of Israel.

From one day to the next, the armed forces in the region grew bigger. As well as Russian armed forces, most of the Western nations of the world also sent soldiers to the Middle East, including America, France, Italy, Britain, Belgium, Spain, Canada, Portugal, Greece and Holland.

In addition, Iran, North Korea, Iraq, Lebanon, Turkey, Qatar, Jordan, Saudi Arabia, Croatia, Venezuela, Switzerland, United Arab Emirates, the Iranian-backed Hezbollah and

Algeria also started to participate in the war in Syria, either directly by sending soldiers, or more indirectly by sending weapons or money.

By Rosh Hashanah 5776 (September 2015), a huge number of soldiers and weapons, including tactical nukes, were located in and around Syria. The war was ostensibly being fought against ISIS (Islamic State), but it increasingly resembled an international war being fought by proxy. With so many countries squaring off against each other, concern was high that even minor security incidents could potentially escalate into a world war. A little later, Turkey blew up a Russian plane that they claimed had strayed across the Turkish border with Syria. Russia retaliated by threatening to wipe Turkey off the map and sent a large number of weapons to the area[i].

As Turkey and Russia faced off against each other, it became even clearer how volatile and explosive the situation in Syria actually was.

When this occurred, Rabbi Moshe Sternbuch immediately sent out the following declaration to his students: "*We have received a tradition from the Vilna Gaon, handed down from one generation to the next, that if Russia will enter and conquer Istanbul, the capital of Turkey, a person should hurry to get his Shabbos finery ready, and to wait for Moshiach. The Russians and the Turks have begun to quarrel with each other. We hear the sounds of war, and all of the nations are shocked: How can Turkey start up with Russia? But we see in this the fulfillment of Chazal's saying that when Moshiach comes, God will provoke the nations against each other, and against their will, they'll go to war.*

---

[i] Russia deployed the guided missile cruiser Moskva armed with S-300F (SA-N-6 Grumble) long-range SAM missiles off the Syrian coast near Latakia[15] and S-400 (SA-21 Growler) mobile SAM systems to Khmeimim airbase.

We're in the year after the Seventh year. We see in these matters great spiritual strengthening, and we need to wake ourselves up. We must wake ourselves up to do teshuva, and if we don't, God forbid, then [the enemies] will 'strengthen' the Jewish people [in the matter of doing teshuva], and we will experience some very great suffering."

At the same time, a video of a secular teenage boy who'd had a clinical death, and who had apparently been shown some violent scenes in Heaven relating to the imminent coming of Moshiach, went viral across Israel and the world, with hundreds of thousands of viewers. Among the many things the teenage boy said was that the IDF would only be able to stand up against its enemies for two days, and that Israel was about to be conquered by literally hundreds of thousands of foreign soldiers.

The prophecy in *Zechariah* speaks of all the soldiers of the nations gathering around Israel, and as 5776 (September 2016) began, it seemed that prophecy was about to come true. At this time, Rabbi Berland was asked if the war of Gog and Magog had started, and he replied, "Yes."

But it still wasn't clear what that actually meant. Would it be a massively destructive conventional war? A nuclear war, God forbid? Or something else completely?

THE THIRD INTIFADA BEGINS

Rabbi Berland once said: "People think that Moshiach can come without prayer. That a person can simply travel to Uman, press a button, and Moshiach will appear. He'll be there at Rebbe Nachman's grave, and he just needs to press a certain secret button, and then Moshiach will appear. Moshiach can't come until we do true *teshuva* with a truly broken heart and have true *Shmiras Enayim*!

"It's time to cry out, 'We are guilty!' and then Moshiach will really come, and Moshiach will be revealed. Moshiach wants to be revealed at every moment. *This is the time that Moshiach needs to be revealed.*"

The Rav concluded that all the wars, the intifada and the dangers that will accompany the coming of the Moshiach are only to get people to wake up and do *teshuva*, so that we'll cry out "We are guilty! That's it," he said. "That's all we need to do."

★   ★   ★

"While the first Palestinian intifada was defined in the popular imagination as the "stone-throwing intifada" and the second as a conflict of suicide bombings and gun attacks, the new surge in violence [in Israel] has been so closely associated with knife attacks that on social media some have dubbed it the "knife intifada."
– The Guardian, October 18th, 2015[i]

---

[i] What's driving the young lone wolves who are stalking the streets of Israel? -https://www.theguardian.com/world/2015/oct/18/knife-intifada-palestinian-israel-west-bank

★ ★ ★

On September 27, 2015, Rabbi Berland wrote an unusual prayer about the so-called "blood-red moon" that was seen in the skies above Jerusalem on the first night of Sukkos. The Rav wrote: *"About this [the blood moon] the Zohar wrote in parshas Shelach 162 that 'the moon will turn to blood.'*

The Prophet Yoel wrote about this, in Yoel 3, and said, 'And I will place wonders in the skies and on the earth. Blood and fire, and a pillar of smoke, and the sun will turn to darkness, and the moon to blood, before the coming of the great and awesome day. And all those who call out in My Name will rule, because the remnants will be on Mount Zion in Jerusalem... And I will gather together all of the nations, and bring them down to the valley of Yehoshaphat, and I will judge them there [in regard to what they've done to] My people. And I will give an inheritance to Israel, which is scattered amongst the nations, and My land they will share."

Immediately after the blood-red moon appeared, the third intifada began, with the cold-blooded murder of Rabbi and Rebbetzin Henkin on October 1, 2015, who were shot to death by Palestinian terrorists in front of their four children as they were driving in the Shomron hills. Just a few days later, on October 3, 2015, Aharon Bennett and Rav Nechemia Lavi were also murdered in cold blood in front of their children, in the Muslim Quarter of the Old City of Jerusalem.

The murder of Aharon Bennett, the son-in-law of one of the Rabbis at Shuvu Banim, was particularly close to home. Little Naftali Bennett, aged two and a half, was also injured in the attack that killed his father and seriously wounded his mother, Adel.

Rabbi Yosef Gal, Adel's father, describes what happened

that fateful day: "Aharon, God should avenge his blood, was murdered in the last moments of Shabbos Chol HaMo'ed, on his way back to our home. The terrorist ambushed them, and first attacked Adel, stabbing her 13 times. Despite the fact that she was trying to fight him off, and that Aharon was also hitting him, the terrorist continued. He stabbed Aharon fatally, and even though he had the knife still stuck in him, the last thing Aharon managed to do before he died was pull the terrorist to the floor."

Rav Nechemia Lavi lived in Beit Wittenberg, a Jewish residence located in the Muslim Quarter of the Old City, directly above where the attack was taking place. He heard the screams coming from outside and heroically risked his life to help the victims. Rabbi Lavi quickly wheeled the two children away from the terrorist in their stroller, saving them from certain death, before he, too, was murdered.

When Rabbi Berland was informed about what had happened, he said, *"It's difficult for us to hear the difficult, tragic news about the terrible murder that happened today, where a holy and pure Torah student from our holy community was murdered by the hands of a depraved evildoer and cut down in the prime of his life. We need to know that the holy Rav Aharon Bennett, God should avenge his blood, and also the father and mother that were murdered the week before with terrible cruelty in front of their children, were an atonement for the Jewish nation. They sweetened the decree and prevented another Holocaust from happening to the Jewish people.*

God woke us up, that we should do true teshuva. We should begin to honestly love and care about one another."

Aharon's wife, Adel, was seriously injured in the attack, sustaining 13 deep stab wounds to her upper body. She was immediately taken for lengthy surgery to try to save her life. The family called Rabbi Berland and asked him what to do, and the Rav told them to bring a *pidyon nefesh* for her, which they did. Adel's situation then improved miraculously, against all odds. The doctor came out of the operating room and announced that there had been a miraculous and completely unexpected improvement in her condition.

At this time, Rabbi Yitzchak Meir Morgenstern said that the intifada had begun specifically then because the nation of Ishmael were already feeling that very soon the Temple would be rebuilt, and that the redemption of the Jewish people was close, and at that time they would lose all of their power. So they were trying to prevent the redemption.

A little before Purim 5755, Rabbi Berland issued a call for every member of *Am Yisrael* to contribute a sum of money, however small, toward a communal *"pidyon haKollel"* that would sweeten the harsh decrees of the so-called Third Intifada that the Rav could see looming on the horizon. The goal was to raise $600,000 — a dollar for each of the root souls of the nation of Israel — and to sweeten the judgments that way.

At that time, he sent out a message saying: "We are in a new intifada, and it's a terrible intifada that will spread around the globe. It's impossible to stop it [by natural means]."

Unfortunately, even though the request to participate in the *"pidyon haKollel"* was repeated many times, with announcements appearing in many of the Breslov yeshivas encouraging people to donate, and many people took the Rav's plea to heart, most of these people were not wealthy, and barely a sixth of the total required was raised.

Then the Festival of Sukkos 5776 arrived, and with it came the beginning of the prophesized upswing in Arab violence. When the shootings, stabbings and other attacks began in earnest in Israel, everyone saw that the prophecy of the Rav had indeed materialized. The Third Intifada, foreseen by the Rav and which he'd hoped to avoid and sweeten, had begun.

At this time, the Rav publicized an important message

that whoever would donate 98 shekels a month for a *pidyon* would be saved, in that merit, along with his whole family, from the terrorist attacks.

The Rav promised this himself, in the following words where he said: *"As long as the intifada continues, everyone is obligated to give, every Jew in every place of the world. Even non-Jews should give 98 shekels — which is $26, or €25, every month, for as long as this continues.*

In every place in the world there are terror attacks. Whoever wants to be saved from this new intifada that is spreading over the entire globe needs to give. Everyone who gives the pidyon will be saved from all attacks, and from all stumbling blocks, and from all types of sin."

The Shuvu Banim Rabbis joined together with the Rav in this important project and tried to organize a group that included all the Rabbanim across *Am Yisrael*.

WHY *PIDYON NEFESH* WORKS TO REMOVE HARSH JUDGMENTS

The language the ancient Torah sages use to describe "money" is *damim*, which literally means "blood" or "bloods" in Hebrew. When there are harsh decrees hanging over *Am Yisrael*, they can only be sweetened by immense amounts of self-sacrifice from the Jewish people, which often entails the spilling of blood.

But there is another way of sweetening the decrees.

Instead of spilling real blood, God forbid, it's also possible to fulfill the requirement to "spill blood" by the self-sacrifice required in giving money, or *damim*. If you give whatever amount you're able to give, with self-sacrifice, then you fulfill the verse that states, "Charity saves from death.[1]" A *pidyon nefesh* where each person gives a fixed amount is called *pidyon haKollel*, or "communal redemption," and this sweetens all of the judgments that are currently hanging over the nation of Israel, which means we won't see any more blood spilled in our country.[i]

As the Third Intifada gathered steam, barely a week went by without reports of another terrible attack in Israel. Perhaps one of the most notably disturbing incidents happened in the Central Bus Station in Beer Sheva on October 18, 2015, when an IDF soldier was killed and 10 others injured 3 in bad condition. IDF soldier Daniel Harush was so badly injured in the attack; the attending paramedics actually initially believed he was dead. This is how Daniel himself remembers the attack and its aftermath.

"I was using the washroom when the attack first started," recalls Daniel. *"I peeped outside in order to assess the severity of the situation, and I saw that a soldier had been wounded by the terrorist and was lying on the ground. I immediately turned to my friend and told him that we needed to try to help the wounded soldier. However, as soon as I came out of the washroom, I got hit by a number of bullets that completely immobilized me — I collapsed on the spot."*

He continues: *"I took five bullets, and I can't even begin to describe how scared I felt. I didn't even have time to weigh the situation that I found myself in. I was wearing my army uniform and I still honestly have no idea how a policeman could end up confusing an Israeli soldier with a terrorist. [Daniel was injured by 'friendly' fire.] And then, the next thing I knew I was lying on the floor, covered in blood, and trying not to lose consciousness.*

Afterwards, they discovered that I'd been critically wounded in the stomach and liver, and also seriously wounded

---

[i] Mishlei 11:4.

in the elbow. They took me straight to the operating room, and when I got there, I didn't have a pulse. I was fighting for my life," he says. "I went through a series of long, complicated operations, and for all intents and purposes I was in a coma and on a respirator for more than three weeks."

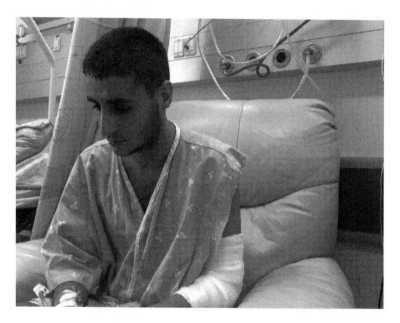

Throughout those long, hard weeks, Daniel's relatives were constantly by his side in the hospital, caring for him throughout the difficult time that he was in a coma. Daniel's good friend, Tzvi Mamon, takes up the tale of what was happening to Daniel during those weeks that he was unconscious and fighting for his life.

"Daniel arrived in the hospital in a state that was described as critical. As soon as we could, we got in contact with Rabbi Berland and told him about the terrible situation," Tzvi explains. "The Rav already knew Daniel from the time that he came all the way up from Eilat to hear a Torah class that the Rav was giving in Beitar Illit. The Rav asked us to immediately

send his attendant, Natan Solomon, a sum of money for a pidyon nefesh for Daniel, and told us: 'He will have miracles and wonders, and he will merit bringing the redemption to Am Yisrael.'

The following day, the Rav sent a bottle of drops to Daniel's family. In the meantime, it seemed as though the whole of Eilat joined us in the mitzvah of pulling together the funds required to immediately arrange the pidyon; everyone gave whatever they could."

And what about the drops? Was Daniel immediately given the drops that the Rav had sent him?

"Unfortunately not," Tzvi tells us. "For various reasons, the drops kind of fell off everyone's radar, and we forgot all about them for a few weeks. But once we remembered them, we had our first big miracle. Around two hours after we gave Daniel the Rav's drops, Daniel opened his eyes for the first time in more than three weeks," says Tzvi.

"I am 100 percent sure that it was the drops that helped me!" interjects Daniel.

"It clearly was," replies Tzvi. "Until we gave him the drops, nothing was moving. It looks like Rabbi Berland wanted to create some sort of natural 'cover' for the enormous miracle that was going to heal Daniel."

Daniel's family informed the Rav's gabbai, Natan Solomon, about the great miracle that had occurred, and how Daniel had woken up right after they'd given him the drops, even though he'd been in a coma for three weeks. When the gabbai told Rabbi Berland what had happened, the Rav answered, "Wow! What amazing drops! We need to distribute them to the whole world!"

★   ★   ★

As the toll from the terrible stabbings, murders and other

terrorist attacks in Israel continued to mount, shortly before the Fast of Esther 5776 (March 22, 2016), Rabbi Berland issued a call for at least 10,000 people to come together at the Tomb of the Patriarchs in Hebron.

Rabbi Berland promised that if a minimum of 10,000 participants would go to Hebron on the forthcoming Fast of Esther to pray, the attacks would stop. A little over 10,000 people — including some of the nation's leading Rabbis — heeded the call and went to Hebron for the prayer gathering.

After the crowd had finished reading through the entire book of *Psalms*, Rabbi Berland was contacted to speak to the gathering on a phone that was attached to a number of loudspeakers. Over 10,000 people heard him say that night: "In the merit of this gathering, the Intifada will stop".

Miraculously from that night on, the stabbings and attacks that had been occurring on an almost daily basis beforehand did indeed abruptly stop.

After the event, Israeli kabbalist Rabbi Yekusiel Fish commented: *"Whoever can't put two and two together is an idiot. Specifically, at the same time that we are under constant attack from the Iranian nuclear threat, Rabbi Berland is being persecuted and is suffering in exile...*

There is no question that Rabbi Berland is fighting them at their source, as well as all the other threats that Am Yisrael is facing. Whoever doesn't put two and two together.... Here's a Tzaddik who is halting the tragedies himself, who is stopping a nuclear attack. He said: "Go and make a prayer gather on the night of the fast of Esther and it will stop the Intifada." They went and did this, and immediately the Intifada stopped after half a year that not one day passed without killings!"

Speaking shortly before Passover 5776, Rabbi Shalom Arush commented: *"After the last prayer gathering in Hebron on the Fast of Esther, we clearly saw with our own eyes the strength of our teacher, Rav Eliezer Berland, shlit"a. After the prayer gathering that the Rav called for in Hebron, the terrorist attacks halted altogether. We suffered so much from those terrorist attacks and now we see with our own eyes that it stopped.""*

Rabbi Berland had requested that another prayer gathering should be organized in Hebron on April 27, 2016, and Rabbi Arush was encouraging people to attend.

Rabbi Arush continued: *"Passover is the time of redemption, and there is no other place that can work salvations like the Tomb of the Patriarchs... Everyone is obligated to make an effort and to participate. It's really important. We clearly saw with our own eyes how the last prayer gathering truly worked miracles on behalf of the Jewish people... We need to [pray to] continue to bring the redemption the sweet way, and that the Rav should return [to Israel]."*

But, before things could get better, and Rabbi Berland could return to the Holy Land, the Rav's precarious position in exile was about to get a whole lot worse.

REBBE NACHMAN'S DREAM

I n December 1809, Rebbe Nachman dreamt a dream that was shrouded in mystery for more than 203 years. Rebbe Nachman taught that dreams should only be written down if you want them to come true. This particular dream that he'd had was so awful, the Rebbe cried for a full day after he'd dreamt it, yet Rebbe Nachman still insisted that it should be written down and even publicized. None of his students or followers had any explanation as to why this should be the case.

There is a tradition within Breslov that the cryptic dreams and stories of Rebbe Nachman would only really be fully understood when the Jewish people approached the end of days. The following dream[i] of Rebbe Nachman bears that tradition out very powerfully:

I was sitting in my room, but not even a single person came to see me. I was very surprised by this, so I went to a different room, but there wasn't a single person there, either. I went to the large house, and the study hall, but there wasn't a single person in either of those places, either.

So, I thought I would go outside. I went outside and saw there rows and rows of people standing around and whispering

---

[i] You can read the full dream for yourself in the book in the book *Tzaddik*, published by the Breslov Research Institute in the section called New Stories.

among themselves. *One person would make a comment about me, and someone else would snicker, and then yet another person would make a face at me. Even my own followers were against me. Some of them looked at me in a very arrogant way, while others were telling each other secrets about me, and so forth.*

I called one of my followers over and asked him, "What's going on?"

He replied, "How could you do such a thing?! How could you do such a terrible sin?![i]" I still had absolutely no idea why everyone was mocking me. So I asked this man to go and gather a few of my followers together. He left me — and I didn't see him again. So I started thinking to myself what I should do next. I decided to leave, and to go to another country.

I arrived there — but things were exactly the same. Even there, people knew about the situation and were standing around and talking about it. So, I thought I would go and live in the wilderness somewhere. Five of my followers joined me, and we went together to live in the wilderness. Whenever we needed to eat something, or so forth, we'd send one of the men out to get us what we needed. I used to ask him if the uproar had died down yet, but he answered, "No. It's still very fierce."

While we were living there, an old man came and called me, and told me he had something to tell me. So I went with him, and he started saying, "How do you dare to do such a thing?! Can't you see how you've put your ancestors to shame — your grandfather, Rabbi Nachman Horodenka, and your great-grandfather, the Baal Shem Tov, zt"l? Think of the holy Torah! Think of the Patriarchs, Abraham, Yitzchak and Jacob! Aren't you ashamed of yourself?! How can you even think

---

[i] The line "how could you do such a terrible sin" was taken out of later printings of the book, but can still be found in the printing by the "Mesech Hanachal" publishers, which was copied from the original manuscript and published in Lublin 1920

about staying here? Can you stay here forever? Your money will run out; you're physically weak. What are you going to do?

"And what's with the idea of running away to a different country? However you look at it, it's not going to help you, because if they don't already know who you are they won't give you any money. And if they do already know who you are, then you still won't be able to stay there because they'll already know all about this situation."

I replied, "If that's how things are, and I'm simply a fugitive, then at least I'll still have the World to Come."

"You really think you're going to have the World to Come?!" he answered. "After sinning like this, you couldn't even find a place to hide yourself in Gehinnom because you caused such a terrible desecration of God's name[i]!"

"Go!" I said. "I hoped you would have comforted me and spoken kind words to me. Now you're only just making things more painful. Get away from me!" So the old man went away.

While I was staying there [in the forest], I thought to myself: "If I'm staying here for such a long time, chances are I could completely forget my learning." So I asked the man who used to go into the city for us to try and find a [Torah] book there, and to bring it back to me. He went to the city, but he didn't end up bringing back a book. He said it had been impossible to do it, because he couldn't tell anyone who the book was for, but it was also impossible to find a [Torah] book secretly. I suffered a great deal, because not only was I a fugitive, I also didn't even have a [Torah] book. Because a person can end up completely forgetting all of their learning.

Later, the old man came back, carrying a book under his arm. I asked him, "What have you got there?" And he replied, "A book." I asked him to give it to me, and he did. I took the book, but found that I had no idea how to position it. I opened

---

[i] These words were also taken out in later printings.

it, but I found I couldn't understand a word of it — it was as though it was written in a different language and a different alphabet. I couldn't understand it at all, and this was very painful to me. I was also afraid that the men who were with me would leave me if they found out about this.

The old man called me over to him again, to speak to me. I went, and he started berating me again, as he'd done before: "How could you do such a thing?! Aren't you ashamed of yourself?! Even in Gehinnom, you'll have nowhere to hide!"

I said to him, "If it was someone from the Upper World who was telling me this, I would believe him." He told me, "I'm from there!" and then he showed me a sign that he was from there. Then, I started thinking about the famous story about the Baal Shem Tov, where the Baal Shem Tov thought that he wouldn't be given any share in the World to Come, but he said anyway, "I love God, even without the World to Come."

In great bitterness, I threw my head down and turned away. As soon as I did that, all the different people the old man said I had shamed appeared in front of me — my grandfather and great-grandfather, the Patriarchs, etc. — and quoted the verse, "And the fruit of the land for excellence and proud beauty" (Yeshayahu 4:2). They said to me, "On the contrary, we will be proud of you."

They brought all of my followers and sons[i] to me (because even my sons had left me when all this had begun) and they spoke kind words to me — the opposite of what had happened beforehand.

As to my throwing my head down in bitterness... If someone who had transgressed the whole Torah 800 times had

---

[i] At the time Rebbe Nachman told over this dream, both of his two sons had already died in early childhood.

thrown his head down as bitterly as that, he would certainly have been forgiven.

Rebbe Nachman finished relating his dream with these words: **"I don't want to tell you the other great goodness contained in this [the dream], but it was most certainly good!"**

SOUTH AFRICA: PART II

THE HIDDEN SCROLL OF REBBE NACHMAN

Breslov *chassidus* has in its possession a secret document called the *Megillas Sesorim* (the Hidden Scroll) that was written in code and contains Rebbe Nachman's detailed description of what would occur in the time leading up to Moshiach.

In the Hidden Scroll, Rebbe Nachman says: "At first, there will be a huge controversy surrounding Moshiach, and people will say [in astonishment], 'That's Moshiach?!'"

Writing in his book *The Workings of the Tzaddik*, Rabbi Eliezer Schick brought down the following: "*Rav Natan once spoke up about Rebbe Nachman's Hidden Scroll and said, 'The war of Gog and Magog is not specifically described in the Hidden Scroll, but what was indicated was that there would be a flood of heresy in the world, and that would be the huge test facing us, and the Moshiach.*"

Rabbi Shick continues: "*So from this we can learn that every time, in every generation, that we see enormous accusations between the people of Israel, and we see that arrogance is increasing — know! The Moshiach is already ready to reveal himself! It's only the heresy and the arrogance that is covering him up and concealing him...*

The war of Gog and Magog includes all the controversy

and accusations that there will be around these same true tzaddikim, who reveal the true will of God, because they [i.e., the arrogant people and mockers] want to devour them alive, may God have mercy.

And they will say every forbidden thing about them [the true tzaddikim] and make fun of them a lot — and by so doing, they will distance the Jewish people from them. And this is what lengthens the bitter exile, may God have mercy. And so I say, woe to them! And woe to the souls of those who have any part in the controversy and the arguments concerning the true tzaddikim, who reveal the true will of God.

For they are the brazen-faced of the generation, those with the face of a dog[i], the soldiers of Gog and Magog, who conceal the truth, and they are the wicked people of the generation… of whom it's said: "When you see that he is so brazen-faced it is a proof that he is wicked", and it's written in the Midrash (Bamidbar Rabbah 18:10): 'He who is brazen-faced, and he who is an inveterate sower of strife and hatred — he is the most wicked of wicked people,' may God have mercy.

And if you would have known, my beloved brother, what is written in the Hidden Scroll about these soldiers of Gog and Magog, who conceal and hide the truth, you would become faint and terribly frightened, and you would fall on your face from the terrible panic and fear, about by who, through what, and why this bitter exile has been lengthened."

Rav Shick concluded: "In all circumstances, beloved brother, run away from *controversy* and disagreements, and don't get into arguments, and take no part in any controversies ever, or arguments about or mockery being made of the true

---

[i] This term is taken from the Gemara, which states that the face of the generation in the time of Moshiach is the face of a dog. It is interpreted by many as referring to false leaders who try to prevent people from finding the true Tzaddik who can really get them out of the bitter exile. Also see Rebbe Nachman's Stories, number 8.

tzaddikim, because we don't know what each day will bring, and you have no idea who and what you may be challenging and making fun of.

And even though they will want to entice you [to join them], saying it's a *mitzvah* to persecute good people, you, my beloved brother, you must protect your soul! And run away from '*mitzvos*' like these, otherwise 'bitter will be your end' — and the opposite is also true. If you help the true *tzaddikim*, you will bring the *redemption* closer, and you will be worthy of all the good that has been prepared for the soldiers of King David."

★ ★ ★

Given the terrible threats to his life that he'd experienced previously, it perhaps seems a little odd that Rabbi Berland decided to return to South Africa after he left Holland. Logically, it would have made more sense for him to go somewhere else, where he knew he wouldn't be actively chased by a violent bunch of gangsters-cum-policemen like the South African Hawks. Or, to go to another country which didn't have an extradition treaty with Israel (according to the claims that he was simply 'on the run').

The simple fact of the matter is that Rabbi Berland returned to South Africa solely because there was still spiritual work for him to do there.

When Rabbi Berland re-entered South Africa, he immediately got on with the work of creating a viable Torah infrastructure so that his followers and students could come and visit him, without disrupting their Torah learning, prayers and other religious devotions

In contrast to his first visit to South Africa, this time the Rav and the 80 Shuvu Banim families who joined him found a place to stay that was an hour out of Johannesburg, where they could keep a low profile and not tread on anyone's toes in the local Jewish community.

Despite the fact that the corrupt South African Hawks had been violently persecuting the Rav for months during his previous stay in South Africa, within a couple of months of his surprise return to the African peninsula, the Rav was granted diplomatic immunity and a South African passport by the government there.

His followers fervently hoped that this would mark the end of the terrible persecution and threats of imprisonment that had dogged the Rav throughout his three-year exile, as his persecutors from Israel tried to stir up one country after another against him. Being granted diplomatic immunity meant (in theory) that the Rav couldn't be arrested and could move around the country as a completely free man, without being subjected to any checks or governmental interference.

It sounded great — in theory. In practice, the Rav's persecutors continued to pour enormous amounts of time, money and energy into finagling his arrest and "deportation" back to Israel. But it would take a few more months before their efforts bore fruit.

On the Shabbos before Tu B'Shvat 5776 (January 22, 2016), more than 400 of the Rav's followers flew out to Johannesburg to spend the festival with the Rav.

The Rav was staying at a holiday village in South Africa, and the premises quickly filled to capacity. Whoever hadn't made prior reservations at the holiday village ended up sleeping on blankets on the grass outside.

Even though his students were flying out to spend Tu B'Shvat with Rabbi Berland, which was on the following Monday, January 25, 2016, the Rav had made a specific point of encouraging his followers to be with him for the Shabbos before, called Shabbos Shira. In a recording that was put out on the community hotline, the Rav announced that over the following days, big things were meant to happen in relation to the forthcoming redemption of the Jewish people.

The whole week beforehand, the Rav had been speaking about his persecutors and their ongoing machinations against him, which was very unusual, for the Rav. He said that because he'd organized another wedding in South Africa, the Hawks were going to try to arrest him again.

The wedding was originally scheduled to take place on Sunday night, January 24, 2016, but Rabbi Berland advised the couple to push the wedding forward to before Shabbos, because he clearly knew what was going to happen next.

That Friday night, the Rav and the community prayed a very long service in the big marquee tent that had been left up from the wedding that had taken place earlier in the week. At 11 p.m., after the prayers had finished, the Rav went to his holiday cottage on the grounds of the hotel with his family, in order to eat the Friday night meal.

About half an hour later, around 60 commandos from the South African Hawks suddenly appeared at the hotel grounds. It was an extremely dangerous and threatening situation. The 60 Hawks policemen were dressed in black and had their weapons drawn and ready to fire as they circulated through the hotel grounds, trying to find the Rav.

One look at their faces told everyone there that they really meant business, and that this time they were determined to stop the Rav in his tracks, one way or another. The situation was so frightening that one of the children there developed breathing difficulties as a result of the fear he experienced and had to be taken to the hospital urgently by his family on Shabbos.

The Hawks had surrounded the entire hotel grounds, and according to the laws of nature there was very little chance that the Rav would be able to escape from the Hawks this time around. The hotel complex consisted of many different holiday cottages, each with two rooms upstairs and another two rooms downstairs.

The South African police moved methodically from one cottage to the next, conducting a detailed search of all the rooms and all the guests as they went along. When they reached the Rav's cottage, they immediately started searching through the lower two rooms. Then, they got ready to climb the stairs to the room where the Rav was calmly sitting, with the door wide open. Everyone held their breath to see what was going to happen next.

The police were already climbing the stairs, just as they'd done in every other cottage that they'd already searched, when suddenly, and for no obvious reason, they decided to turn around and leave without searching the upper rooms.

A few minutes later, the Rav left his room and started to walk down the stairs. One of the policemen was standing directly opposite him and was looking straight at him — but the policeman didn't see a thing! God had blinded his eyes, and the Rav walked past him without being seen, in what appears to have been a remarkable, open miracle. Rabbi Berland then proceeded to leave the hotel grounds undetected.

★   ★   ★

Over the next three months, the Rav continued to be persecuted by the authorities in South Africa. Sadly, the poisonous stories that continued to appear about the Rav and his followers in the local media also succeeded in causing tensions to rise between the Rav's followers and some members of the South African Jewish community.

Shortly after the media made the fantastic claim that Rabbi Berland was urging his followers to violently attack the

South African Chief Rabbi, the Rav released the following statement:

"I've come to make it known to everyone that the Chief Rabbi is my most faithful friend. He is with me in heart and soul. He is, thank G-d, taking care of me and our kehillah here in Johannesburg, physically and spiritually. I have never had a friend like Rav Goldstein my whole life, a friend so faithful. The kehillah feels the best under his patronage. He takes care of all of the affairs of our kehillah. I only respect him and pray to G-d that He should prolong his days and years. G-d forbid that things which were never said and have no foundation or basis should be publicized in my name — to say that I want to, G-d forbid, take his life. I only pray for his well-being.

G-d should prolong his days and years and establish his kingdom forever and ever, him and his family and children for all generations until the coming of our righteous Moshiach."

By Rosh Chodesh Nissan 5776, a little more than three years after he first left Israel, it seems that Rabbi Berland had finally been given permission from Heaven to start the process of ending his exile in and returning to Israel.

In a statement he released a little later, on May 26, 2016), the Rav wrote the following:

Bs"d
(May 26, 2016)
To whom it may concern,

Today, Lag B'Omer, is a great day for sweetening judgments in the world and today I was told that I could return to Israel. From Rosh Chodesh Nissan I already decided to return to Israel. I myself called the Gaon Rav Yitzchak David Grossman, the head of Migdal Ohr, to take care of all my concerns and to prepare the ground for my return to Israel.

I am asking for everyone to unify, and to unify all of our organizations, and not to accept any evil speech about anyone in the world that they persuaded me to return to Israel against my will. For it is my exclusive will, and the choice to return to Israel came only from myself alone.

On April 7, 2016, on the way to voluntarily handing himself in to the South African authorities, the Rav felt unwell, and was taken to the local hospital in Sunninghill, Johannesburg. While he was there, Interpol showed up and took the Rav into custody, at the urging of the Israeli government and the Rav's other persecutors.

Rabbi Berland was officially under lock and key.

Passover in Johannesburg Prison

"The elite priority crime division of the SA Police, The Hawks, have confirmed that they arrested the 78-year-old Rabbi Eliezer Berland in Sunninghill in northern Johannesburg on Thursday. The Hawks refused to say where he was arrested or how they had found the elusive rav-on-the-run - but he will remain in custody and appear in court next Thursday."
— South African Jewish Report, April 8th 2016[i]

"The night time is when most of the dangerous incidents occur, ranging from inmates igniting fires in and to the prison, to attacking other inmates, threatening other inmates and gang activities,"
- 'Sun City' prison inmates go 20 hours between meals, News 24 website, January 31st, 2018[ii]

★ ★ ★

Rabbi Berland was first arrested on April 7, 2016, when he went to the Morningside Clinic in Johannesburg for medical attention, on the way to voluntarily turning himself in to the South African police.

---

[i] https://www.sajr.co.za/news-and-articles/2016/04/08/hawks-nab-r.-berland-sajr-nabs-the-news
[ii] https://m.news24.com/SouthAfrica/News/sun-city-prison-inmates-go-20-hours-between-meals-20180131

From that time until he had his first court hearing on April 14, 2016, he was kept in a cell at the Randburg police station in South Africa. The Hawks continued to persecute the Rav even when he was in police custody and pressed the South African judges to place the elderly *tzaddik* in a maximum security prison in South Africa while the court hearings were being held, prior to extraditing him to Israel.

Rabbi Berland's South African lawyer, Themba Langa, told the court that the Hawks were not acting in the interest of justice and had ulterior motives. Langa said, *"This 79-year-old Rabbi is not a threat to anyone. He's just a spiritual man who probably differs in his teachings from the Israeli government."*

The hearing was adjourned to April 20, 2016, and Rabbi Berland was returned to his cell in the Randburg police station. When his lawyers again tried to get the Rav released on bail — because Rabbi Berland had been arrested while he was on the way to *voluntarily* turning himself in to the police — the South African judge decided that the

elderly *tzaddik* should be sent to the Johannesburg Correctional Center, more commonly known as 'Sun City', together with some of the most dangerous criminals in the world.

Bad as African prisons generally are, Sun City Prison in Johannesburg was still renowned for being the worst of the worst. It was home to a number of violent, murderous and disturbed individuals, it had a large prison population of radical Muslims and prisoners in Sun City were frequently beaten up, abused and even murdered by their fellow inmates on a regular basis.

As Jews around the world sat down to their *Seder* on the first night of Passover 5776 (April 22, 2016) to celebrate their emancipation from Egyptian slavery, the generation's *Gadol HaDor*, Rav Eliezer Berland, found himself spending Passover alone, in a filthy, tiny South African prison cell.

As the news of the terrible conditions Rabbi Berland was being kept in filtered back to Israel, a number of prominent Rabbis decided to start speaking out. Rabbi Yekusiel Fish made the following public statement about the terrible way Rabbi Berland was being treated:

"The heart is bleeding, that one of the tzaddikim of our generation, one of the famous Torah greats of Israel from the past 50 years, was thrown into jail in South Africa, and sent to a two-by-two-meter cell, without a bathroom, where he's already been for a few days. We don't know when he'll leave there. He's suffering such terrible tribulations, at the advanced age of almost 80 years old.

This situation is one of mortal danger and danger to live and nobody is speaking about it. The heart aches...

I heard the gaon and kabbalist, HaRav Morgenstern, shlit"a, say that he researched the issue, and demanded details [from those speaking against the Rav] and that everything is false, deceit and a big story. Rabbi David Abuchatzeira from Nahariya also said that everything is a plot to frame the Rav, and we heard similar things from big tzaddikim like Rav David Chaim Stern, Rabbi Arush, shlit"a, and more tzaddikim. Everything is based on one person who claims that he climbed up to the Rav's apartment and saw what he saw.

Rabbi Gumbal, shlit"a, is the learning partner of Rabbi Yitzchak Meir Morgenstern, shlit"a, who said that Rav Morgenstern researched all the people who came with complaints. Afterwards, he sat and reviewed the evidence one by one, and he saw that everything is falsehood and deceit, and according to Torah law there's no validity, and it's forbidden to believe any of it.

We have a clear halachah: It's forbidden to accept evil speech about any Jew, and definitely about the Tzaddik of the generation... Say Psalms for the success of Rav Eliezer Berland ben Ettia, learn for his success, and at least think of joining in his pain... We have to protest."

Rabbi Fish explained that in recent years, everyone could see how the Iranians had been threatening the Jewish State with an imminent nuclear attack, and how anyone who had eyes in their head could recognize the link between Rabbi Berland's terrible exile and humiliation and the way the Iranians had been stopped in their tracks.

Rabbi Fish continued: "On the night of the Fast of Esther, Rabbi Berland said, 'Go and make a prayer rally to stop the intifada.' People went and made one, and immediately the intifada stopped! Half a year passed in which there were no killings. Is it possible to stand blind in front of all this? Is it possible to be quiet in front of everything they are saying? Woe to us from the day of judgment."

"It's known that well over 25 years ago, [Rabbi Berland] told his wife that he's going to establish an institution for 25 years, and that afterwards he's going to dismantle everything, and he asked her if she agreed to this. Several years ago, he said that a difficult expulsion had been decreed upon him, and asked people to pray for him. It's known that he told those close to him [in South Africa], 'I'll be in jail for Passover.' Heaven forbid, we can't think anything negative about him."

Rabbi Fish concluded: "Rabbi Shalom Arush, shlit"a, testified that he started undertaking activities with the Rabbinical Court on behalf of the Rav, shlit"a, but that he got a message from the Rav himself to stop. And we remember that before he went into exile, the Rav told us that he would *be going into exile for three years, and then, thank G-d, there would be the complete redemption. We are anticipating the beginning of the redemption, to see HaGaon Rav Eliezer Berland here, healthy, alive and whole, happy with us in the coming of Moshiach, speedily in our days, amen."*

Immediately after Passover, Rabbi Yitzchak David Grossman, the Chief Rabbi of Migdal HaEmek and founder and dean of Migdal Ohr educational institutions, packed his bags and flew to Johannesburg to see what he could do to ease the suffering of Rabbi Berland.

"I left Israel immediately, the day after Passover, together with the grandson of the Rav, Reb Chaim Reicher," he said. "We already did a lot of work before the holiday, just to bring the Rav matzos. It was a major operation. I arrived in Johannesburg on Sunday [May 1, 2016] from Israel because I decided that I just couldn't stay in my home."

Rabbi Grossman was shocked to see how bad things were for Rabbi Berland in prison when he went to visit him. *"Rabbi Berland is so happy in learning, he was dancing and crying, I can't explain it. I took his hand and I told him, 'Your hand is so cold!' and then I discovered that he hadn't eaten in two days, because they didn't let any [strictly kosher] food in.*

I went and told the lawyer that we need to bring food to the Rabbi immediately, and he went to ask permission — but they said no. So then I said, 'I am not leaving this jail until I meet the chief warden of the jail!' I explained to him that this is a holy Rabbi, who only eats what is especially kosher. So [the chief warden] called over one of the non-Jews who was in charge of the food, and he told me, 'This man says that it is kosher.' For them, if it's not pork it's kosher!

So I explained to the chief warden of the jail that this is a holy Rabbi, but he replied, 'Only the court can give permission to bring him [kosher] food, only the court.' In the end, I told the chief warden that Rabbi Berland hadn't eaten in two days, and that his feet and hands were cold! I convinced him to make an exception for that day, and I went and got food and gave it to the Rav. But then the chief warden told the lawyer, 'No more!'"

Next, Rabbi Grossman tried to get the South African Jewish community mobilized to offer Rabbi Berland more help and support while he was behind bars in Johannesburg. He recounts:

"I spent the whole day with the Chief Rabbi [of South Africa] and his people to convince them to give Rabbi Berland [properly kosher] food, and they all said that we needed to wait for Monday for the court, and that we needed to pray that the court will allow them to bring him food. Anyone who understands what it means to be in jail in Africa, it's unbelievable."

Rabbi Grossman then went to speak to the Jewish chaplain in Sun City Prison, Rabbi Michael Katz, to see if he could help. Rabbi Grossman asked the chaplain, "Do they have to wait until Monday just to put in a request with the court that the Rav should have kosher food? Right now it's Thursday!" Rabbi Katz replied that once a week, on Friday, during family visiting hours, Rebbetzin Berland would be allowed to come and give him food, but that it wouldn't last for two days without a refrigerator.

On the following Sunday after Rabbi Grossman had already left to return to Israel, the South African prison guards stuck to their position of refusing to allow kosher food to be brought in to the Rav. When Nachman Shitrit, the Rav's assistant, tried to bring him food, he was arrested and interrogated for a few hours before being told, "There is no difference between an 80-year-old prisoner and a young prisoner. Everyone will eat the same food. Make sure we never see you again here."

Rabbi Grossman continued that the South African Jewish community was steering clear of helping Rabbi Berland because *"they think that if Israel wants the Rav to come back and he doesn't, then that means that he ran away from court. It makes the whole situation look bad."*

Rabbi Grossman continued: *"I was with Chief Rabbi Warren Goldstein for a few hours, explaining who Rabbi Berland really is, who his people really are, and what happened. I got all the people who are working with Rabbi Berland to meet the Chief Rabbi, and at the end he said, 'Let's make a cease-fire so that we can do everything to help the Rav.' The Chief Rabbi himself said he will see what he can do."*

Before Rabbi Grossman left South Africa, he met with some of the biggest lawyers in Johannesburg to arrange another appeal for the Rav to be released on bail, until he was sent back to Israel. The appeal was ultimately unsuccessful, and Rabbi Berland ended up spending more than three months in prison in South Africa.

Rabbi Grossman also spoke in a Johannesburg shul to try to arouse the community: *"Rabbi Eliezer Berland is a holy man, and an incredible Torah scholar who knows the whole Torah. He's devoted his whole life to helping people, and to making hundreds and thousands of returnees to Judaism. He is working for God day and night. Everyone should learn more, pray more, and do more kindnesses in the merit of Reb Lazer Berland, which is the biggest thing, because when he hears that people are praying and learning, this gives him strength."*

★ ★ ★

Meanwhile, back in Israel, other students and followers of Rabbi Berland, most notably Rabbi Shalom Arush, were also desperately trying to raise public awareness about the terrible, life-threatening situation Rabbi Berland was now in, during his stay in Sun City Prison in Johannesburg.

In an interview he gave to the Kol B'Rama radio show, Rabbi Arush said the following:

"It's terrible the way people believe the media today… if only they would believe the Torah as much as they believe the media!

The man is not a man, he is an angel! He is an angel of God who can stand 16 hours without moving for the Shemoneh Esrei prayers. He knows what people are thinking. I always used to ask him questions in my mind and he'd turn around and answer me! And many more miracles which I promised the Rav I will never speak about. It would take 10 hours straight for me to relate all the stories that I saw with my own eyes."

Rabbi Arush explained that people had paid money to women to speak against Rabbi Berland, and that the Rav had taken upon himself the disgrace of being libeled as an adulterer in order to cancel out the terrible Heavenly decrees against the Jewish nation. *"The leaders of the generation,* many of the people that I'm connected with, said that the Rav is atoning for the entire generation," he said. "So what can we do, there are people who believe the media that an 80-year-old person... [Laughs]. It's insane!"

Rabbi Arush continued by trying to urge the Israeli public to act to get the Rav out of prison. He said, "He's in a life-threatening situation right now! He's in prison, and even the prisoners are saying that he is an angel of G-d. He only studies Torah and prays all day! He barely eats!

We must get up and demonstrate! We need to stand in front of the South African consulate and bring politicians and public figures who will stand up and declare, 'What's going on here!? What are you holding him for?! What are you doing to him?!'

Who knows what kind of Heavenly judgment is hanging over the Jewish people due to the way we are dealing with the situation, that this great, awesome tzaddik is sitting in jail and no one is opening their mouths! This thing cannot go on! This is a huge Heavenly judgment on the nation of Israel!!!"

Rabbi Arush concluded: "We call on people to help, whoever can help in any way possible, they should come and do whatever they can. Whoever does will be blessed, God will guard him, will watch him, and will make him successful... We should have the merit that the Rav should lead the people of Israel, and merit to see his redemption together with the redemption of the whole nation of Israel. Amen."

Rabbi Michael Katz, the Rabbi of the Johannesburg Prison Service, related that the Rav made an enormous impression on his fellow prisoners while he was incarcerated Sun City Prison:

"As part of my duties as the Rabbi of the Prison Service, I met with the gaon and tzaddik, Rav Eliezer Berland, shlit"a, on many different occasions," begins Rabbi Katz. "Rabbi Berland was imprisoned under really terrible conditions, but he was always happy.

The prison cell the Rav was kept in was very small, less than three square meters. It had an untiled, dirt floor, with an open toilet in the corner that was only partitioned off with the Rav's blanket as a makeshift divider[i]. The cell also contained a very small writing table, and a crate of the Rav's holy books in one corner."

Rabbi Katz continued: *"Every time someone came to visit the Rav, they would bring him more holy books."*

The Rav was imprisoned during the winter months, and during the night the temperature would frequently fall below zero, and the cold would permeate the walls and the floor of the cells in the giant subterranean prison building.

The Rav was incarcerated there with literally thousands of other inmates, including the worst dregs of South African society. *"I didn't know whether or not the Rav had his own heater, but when I went to see him I saw that he was keeping himself warm by moving around his cell a lot, and learning Torah,"* says Rabbi Katz.

"I have no idea what the Rav's praying times were, because each time I visited him, he was happily wrapped in his tefillin and tallis, and always had a holy book in his hand. The wardens, prison guards, and even the other prisoners in the prison facility all called the Rav 'the Holy Man,' and would come at all hours to ask for his blessing, and to ask for his advice about how to deal with the many problems they had in their personal lives.

The other prisoners treated the Rav very respectfully and honorably and tried to look out for him, to make sure that he had what he needed, and would frequently ask him if they could do anything for him."

Rabbi Katz said that what amazed him the most about

---

[i] Halacha forbids a person from studying holy works in an unclean place, such as in a bathroom or next to a toilet. Rabbi Berland chose to forgo his blanket - in the middle of winter - in order to be able to continue studying his holy books.

the Rav's time in the Johannesburg prison, though, was the way he was always smiling and in good spirits, and didn't complain about his living conditions, unlike the vast majority of the other prisoners there. *"He told me repeatedly that everything was good, everything was okay, and that everyone was helping him. He also told me that finally, he had the opportunity to spend lengthy hours in hisbodedus, the way he'd always wanted to.*

The Rav asked me to give over a message in his name that he is always with us, both in our materialistic endeavors and our spiritual endeavors, and that we need to strengthen ourselves in emunah and bitachon that everything that's happening is all for the good."

Many of the prisoners in Sun City started to revere Rabbi Berland and would regularly visit him for advice and blessings. But in such a large population of violent and psychotic individuals, there were inevitably some who still wished to harm the obviously Jewish, elderly prisoner.

In order to try to keep the Rav safe, his family and attendants arranged for one of the more physically imposing inmates to be paid to become the Rav's bodyguard, and to protect him from his fellow inmates in Sun City, many of whom were radicalized Muslims.

While this arrangement originally worked out well, by the end of the Rav's sojourn in Sun City this "bodyguard" had started to extort more and more money out of the Rav's attendants for his services and was also very unhappy about the prospect of losing his lucrative salary if the Rav should be extradited back to Israel.

As rumors started to circulate that the Rav was about to be released back to Israel, the erstwhile bodyguard became the biggest threat to the Rav's safety. He locked the Rav in his cell and started threatening the Rav's life if the prison authorities dared to try and remove him.

When the Rav was ready to leave prison, his attendants had to trick this "bodyguard" into releasing the Rav from his cell without harming him.

As difficult as the situation was throughout his exile, nothing fazed the Rav or took him away from his Torah learning and other devotions. Even when the South African police first arrested him at the Morningside Clinic, the Rav remained engrossed in the *sefer* he had with him at that time, the *Ketzos HaChoshen,* and continued studying from it even while he was inside the police car.

In every court appearance he had to attend, wherever that happened to be in the world, his head was always in a holy book, and he continued to toil in Torah even in Sun City Prison. Just as Yosef HaTzaddik had spent his time singing and dancing in jail and clinging to God, so too Rabbi Berland accepted all the suffering he was being sent with joy, peace and a calm spirit.

In one of Rabbi Berland's many court appearances before the South African judges, his lawyers were fighting to get the Rav moved out of Sun City Prison to somewhere with easier conditions, where his physical needs would be attended to and he would be able to receive suitably kosher food and drink.

At the end of all the arguments, the judge ruled that the Rav could be moved to a holding cell in the local police station. As soon as the Rav heard this decision, he took his head out from the holy book he was absorbed in and told the judge, "No, I want to stay where I am. I can learn better here, without any interruptions." The Rav knew that the police station he'd be sent to would be crowded with people, and that there would be too many distractions and disturbances that would make it much harder to learn.

Once the judge heard the Rav's amazing comment, he responded, "If his studying is more important to him than food, then he will have his way," and the Rav stayed in Sun City Prison despite the horrible conditions, and the difficulty of meeting even his most basic needs there.

The Rav often went for many days without food or drink while he was in Sun City Prison — but he barely noticed, because he was able to learn day and night. At that time, he told one of his students in a phone conversation: *"I am in the Garden of Eden here! I haven't had the settled ability to learn Torah without interruption, day and night without end, without having to deal with the needs of the community, for 50 years already. My mind has opened up like it never has before."*

Despite the awful conditions in the Sun City prison in Johannesburg, despite the fact that the Rav wasn't being given kosher food or drink, his main request from his visitors was that they should bring him more holy books. Even though he'd barely eaten for days, his greatest hunger continued to be for the wisdom of the Torah.

When Rabbi Berland finally left Sun City Prison in the middle of July, it took the prison wardens a couple of hours to clear his tiny prison cell of the 600 or so holy books he'd amassed in the two months he'd spent there.

★ ★ ★

As word continued to spread about the terrible conditions that Rabbi Berland was being kept in, *tzaddikim* from across the world contacted the Rav's community to show their support.

The Rebbe of Berdichev, Rav Aharon Boymill was frequently in the middle of many of these communiqués. He says: *"Don't think that only Breslover chassidim are praying for Rav Eliezer Berland, shlit"a. All of the big Rebbes, Rabbis and tzaddikim around the whole world are praying for the Rav, shlit"a!*

From Rav Steinman to the Belzer Rebbe, to the Gerrer Rebbe and Rav Kanievsky, everyone is praying for Rabbi Berland, shlit"a, and they're always interested in what's happening with him. The attendant of Rav David Abuchatzeira, shlit"a, called me personally last week and told me that the Rav wanted to know what's happening with Rav Eliezer Berland, shlit"a. The house of Rav Steinman called and wanted to know what's happening with the Rav. The son of the Belzer Rebbe himself called me to find out what's going on with the Rav and said that his father wants to know."

Rabbi Boymill continued: "It's not that Rav Eliezer Berland, shlit"a, is alone in the world and that only his chassidim care about him. All the Torah giants across the whole world, care about the Rav and are praying for him.

A minyan of us chassidim went to the gravesite of Rebbe Yossi HaGalili [to pray] for the success of the Rav, shlit"a. On the way home, we stopped in Tiberius by the tzaddik, Rabbi Dov Kook, shlit"a, but it was very hard to reach him because of all the students surrounding him. I banged on the pulpit and said, 'HaRav Kook, HaRav Kook, HaRav Eliezer Berland is in exile and is suffering so much. If you had been in this situation like the Rav, Rabbi Berland, shlit"a, would turn the world upside down for you. Why don't you overturn the world for him?'

The whole synagogue stood silent. Then, three members came up to me and told me to leave immediately," says Rabbi Boymill. "But then HaRav Kook came up to me, hugged me, and told me, 'I need this kind of gabbai.' He said to me, 'HaRabbi Berland, shlit"a, is an expert in performing miracles, and the same wonders and miracles will happen. Those miracles will accompany him and he will get out of everything, with G-d's help.' Then Rav Kook informed everyone in the synagogue that they would pray for ten minutes for the success of the gaon and tzaddik, Rav Eliezer Berland."

As the extradition hearings in the South African court dragged on and on, and as the judges repeatedly refused to allow the Rav out on bail or to be placed under house arrest, the Rav decided to make a deal directly with the Israeli police.

He would return to Israel voluntarily, on July 19, 2016.

Two South African police marshals accompanied the Rav on his flight home, but the rest of the plane was filled with his *chassidim*. The Rav was flying home to his family and thousands of students, and it seemed that the end of his three long years of exile was finally in sight.

RABBI BERLAND
RETURNS TO ISRAEL

"Sometimes, the controversy surrounding a tzaddik
is the greatest proof that he is a tzaddik."
                                    – *Rebbe Nachman of Breslov*

★   ★   ★

At the beginning of the Rav's exile in February 2013,
the great kabbalist from Tiberius, Rabbi Dov Kook,
released the following statement via his nephew, who
added: "I don't remember Rabbi Kook ever saying something
similar to this before."

This is what Rabbi Dov Kook said:

*"Heaven is very angry about the people who are disgracing
the gaon and tzaddik, Rav Eliezer Berland. I am very concerned
about the situation. Who knows what will be with us?*

*God is very angry, like the time the Jews sinned by making
the Golden Calf. If it wasn't for God's mercy, who knows what
would happen to us? The main claim is not against the Jewish
people, who don't know the Rav and therefore believe the lies of
the media, because when a Jew doesn't keep Torah and mitzvos
and sees words like this in the media, it's unfortunately only
natural that he's going to believe them.*

*But what God is really upset about is that not all of the
Breslov chassidim believe, with all their hearts, that [Rabbi*

*Berland] is a tzaddik. If all of the Breslov chassidim would
believe that Rabbi Berland is a tzaddik, then Moshiach would
come. But since the Satan knows this, he's trying to torpedo it.*

*The fact that Rabbi Berland is unable to be in Israel is soul-
destroying. The president of Iran has an atom bomb, and God
could arrange for it to be dropped on us in a second. But He's
not doing that, because He has mercy on us."*

On a separate occasion, when some of his students were
trying to question him about Rabbi Berland, Rabbi Kook
responded: "How can you even have any thoughts against
Rabbi Berland?! I myself am not even able to grasp him."

Three years later, when Rabbi Berland was being chased
by the South African police prior to returning to Israel, Rav
Kook made the following statement on Purim night, March
23, 2016: "There will be tremendous Divine Providence. He
will return to Israel and redeem us! His return will usher in
the redemption[i]."

Hopes were high that all the terrible suffering the Rav,
his followers, the Torah world generally and the nation
of Israel had endured over the past three years would be
replaced with great joy, miracles and happiness. But that's
not exactly what happened.

On July 19, 2016, Rav Eliezer Berland finally returned
to Israel from Johannesburg, after an absence of more than
three years.

Again, it should be stressed that Rabbi Berland was not
formally extradited from South Africa, and that he returned
to Israel of his own free will. During the flight, the Rav
learned Torah, prayed with his followers, and then spent
many hours joyfully singing and dancing with his students.

---

[i] You can see the clip of Rav Kook saying this at: https://www.
youtube.com/watch?v=cZyqRT4Fzgg

As soon as the Rav stepped back onto the holy soil of Israel at Ben Gurion Airport, he kneeled down and kissed it reverentially. Then, he was immediately surrounded by the Israeli police.

Given the fact that there was no case to answer, no credible evidence to dispute, no possible legal justification as to why the Rav could be prosecuted in Israel, his followers plus many of the nations' leading kabbalists and Rabbis were sure that after a day or two, the Rav would be completely exonerated of all charges, released — and then the redemption would begin in earnest, as Rabbi Dov Kook had predicted.

In addition, the Rav himself had given permission on July 11, 2016 for his assistants to file a libel suit against Israel TV's Channel 2, one of the first media outlets that had aired allegations against the Rav back in March 2013.

It seemed as though the tide had finally turned against the Rav's persecutors, and that after a few legal formalities, he'd finally be a free man. Rav David Abuchatzeira said at this time: "The rectification is over. Everything is going to go quickly now." On another occasion, Rav Abuchatzeira commented: "[Everything related to] Rav Eliezer Berland is secrets. It's above our understanding. He's fixing the whole world."

But was the process finished, or was there still more "fixing" required?

★ ★ ★

Immediately after he bent down to kiss the holy ground of Israel, Rabbi Berland was surrounded by group of police officers who led him to a room where five of his followers were waiting to see him. Thousands more of his followers were waiting in the Ben Gurion airport arrivals hall, where they were singing and dancing.

Before the Rav got to Israel, it had been agreed in advance that he would allowed to speak to five of his followers in a small room in Ben Gurion airport, to ensure that he was in good health and being treated appropriately. When the Rav entered the room, he was told that he had 20 minutes to speak to his followers before going on to the court.

The Rav started speaking words of Torah - but not to his five students. Instead, he directed his words to the eight police officers who were guarding him. One of the police officers said to him: "We brought you here to speak to your students who you haven't seen in a long time. Sit down, and talk to them. You can talk to us later."

The Rav replied: *"No, I only came to Israel to speak to the police and the judges! These people (pointing to his students) I already brought to teshuva. No, I'm here to bring all of you to teshuva. Lock me up as long as it takes, I will not leave until every police officer and every judge does teshuva"*.

Rabbi Berland then continued to speak to his police guards about Torah topics, but also surprised them with his vast knowledge of Israel's wars, and his insights into the intelligence and security layout of the country. By the time he'd finished, he'd clearly demonstrated how Israel's security was actually very fragile, and how only the Torah could truly secure the Jewish nation in its homeland.

After this prelude, which lasted a half an hour, the Israeli police took him straight to court in nearby Rishon LeTzion.

While he was talking with his followers in the airport, the first thing the Rav told them was: "That's it, now we're already in the *redemption*," although this would be far from evident over the coming weeks and months. After hearing this statement, one of his followers asked the Rav if things were going to be somehow different, now that we'd entered the next stage of redemption. The Rav replied: "No! Moshiach is already with us." And that was that.

The first judge to hear the details of the case against the Rav decided that there was no evidence against him, and that he needed to be released immediately. But he gave the police prosecutors a day or two to appeal, as they claimed they needed more time (after three years of waiting…) to pull their evidence together.

The case went to the appeals court — and the Rav's unconditional release was overturned. This set the pattern for more than 10 hearings over the following weeks where the Rav would be released by one judge, but the decision would then be overturned by the appeals court. It later transpired that this is a common tactic used by the Israeli authorities to keep people in prison, and that the appeals court rarely if ever goes against the police prosecutors.

In the meantime, the Rav was kept in prison in Ramle, and ferried between the court in Rishon L'Tzion (which routinely freed him) and the appeals court in Ramle (which routinely overturned that decision).

The Israeli police were having enormous difficulties pulling even a semblance of a case together because the 'evidence' they claimed simply didn't stand up and the police officers who had been responsible for bringing the claims in the first place were now all out of the picture.

One police officer who'd been involved in putting together the original claims about Rabbi Berland had killed himself back in July 2015, on the same day that the Rav had left Holland. Another police detective who'd been responsible for turning the claims into the court papers that had been sent to the Dutch court had also now 'disappeared'.

And then, the Head of Investigations who'd been assigned Rabbi Berland's case went abroad on "vacation" when he heard that Rabbi Berland was returning to Israel — and no-one knew when or if he was planning on returning.

Back in January 2016, another police chief (who wished to remain anonymous) had visited Rabbi Shalom Arush and told him that[i] his superiors had threatened him that if he didn't forge a false case against Rabbi Berland, he would lose his position. The anonymous police chief acknowledged that in reality, the case against Rabbi Berland was completely devoid of any evidence, and that all of the things that were being said about Rabbi Berland were lies.

The police chief continued that from the moment he'd begun trying to create a case against the Rav, he'd been suffering. He'd had a major car accident, and he'd got divorced, etc.

While this police chief had formally been completely secular, he'd started to do *teshuva* and return to his religious roots as a result of all the suffering he'd endured, and he felt terrible about his part in falsifying the case against Rabbi Berland.

Rabbi Arush told the anonymous policeman that he could only fix the situation if he came clean and publicly admitted what he'd done. But the policeman told Rabbi

---

[i] As heard from Rabbi Arush's attendant, R' Chaim Barzilai.

Arush that he simply couldn't do that. If he admitted that he'd been trying to fabricate a case, he'd be sent to prison for at least 13 years…

But having worked so hard to chase him all over the world, blacken his name and arm-twist the South African government into extraditing him, the Rav's persecutors weren't about to let him go so easily.

If they couldn't make a case against Rabbi Berland in court, then they would fall back on their tried-and-tested strategy of subjecting the Rav to more "trial by media."

From the minute the news reached Israel that the Rav was returning to the country, the Rav's persecutors started working on trying to blacken the Rav's name further, with the aim of giving the Israeli police more ammunition to press for the Rav to be kept in prison indefinitely.

One story after another appeared, quoting the same lies in identical words, but that didn't stop many news outlets from simply airing these scandalous lies as if they were true.

In the days leading up to the Rav's return on July 19th, 2016 the anti-Torah media in Israel continued to feed its audience a steady diet of deceit, libel, lies and fantastic tabloid headlines designed to make it look as though the Rav was guilty as charged.

But the worst was still to come. At the same time that the Rav's lawyers were successfully arguing that there was no case to answer and that the Rav should be freed — or at the very least, released to house arrest — some "Breslov" zealots from Meah Shearim began to unleash another barrage of awful, slanderous stories via the media.

On July 17, 2016, before the Rav had even left South Africa, the Breslov zealots falsified a statement from Rabbi Yaakov Meir Shecter, plus two other Breslov Rabbis from the Meah Shearim community, effectively stating that the Rav and his Shuvu Banim community should be ostracized.

Sadly, even the so-called *frum* media was more than happy to publish the most brutal and scurrilous lies about the Rav and his community, without first checking the veracity of what they were printing.

Rabbi Shecter immediately wrote a rebuttal, which was hastily pasted up all across all the walls in Meah Shearim.

Then on July 18, 2016, the zealots released another falsified statement, this time claiming to be from the Rav's son, R' Nachman Berland, to the effect that the Rav's own son had turned his back on his father and wanted nothing more to do with him.

Again, R' Nachman Berland immediately made a statement and recorded an interview rebutting this falsehood, where he clearly stated: "**The recording is forged. There is a war against us. My father is the *Gadol HaDor*.**" But again, the media chose not to cover R' Nachman Berland's statement, nor to retract the false stories they'd printed.

The following day, July 19, 2016, the well-known Sephardi halachic decisor, Rabbi Shimon Badani released the following widely-reported statement about all the false media reports circulating about Rabbi Berland and his community: "It's defamation, malicious and strictly forbidden," said Rabbi Badani.

He continued: "*To slander a* Torah scholar *such as this is showing complete contempt for Torah scholars. It's not up to each individual to make a judgment about whether someone else is okay or not. This is malicious. Anyone who is doing something like this — let the Jewish court decide. It's forbidden to tell it all over the place, it should be said only in court, and then the court will decide. This is a very grave [sin]. A person who does this will end up in purgatory, if they speak false, evil words against a Torah scholar.*"

In the meantime, the Israeli authorities were only too grateful for all the fake news appearing in the media, which helped to paint a sordid and deceitful picture of Rabbi Berland.

But the most terrible deceit of all occurred a few days later, on July 26, 2016, when the zealots released two very poorly-doctored videos to the media that simply overlaid a false audio on the images being shown.

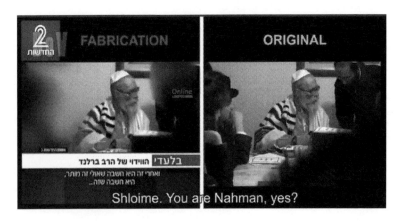

In one video, they had it appear as though the Rav was condoning murder, while in the other, infamous, video they had the Rav apparently confessing to committing a terrible crime. It was blindingly obvious that both videos had been falsified in a very amateurish way, with a fake audio track placed over old video footage[i], but once again the media eagerly lapped up this new "evidence" against the Rav, splashing their terrible headlines over their front pages.

These recordings appeared at a crucial juncture in the many court hearings the Rav was undergoing where his lawyers were trying to win his freedom, or at the very least, to have the Rav released to house arrest pending going to trial in order to clear his name.

Now, thanks to the falsified videos put out by the

---

[i] You can see the fake VS real video for yourself here: https://youtu.be/u1W6XMdLzPI

Breslov zealots, the Israeli government came up with a new strategy for keeping the elderly Rav behind bars. He was now, officially, a threat to national security. His court papers categorized him as belonging to the highest level of dangerous criminals, a status usually reserved for mafia leaders and senior terrorists.

ISRAELI 'ADMINISTRATIVE DETENTION'

Given the ongoing historical threat from Arab terrorism, the Israeli justice system has developed a peculiar set of laws that can be used to keep those who are designated as threats to the country's national security in prison for large stretches of time, without any evidence or trial.

This system of Israeli "administrative detention" is meant to give the Israeli police force, IDF, Mossad, and any other Israeli agencies involved with national security a period of time where they can collect enough evidence against a suspected terrorist to bring them to court, while also keeping the suspected terrorist off the street, in the meantime.

Thanks to old laws that were kept on the books in Israel from the British Mandate period, the Israeli government can imprison someone for months, and even years, before they're even obligated to bring charges.

★ ★ ★

It's well known that the Israeli judiciary unfortunately continues to be an almost exclusive enclave of liberal, left-leaning Jews with pronounced anti-religious bias.

The Israeli judiciary appoints its own judges. Very few center, center-right or religiously-observant candidates ever make it through the selection process. So, while loudly proclaiming its commitment to the highest ideals of impartiality, independence and truth, the Israeli judiciary often views things through a narrow lens of left-wing, anti-religious and "liberal" values.

Judge Shelley Timan was formerly one of the senior judges in the Tel Aviv District Court, until he quit in 2016 citing corruption within the Israel justice system. In an interview he gave to the Israeli TV Channel 2[i], Judge Timan said: *"I left my job absolutely convinced that I'm doing the right thing, because I felt I couldn't serve the cause of justice anymore.*

There are people who are rotting away in prison. Many of them still haven't even been brought to trial yet or convicted [of any crime]. Others are completely innocent of doing any crime," he explained.

Timan continued: *"In a democracy, a person's case should be judged in a prompt fashion, but you see how many cases here (in Israel) have a huge delay before they come to trial. I tried, I really tried, but I can't stand it anymore. The prosecutors have enormous egos, and they want to see a conviction at any cost.*

There's also a lot of errors and omissions [in the evidence], because the Israeli police aren't doing their job the way they're supposed to, again because there are a lot of ambitious people who want to win a conviction at any cost. And so, people are rotting away [in prison] for the rest of their lives, or for very long stretches of time.

I'm very sorry to say it, but the Israeli police are stitching people up, and fabricating charges. Also, the pressure from the media is also very hard for the judges to bear, and its skewing their decisions. Lobbyists and the media are determining the fate of the accused."

Writing in the Hamodia newspaper on March 8, 2018,

---

[i] Judge Timan's interview, with English subtitles, can be seen here: https://youtu.be/qLJUWDziGSA

columnist Joel Rebibo had this to say about the increasingly sorry state of the Israeli judicial system in the wake of the Bezeq corruption case[i]:

"Many in Israel don't believe the courts are impartial, or willing to give them a fair hearing, and for good reason. Judges and prosecutors tend to be cut from the same elitist left-wing secular Ashkenazi cloth, and don't relate to or respect the values and priorities of most of the Israeli public....

"It is mind-boggling that the Israeli judicial system needed 70 years to understand that there's a problem with judges meeting alone with government lawyers.... It isn't just defendants who are hurt by this reckless disregard for fair play. The courts undermine their credibility with the general public."

Despite the obvious lack of evidence against Rabbi Berland, despite his failing health (which already at that point had required him to have surgery to remove a tumor), and despite the spiritual toll remaining in prison would take on the elderly, 79-year-old *tzaddik*, both of the judges assigned to the case by the Jerusalem District Court repeatedly ruled that the Rav should continue to be kept in prison.

After the seventh hearing to try to get the Rav freed, one of the judges refused to consider him for house arrest, because she said that: "Rabbi Berland is focused on himself, has a big influence on his surroundings, and there's a risk he may try to escape."

Shortly after this occurred, these two judges were back in the press for all the wrong reasons. They happened to be the judges who had freed a convicted Arab terrorist and then lifted the restrictions on him entering Jerusalem shortly

---

[i] Two suspects in this case appeared before a judge in the belief they could convince her to release them to house arrest. It was subsequently discovered that the judge and a government prosecutor had arranged the outcome of the trial beforehand, which lead to a huge public outcry.

before he went on to murder two people and injure five more in a shooting attack in Jerusalem on October 9, 2016.

The Israeli public was outraged at the poor judgment shown by these two judges that then led to the murder of two Israelis, and there were many calls for the judges to be fired from their posts. But in the meantime, the damage had been done. While a known terrorist had been freed to kill again, the elderly, increasingly unwell *Tzaddik*, Rabbi Berland, continued to sit in prison.

★   ★   ★

It's hard to describe the blow that Rabbi Berland's persecutors managed to deal at this time to the Rav, to his community, and to the nation of Israel, generally.

In the aftermath of their shocking activities, many of the Breslov leaders and other rabbis tried to repair the damage by issuing a number of statements in clear support of Rabbi Berland, which publicly explained for the first time how these persecutors had been chasing the Rav for many, many years.

A close family member of Rabbi Yitzchak David Grossman had the following to say about the matter:

"How is it possible to believe all these stories about the Tzaddik that are being spread around by criminals and sinners? By people who have sold him out for money? They took the Rav from Torah class to Torah class, and then charged people thousands of dollars just to speak to him. And these are the same people that we're now meant to believe, when they started to spread all these stories about the Rav?!

These people are thieves and liars, and they have no connection to holiness. They completely damaged the community, and they kept the Rav under lock and key and didn't let him speak to anyone — only what they themselves wanted. And these people are the ones you're going to believe?!

These wicked people paid tens of thousands of dollars to a false witness, in order for her to agree to lie on their behalf — and these people you want to turn into Tzaddikim?!

How can people believe these lies? [He is a holy Tzaddik] and they are criminals and sinners who are exploiting his complete nullification to God's will [i.e., by not taking steps to silence them or to defend himself publicly]. They are exploiting this, and they threatened him that if he doesn't agree to do what they want him to do, they will spread stories and lies about him."

Which is exactly what happened.

Rabbi Shalom Arush also released the following statement:

"We are stunned and pained, to the depths of our heart, to witness the terrible rumors and the controversy occurring in our community, which are describing things that are just completely impossible, have no logical basis, and are completely disconnected from reality.

"[We are shocked that] spiritually unrefined, brazen, chutzpadik people with coarsened hearts are opening their proud, arrogant mouths against the holy honor of Rav Eliezer Berland, shlit"a, who is a true Torah scholar and one of the pillars of the generation, whose whole world consists of Torah, prayer, holiness, abstinence, judging others favorably and sacrificing himself for another Jew, whoever that other Jew might be.

People are saying falsehoods, and spreading evil rumours concocted by malicious, accursed baalei machlokes [troublemakers, people who create division and strife] who are trying to harm the Rav.

AND THE COMMUNITY SHOULD KNOW THAT THE THINGS BEING SPOKEN OF ARE ABSOLUTE

LIES, AND WOE TO ANYONE WHO BELIEVES ANY
FALSE STORIES OR FALSEHOODS ABOUT HIM,
EVEN JUST IN THEIR HEARTS."

Meanwhile, the terrible circumstances also prompted the normally reclusive Rabbi Yaakov Meir Salmanovitch, one of the leaders of the present generation of Breslov *chassidim* and the former Rebbe of two of the Breslov zealots, to make the following public statement, after he'd been approached by his former students and asked if he'd be willing to sign something condemning Rabbi Berland and his community:

"How can we continue to be silent, when there's already been so much suffering, and so much spiritual misery, and so much strife and contention, and so much pain? How are you able to continue to conduct such a cruel war? You have claims to make? You have things to say? Only in a good way! Only act in a merciful way!

How are you willing to cause so much pain to the world? Stop now! Stop now! Woe to you, from the Day of Judgment. If you have cause for complaint, speak to the other person in a peaceful way. [This is] terrible hatred, something that hasn't been seen since the creation of the world. This is delaying the redemption!

You want to try to cause our tzaddikim to stumble even more, with another signature, and another signature? Woe to you, from the Day of Judgment! ... Aren't you scared to go after such big tzaddikim and cause them to stumble? To go after such big tzaddikim and cause them to hate?

... How can it be that in Breslov, something as painful as this could be happening? Something as evil as this? It's already been four years of this wickedness, four years of people crying, four years where thousands of people have had their souls trampled. If you want to rectify things, even the most profound things, everything can be done peacefully! Not with wickedness! There's so much hatred going on here, so much

hatred, hatred without end. If each person had love [in their hearts instead], we could have rectified everything.

... What are these terrible things that are going on? All the people who made trouble for Rav Shecter and involved him in disputes in the past already regretted what they did, and Rav Shecter, who is the holy of holies, stumbled into a controversy in the past because of other people [who told him lies], for which he's already asked forgiveness. Now, you come again, with another set of signatures, and call in other people, and you want to involve him [in another controversy] again. Shame on you!

... Who knows if the final redemption of our people hasn't been delayed solely because of this terrible controversy, which has spread strife and the defamation of God's Name across the whole globe? I've heard so much desecration of God's name coming from every corner of the world as a result of this conflict. People are saying, even if what happened actually happened (God forbid, as though that could actually have happened) — where is all this terrible, murderous hatred [lit., murder] coming from? They say only in Breslov do you find this sort of murderous hatred!

... There are literally thousands and thousands of people who are deeply connected to Rabbi Berland across the whole world, and they are crying out, and their cries have pierced the hearts of the Heavens. Shame on you!

... Regret what you did, do teshuva, and you'll be accepted with love. There is no hatred here, even though you did what you did, there is still no hatred [toward you]. Thousands of people have already been torn and broken by this terrible affair.

God should help us that Moshiach should come and he will conclude matters... This is the first time that I've ever done something like this, and you should know that this wasn't a simple decision at all. If you stop now, with all your strength, there is still a chance that the redemption will still come."

★ ★ ★

Another of Breslov's leading lights, Rav Mota Frank, also released a statement at this time, where he said of the Breslov zealots:

"… They're not embarrassed to stoop to the very lowest of levels, and to raise their hands against the Torah. And they're trying to make other people go to secular court, too, to testify against Rav Lazer, to participate in the investigation by the police, who are known to hate religion [i.e., Judaism], about issues that have nothing to do with the investigation, solely with the aim of trying to make more trouble for him.

And the most terrible thing of all was to go to such a low level to publicly cause the embarrassment and humiliation of Rav Lazer and all of his people in this way, to pass around a recording of a false video (as is evident to everyone who really knows Rav Lazer), which they brought out in a backhanded, deceitful way, made up of old footage of Rav Lazer.

And they passed this video recording to whom??? Not to the Rabbis who sit on the throne of justice, with level heads and with pure fear of Heaven, and who make decisions with full cognizance that the 'gates of purgatory are open below them' should they make a mistake; and not to a religious Jewish court of law that's made up of at least three judges, who sit together and act in accordance with the halachic laws of investigations.

Not only did they pass this recording to the police investigators behind closed doors, but to our great regret and embarrassment, they also passed this recording to who??? The Israeli television stations!!! In order to persuade the haters of Israel to aim their poisonous arrows of hatred against hareidi Judaism, and to debase a Rabbi and his community in such an evil way, and to cause millions of people to speak profanities in the worst way, and to have thoughts that he [Rabbi Berland] committed a terrible sin…. God should have mercy.

Who are the people [who are guilty of] spreading around profanity and false accusations of sin, in a way that has never been seen before? Rabbi Berland or [the Rav's persecutors]???

… Anyone who has even a little bit of understanding about everything that is happening around us knows with certainty that the Rav is being persecuted and is an innocent man. And more than this, that there is a lowly group that will not stop at anything, even the most degrading things, against this tzaddik, the foundation of the world."

But it wasn't only the Breslov leaders who were shocked into openly speaking out. The great kabbalist known as 'the Milkman', Rav Chaim Cohen Perachia, also released a statement on August 8, 2016, where he said:

"I'm issuing a warning about [one of the Breslov zealots][i] *that a dangerous spirit of insanity has possessed him, and he is no longer in control of himself. Therefore, it's completely forbidden to speak to him about anything whatsoever in connection to Rabbi Berland, shlit"a, because he has the ability to convince and persuade people [that falsehoods are true], even including those people who don't engage in lashon hara. And this ability is coming from the dangerous spirit that's entered him, God should have mercy."*

Meanwhile, the leading kabbalist from Bnei Brak, Rav David Chaim Stern, had this to say publicly[ii] while speaking in Bnei Brak on August 11, 2016:

"I know Rabbi Berland, we have a strong connection. He is an exalted Jew who stands above all others. There is no man who is completely kindness and mercy [as Rabbi Berland is]. Whenever he had money he immediately distributed everything to charity…

---

[i] The Milkman specifically named the person, in his original statement.

[ii] You can see the video of Rav Stern speaking here: https://youtu.be/Wtj6PWBOSjM

Others don't know Rabbi Berland, like I know him. And they didn't ask the Steipler what I asked about him.... He's holy and pure — that's it! We need to wake up the masses! A holy tzaddik is suffering in prison. I believe that every single action is the greatest mitzvah, to save this tzaddik as quickly as possible. He's not guilty — he didn't do anything!"

On another occasion, Rav Stern said: *"Woe to whoever speaks ill of Rabbi Berland, for they will be punished severely. All those who dare to speak ill of this tzaddik should fear for their lives, for they will all, without exception, receive severe punishments from Above. I've known him for more than 50 years, and the way he learned with the Steipler was unmatched by any other. He is entirely holy.*

The final test before Moshiach comes is Rabbi Berland. Anyone who talks against him, or who believes the rumors being circulated about him, won't merit to witness the imminent redemption of our people."

Rav David Abuchatzeira had this to say:

"Rabbi Berland is all Torah, and he's in prison by unnatural means, and his salvation will also be by unnatural means. The suffering that he's enduring now is the hardest, but the salvation is close, because the Rav is now undergoing the harshest degradation, so the salvation has to come, and all of his accusers will fall."

As the statements of support for Rabbi Berland continued to pile up, more and more notable Rabbis came forward, warning people from believing any of the terrible lies being told about the Rav.

Rav Yehuda Sheinfeld, a leading kabbalist and *Rosh Kollel* of the Shimon HaTzaddik Kollel, added his voice to the fray. In an open letter to the Badatz, Rav Sheinfeld wrote:

"To all the honored Rabbis of the Badatz and all the other Rabbis involved with judging matters in beis din.

It has come to my attention that certain people want to try to include the Badatz in a letter of excommunication against the gaon and tzaddik, Rav Eliezer Berland, shlit"a, and his community.

I'm here to tell you that I know all the background [about this matter] from the inside out, and how the person responsible has devised a number of cowardly, negative rumors and intrigues.

I'm writing to warn you to not believe any libels or false claims, without first verifying the other side's account, in accordance with Jewish law, and particularly when we're dealing with an individual like this... who is delusional, and who is deluding other people along with him.

So, my fellow Rabbis, you should proceed extremely carefully. I have examined all the details of this case minutely, and spoken to both sides involved, and you can clarify any matters pertaining to it directly with me."[i]

★ ★ ★

In what appeared to be a ruse to make it as difficult as possible for the Rav's followers to picket the prison where he was being held, the Israeli prison authorities regularly shunted the Rav from prison to prison, despite his advanced age and increasingly serious health issues.

He started off in the Ramle prison in the center of the country, but then he was moved to the prison in Beer Sheva

---

[i] Some of Rabbi Berland's supporters tried to rally the generation's leading Rabbis to begin publishing letters of support for the Rav, to try and redress the balance and inform the public about what was really happening. One Rav who was asked responded, "If I come out against them, then tomorrow [his persecutors] will turn on me, and they will also start telling lies about me, too." This same concern was heard many, many times from other leading Rabbis in Israel.

— about as far south as you can get. Undaunted, hundreds of the Rav's followers followed him down south and set up a tent city on the prison's periphery, where they intended to stay and learn Torah until the Rav was released.

(For reasons of modesty, the Rav requested that only men should come and camp out in the tent city in Beer Sheva.)

Once the authorities realized that their attempts to sever Rabbi Berland from his community weren't working, the Rav was moved to a different prison, this time way up north, in Tzalmon.

Once again, his followers had to dismantle their tent city in Beer Sheva and take the time, trouble and expense to rebuild it somewhere else, but they did so uncomplainingly. After following the Rav literally all the way around the world and back, moving up north was the least of the challenges they'd faced to stay close to their Rav throughout his three-year exile.

As the terrible miscarriage of justice against Rabbi Berland lengthened into weeks and even months, a palpable sense of despair fell on large swathes of the Breslov community. What else could be done to turn things around? What more was needed, to get the breakthrough that would force the Israeli government to finally release the Rav?

Around this time, Rabbi Yosef Palvani[i], author of the *Hemdas Yosef* and *Darchei Ayun* sefarim, made the following statement:

"Who can dare to say something against this person, whom no one can even come close to! And the amazing people he brought close to Judaism, and the tens of thousands of people he inspired to do teshuva, and the amazing synagogues that he built! Who can dare say something against him? He's the Leader of the Generation!

Who knows, God forbid, what could happen? The people who are talking against the Rav, if they don't care about their own lives, they should care about their children and the families' lives. Who knows what's going to happen to them?! People got terrible diseases from speaking badly about other Jews!

Someone came into [the secular] court and was saying a lot of insults against the Rav. They asked the Rav to respond, and the Rav said, 'I just want to give him a kiss on his forehead.' Who else would say something like that?! When the Rav was being interrogated by the police a few weeks ago, they brought in someone who said the most terrible, disgusting things against the Rav in front of him. As he was leaving, the Rav thanked this person for coming - and he said it so sincerely, 'thank you for coming' - as if he came to do him a favor!

When we hear a story like this, how can we not cry?

How can anyone say anything bad against him? What can we say about him? This person put [the Rav] in the most terrible torture and pain, caused him to be in disgusting prisons

---

[i] Rav Palvani was a Sephardic Talmid Chacham, and posek. He was very close to Rabbi Abba Shaul, and Rav Ovadia Yosef. You can hear the whole interview with him at: https://goo.gl/otm8b6

in Africa, the worst places in the world, caused him so much suffering and pain — and after all this, to come and give him a kiss on his forehead?! This is not a person! This is an angel of God!

The Gemara (Yerushalmi) says that the degree of the tzaddik's suffering indicates the degree of his greatness afterwards. The more he suffers, the higher he'll go. It's like a bow being pulled back — the further it's pulled back, the higher the arrow will fly when it's released. The Rav is suffering for our sins. We should be zocheh this year to see the full redemption, amen."

Between July 19, 2016 and the end of October 2016, the Rav's lawyers had accompanied him through more than 10 different legal hearings, in many different courts and locations around the country.

The cost of mounting so many different appeals to get the Rav freed was enormous. At the beginning of the hearings in Israel, the presiding judge asked Rabbi Berland to post NIS 700,000 in bail. The Rav's followers managed to raise the money within the very tight deadline they'd been given — but the judge still refused to grant bail.

Another round of fundraising occurred at the beginning of November, to pay for the astronomical legal costs involved in getting the Israeli courts to re-evaluate the Rav's unwarranted detention, which involved hiring a new team of top lawyers to try to secure the Rav's release.

On November 9, 2016, after the Rav had already spent more than 220 days in prison, the Rav gave a recorded *Torah class* from Tzalmon prison where he spoke about the great benefits of taking on suffering and disgrace for the sake of the Jewish people. But he concluded the Torah class with these words: "But now it is time to cancel the decree, I am now in a life-threatening situation. It is true that we merited great things, but now it is time to sweeten the judgments."

As the authorities continued to use every legal procedure[i] they could think of to keep the Rav in prison without a trial for as long as possible, other leading rabbis became increasingly concerned about the toll the situation was taking on the Rav's health.

Rabbi Berland's family and attendants had a strong suspicion that the Rav's cancer had returned, yet the Israeli Prison Service wasn't co-operating with allowing the Rav's attendants to have his condition properly diagnosed or treated. The need to get the Rav out of prison was becoming a very serious race against time.

At the beginning of November 2016, this group of leading Rabbanim decided to intervene by sending a new legal team, which they hoped could find a way around all the legal arguments the State of Israel was using to keep the Rav imprisoned indefinitely without a trial.

This team of lawyers, headed by attorney Ephraim Dimri, suggested that the only way the Rav could avoid spending the next two years in prison, despite the lack of evidence against him, was if he agreed to a plea bargain.

Rabbi Berland's decision to make a plea bargain was not taken lightly. The Rav's lawyers and attendants consulted with many of the Jewish nation's most well-known Rabbis and Rebbes to ask for their agreement before proceeding. Attorney Dimri later explained why his team had pushed the Rav to make a plea bargain:

"The State of Israel spent 10 million shekels in order to

---

[i] The judges in Rabbi Berland's hearings agreed to allow the State to use the "remand until the end of proceedings" rule in his case, which meant he'd be forced to stay in prison until the end of the proceedings, even if that process took many years, and even if the final verdict was "not guilty."

bring him back, and from the moment that we'd try to leave the State of Israel with nothing to show for this, it was going to

be very dangerous," he explained. *"The State was not going to give up on him, not the prosecutors and not the judges. That's how it is with the State of Israel — what can you do?"*

Dimri continued: *"Real justice only happens by God, in His Heavenly Court. Here [in Israel], don't go looking for justice. I told this to Rabbi Berland, and Rabbi Berland knows that it's true. Because if there was justice, Rabbi Berland wouldn't have needed to spend even a single day in prison. There is no justice!*

So, this [i.e., the plea bargain] was the minimum that was possible. We were up against a large group of people, including police prosecutors and his enemies from within the [Breslov] community. The people who caused all this enormous damage to the Rav are people from within the community, and they haven't ceased [their activities] for a second, and they won't rest until, G-d forbid, they cause the biggest damage of all to the Rav. They want to take the Rav apart — and we weren't going to let them do it!"

On November 22, 2016, the plea bargain was finalized. In return for falsely "confessing" to three very minor counts, the State of Israel would give Rabbi Berland a shorter sentence of 18 months, with a third of that time possibly being knocked off for 'good behavior'.

As news of the Rav's plea bargain leaked out, many of his supporters and followers were again shocked by the latest turn of events and couldn't understand why the Rav would plead guilty to crimes he'd never committed.

It was only a little while later, when news of the Rav's serious illness was made public, that they started to understand that if the Rav had chosen to sit in prison to try and clear his name, it would probably literally have cost him his life.

★   ★   ★

Dudu Elkayam was part of Rabbi Berland's legal team for years, and initially, he was completely opposed to the Rav making a plea bargain. He later explained what the Rav had said to him to get him to change his mind.

"The Rav is completely innocent," explained Elkayam, *"but he took something on himself that was really beyond our understanding. You could try to blame different people for what happened, all the lawyers, and say that they pushed him to make a plea bargain.*

Attorney Rachel Toran, Attorney Feldman and I[i] were absolutely against making a plea bargain. We had the information in our hands, and it clearly showed that the Rav was completely innocent, beyond the shadow of a doubt. The Rav was up to date on all the details related to his case and the police investigation, and he understood that after the 22nd of November[ii], from the moment the court would actually start examining the evidence, there would be a 180-degree turnaround in his case.

The day before he made the plea bargain, I spoke with the Rav who explained the situation to me in the following words:

---

[i] This was Rabbi Berland's first team of lawyers, which was subsequently replaced by the team led by Ephraim Dimri.

[ii] The proposed date of the first court hearing where the judges would start hearing the actual evidence against Rav BerLland.

'Dudu, I'm pleading with you [to understand] that I need to take this upon myself.' From the moment the Rav told me this, I responded, 'I'm standing behind you, and I'll do whatever you decide. I'm with the Rav, and I always will be.'"

"I didn't say this because I'm a fanatic," Elkayam continues. "I said this because I'm almost the only person who knows, definitively, the whole truth about the matter. I want to tell the community straight out — and I'm prepared to swear to this under oath and in front of witnesses — **Rabbi Berland has admitted to things that he never did, and he did this deliberately. But our understanding is too limited to grasp why he took this upon himself. If I believed in the Rav before his plea bargain, my faith in him has only increased tremendously after the fact, because I know that he has taken things upon himself that are beyond my intelligence [to grasp], and beyond the understanding of all the nation of Israel. We simply can't understand what's going on.**"

Elkayam continues: "Anyone who searches their heart will understand that what I'm saying is the unvarnished truth. He's innocent. They concocted a very terrible slander against him that we successfully unpicked. We effectively overturned the whole case against him.

[One of the things] they were claiming was that the complainants against the Rav were scared to testify in court [which is why they had no witnesses]. We showed that the only thing they were really scared of was the witness stand. I asked Attorney Rachel Toran to ensure that every complainant would be obligated to come and testify. We had all the evidence required to show that the Rav was completely innocent, beyond even the shadow of a doubt.

The libels against the Rav were very convoluted, and every action they took to smear and sully the Rav succeeded in blackening his name and increasing the time he was being detained in prison. However, we knew — and the Rav also knew — that the week after his trial began, he'd already be acquitted. We weren't just working to get the Rav freed, we also wanted him to be completely exonerated from all the charges.

They were in a hurry to press charges and produce a bill of indictment because they knew that all the material they had was only good enough to blacken the Rav's name, but wouldn't stand up for a moment in court.

Indeed, we publicized one of the recordings we had where you could hear [one of the Breslov zealots] lamenting to [another Breslov zealot][i] that they couldn't find a single complainant to come and testify [against the Rav]. Even the wife of [one of the persecutors], the main false witness against the Rav, told [one of the Breslov zealots] that she didn't want to come and testify.

She was the last complainant who they believed would be prepared to testify, and ultimately she also backed out. From our side, we really wanted her to take the stand, so that we could rebut the whole web of lies that she and her husband had told. The police prosecutors themselves knew that their witnesses weren't at all credible and had even tried to coordinate their testimony by coaching them about what to say, which is completely against the law.

Believe me, if this couple had got to the witness stand it would have been the biggest circus in town. But what can we do, we're dealing with a tzaddik who took things upon himself to sweeten the judgments upon Am Israel.

Legal counsel had nine secret files on people who didn't want to be exposed under any circumstances. I have no doubt that as soon as those files would have been opened, the whole web of false testimony would have been destroyed. But the Rav accepted on himself to be 'burnt.' Anyone who understands

---

[i] The names have been omitted to protect their anonymity, as per Rabbi Berland's request.

that the Rav is the true Tzaddik [of the generation] has to wholeheartedly go with his decision."

Another of the Rav's original legal team, Attorney Rachel Toran, gave over the following message when news of the plea bargain became public: *"My heart is broken, because the Rav would have been found innocent. Attorney Naama Elchadad went in to see the Rav and pleaded with him, with tears in her eyes, not to make a plea bargain, as he would certainly be going home the following week [after the trial began]. She said that the Rav lowered his face and told her that he knew that, but that he was obliged to take this upon himself."*

★   ★   ★

In order for the Rav's plea bargain to be accepted and for him to be able to get out of prison within the next few months, the Israeli court required the Rav to make a public confession and full public apology. If it wasn't "convincing enough," then even with his plea bargain the court still wouldn't reduce the Rav's sentence.

This appalling and humiliating "show trial" occurred on Tuesday, November 22, 2016. When the time came for when Rabbi Berland was supposed to make his formal admission, the judge asked him what he had to say, and he then he quoted the verse from *Parshas Vayeshev*, 38:24: "[And Yehuda said to Tamar] take her out and burn her". The Rav continued, "In biblical times, people would be burnt for these kind of things"[i].

At precisely the time he said these words, the first fires

---

[i] This was an idea that the Rav repeated when Channel 2 journalist Amnon Levy interviewed him. On that occasion, too, Rabbi Berland said: "I told the judge that **if** what they are saying is true and **if** I would have done what they accuse me of, then the punishment is too light, I would have deserved to have been burnt."

were reported around the Israeli city of Zichron Yaakov, in the north of the country. Despite the size, number and ferocity of the supernatural fires that occurred in Israel, miraculously, no one was killed.

These fires began as Rabbi Berland left the court in Jerusalem to be taken back to Tzalmon prison, located near Zichron Yaakov. Shortly after the fire in Zichron Yaakov became national news (and before any other major fires had occurred in Israel), the kabbalist Rabbi Dov Kook from Tiberius made the following statement:

"All the terrible forest fires that are happening now around Zichron Yaakov are because of the persecution and suffering of the holy tzaddik, Rav Eliezer Berland. The measure of justice is being weighed out primarily against us in the north, and we need to know that the terrible fires that are burning there in a few different places are because Rabbi Berland is being held in the north, close to Tiberius.

The Midrash says that when people persecute and shame tzaddikim, then the Holy One brings fires to the world! All the slanderers and people who are speaking libels and falsehoods about this awesome, holy tzaddik should be aware that soon, judgment will occur, and that there is a Judge mamash, who will reveal his [Rabbi Berland's] honor and innocence to every eye."

It was only after Rabbi Kook's statement that the north was really hit particularly hard by raging fires. Fires were reported in and around a number of northern cities, including Hadera, Zichron Yaakov and the northern metropolis of Haifa, where more than 75,000 residents had to be evacuated.

More than 250 separate fires continued to rage for more than five days across every part of Israel. While the Israeli government was quick to blame the fires on Arab terrorists, Israel's Home Front Command stated that no more than 5 percent of the fires appeared to be deliberate acts of arson[i]. The rest had occurred spontaneously, with no obvious cause.

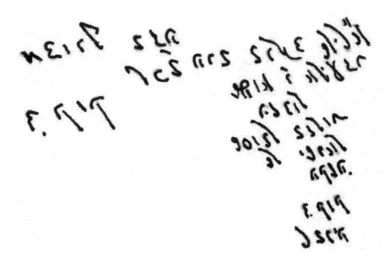

Rabbi Kook once wrote out a statement, and signed on it, that Rabbi Berland is a spark of Rabbi Eliezer HaGadol, a Jewish Sage who lived 2,000 years ago. Despite the fact that Rav Eliezer HaGadol was the Tzaddik of the generation and on the highest spiritual level, the Sages of that time couldn't understand him and actually excommunicated him. They only rescinded their decree when he was on his deathbed.

As the fires continued to rage out of control, the *Daf Yomi*[7] being learned that day recounted how every place where Rabbi Eliezer HaGadol gazed used to get burned up, as a result of his holiness.

Despite his tremendous suffering and his failing health, the one person who appeared to be managing the Rav's

---

[i] Two weeks after the fires, the Israeli government admitted that they'd only been able to press charges against three Arab arsonists. All the other fires were "unexplained."

prolonged and unjust incarceration the best was... the Rav himself.

Rabbi Berland's grandson, Rav Chaim Reicher, paid him a visit in the Tzalmon prison in November 2016, when the Rav had already been incarcerated for around eight months, including his stay in Sun City Prison in South Africa. He reported back that something very peculiar was happening in Tzalmon.

"It's a very strange situation," he began. *"Apparently, we who are coming to visit the Rav, shlit"a, are supposed to be happy and uplifted, and we are meant to be giving strength to he who is inside, who is should be broken and torn. But in fact, the opposite is true. The Rav is always in the best of moods. We come broken and depressed and he comes full of energy and good spirits and uplifts anyone who comes to visit. He always comes out wearing his tallis and tefillin and carrying piles of holy books, until you forget you came to visit him in a prison at all...*

"You sit in front of the Rav, who is already 80 years old, and you... see his holiness, the light that he projects, and you hear from him that everything is fine, there are no complaints, 'I'm just learning here, nobody bothers me.'"

Rabbi Reicher continues: *"If there's anything that strengthens the Rav it's when he hears that people out here are praying for his success and continuing their service of God, their Torah study and their prayers, and that the community is growing and prospering more day by day. I spoke to the Rav about the status of the community and the students out there, thousands of people who just recently arrived and joined the veterans who stayed with the Rav.*

Thousands more new people are drawing close, Lithuanian Rabbis, Rebbes that I talk to and I am in constant touch with. It's like a new world of tremendous wisdom and singing melodies, of real Breslov, opened up for them. Not a Breslov that speaks badly about others, not a Breslov that says we are the best. Rebbe Nachman is prayer, Torah, melodies and holy sons, and to accept insults with love and joy, and so forth — and all this we see in the Rav...

The prison commander says he doesn't understand what's happening here, that whenever the Rav begins to pray, the entire prison is quiet. From 5:00 a.m. the Rav is singing and no one complains that he's bothering them. I heard that all the prisons are asking that the Rav should come to them and help their prisoners behave, too...

The Rav is entirely absorbed in his devotion to God."

Rabbi Reicher continues: "The righteous can never be locked up, like Joseph the Tzaddik, where all the awesome things he attained, he achieved them specifically in jail... Leading Rabbis speak to me privately and tell me that they have explicit instructions from the Rav not to support him openly, except for some things he permits because of the desecration of God's name. The Rav feels that he must take this disgrace upon himself in order to mitigate decrees and ignite the light of teshuva amongst the whole Jewish people.

I told the Rav that they are talking badly about him and asked him if we should act against it, but the Rav said we should do nothing, just pray, just learn, just dance and be happy. The Rav already told me some of those secrets that I must not tell, about why some things happened, and how the Rav filtered out the kind of people connected to him who were only looking for money, pride, status and dignity.

What other Rabbi or Rebbe has these kind of students, who after five years of persecution and torment are still sacrificing themselves? We see clearly that there are people here who learned the ways of the Rav. And anyone who isn't comfortable is welcome to leave. There are enough students already, there are thousands of new ones, there are hidden things happening that we do not understand.

Despite the fact that he studies Torah 24 hours a day, the Rav also has complete mastery of every subject: how to build airplanes, nuclear bombs, science, health, physics, history... He even sat with the Druze prisoners and told them about their holiday and the history of their religion, things that they didn't even know. Everything comes back to his holiness, his love of every Jew, and that he forgives everyone wholeheartedly."

"When I was a bit younger, many times I would find the Rav with his arms and legs sprawled out, crying outto God. I would stand next to him for four or five hours and hear him crying the afternoon prayers. We cannot talk about these things because it just detracts from his true greatness, which is beyond description.

After everyone else left, I was with the Rav in private, and I asked him if I could nevertheless do something to help him. The Rav answered me that I should invest in an additional hour of learning every day. With all my connections in politics, the Rav did not have any other request from me," Rabbi Reicher concludes.

TOWARDS FREEDOM

"Reporter behind anti-haredi video dismissed: Reshet TV dismisses two workers behind video which turned out to be a fake news item targeting haredim."
– Headline on Arutz 7 News, May 1st, 2017.[i]

"Media anti-haredi bias made it easy to spread fake news: As the screaming headlines told us, a group of haredim began to riot on the flight to Israel after it became clear that they would not arrive before Shabbat began. The haredim allegedly pushed flight crew, cursed stewardesses, and threatened to forcibly break into the cockpit....

The story hit on every possible anti-haredi narrative. Violent haredim? Check. Religious extremism? Check. Social media boiled and seethed. "What kind of people are these, who are willing to run wild over their religious beliefs?" people asked.

Yet it only took a few more hours for the entire story to be revealed as a cynical piece of fake news designed to hide El Al's scandalous behavior...

It's important to stress that the libelous stories did not appear in fringe publications, but in Israel's most prominent news platforms, including Channel 2 and Ynet. In other words, for a few hours, almost all of Israel's media edifice was propagating totally false information that smeared an entire community.

---

[i] http://www.israelnationalnews.com/News/News.aspx/228865

> *In an even more serious case of media malpractice,*
> *Channel 10 published videos taken by passengers of*
> *the flight, but with background screams artificially*
> *inserted into the audio. Instantly, a forceful*
> *conversation between passengers and crew sounded*
> *like a violent bar fight. Channel 10 later apologized*
> *and attributed it to a "technical problem."*
> — Arutz 7, November 23rd, 2018[i]

★ ★ ★

On Wednesday, November 16, 2016, Rabbi Berland took the advice of his new legal team to enter a plea bargain with the State of Israel prosecutors. The plea bargain was formally agreed by the court on November 22, 2016, and under the terms of this deal, Rabbi Berland was given an 18-month jail sentence, which his lawyers hoped meant he'd be free by Passover 5777. Many people were stunned by this turn of events, but Ephraim Dimri, one of the Rav's new attorneys, explained why they'd recommended this course of action.

Dimri explained: *"Rabbi Berland accepted this decision in order to end all of the legal circling that's been going on around him. Because right now, until he gets a chance to prove his innocence, he could be sitting in prison for another one and a half or even two years. We needed to act according to the reality which we found ourselves in, and that reality was to free Rabbi Berland, ASAP."*

Dimri continued: *"The Rav is completely innocent. But we needed to be realistic and intelligent, if not necessarily correct. The process of defending the Rav could have taken a very long time, and the Rav is unhealthy and not young at all. Obviously, if the Rav, would have been out, even under house arrest, we would have managed the case to the end and*

---

[i] http://www.israelnationalnews.com/Articles/Article.aspx/23050

we wouldn't have settled for a plea bargain. We would have definitely got the Rav acquitted.

But we can't leave him suffering behind bars. The Rav has piles and piles of holy books in his cell, shelves upon shelves, and all day and night he is sitting and learning. This is not a place for him."

Attorney Dimri continued: *"I was extremely impressed with him. Personally, I call him an angel. He simply has awesome spiritual powers. He's an amazing person. I have merited representing many big Rabbis and kabbalists in my career, but someone like Rav Eliezer Berland, I don't think there is anyone else like this. In my opinion, he is one in the generation."*

Attorney Dimri then shared some of the miraculous occurrences he witnessed while visiting the Rav in prison.

"I'm going to tell you some stories that you're really not going to believe. The Israel Prison Service has now set up a commission of inquiry to find out how prison doors could open without any prison wardens pressing the button… But all these things happened to me, and they're true.

I was standing outside in the lawyers' room, and I was waiting for the prison wardens to open the door, a big iron door, [so I could get in to see the Rav]. Everything there is connected by a closed circuit system, and it's impossible to open the next door along the passage until the first door is completely closed.

I said to the Rav [who was waiting for me behind the next door] that the door wasn't being buzzed open, and that I thought that the prison guard [who was meant to open the door] had gone somewhere. The Rav told me: 'Push!' so I did, but it didn't open. So he told me again: 'Push!', so I tried again – and this time the door opened. This door literally weighed a ton, but it opened.

Then the prison warden showed up, and he said to me: 'How did you get in here?!?' So I told him that I'd pushed the door open. *He went and checked the CCTV, and then he called his superior, because he couldn't understand what had just happened. I said to the Rav:* "They're confused!" *He replied:* "Let them be confused."

Attorney Dimri continues: "*Later on, one of the prison officers contacted me and asked me:* 'Is the Rav normal' (I.e. sane)? *I told her:* "More than you are!' *So then she asked me:* 'Why then is he sitting on the floor every night and crying his eyes out?' *I told her:* 'He's reciting the midnight lament, and the Tikkun Rachel and the Tikkun Leah (deep kabbalistic prayers). He's praying on behalf of all the nation of Israel, and crying for us.'

This prison officer told me that she'd sent the Rav to be evaluated by a Russian psychologist. She told me: 'She examined him and told me that his intelligence is off the charts – above what a human brain is meant to be capable of. He knows history, he knows mathematics etc...'

"*One day, the prison commandant asked me to view some of the footage from the prison CCTV with him. He showed me how the Rav is always surrounded by a hila, or aura or light. This is all true! The commandant thought that maybe the CCTV was malfunctioning, because it's a very advanced piece of equipment, and he couldn't understand what that aura of light surrounding the Rav really was.*

The prison commandant told me: 'Do you see that?' *I told him:* 'This is a holy Jew, a Tzaddik who learns Torah and prays all day long. What you're looking at is his halo, or aura.' *After that, the prison commandant – who happens to be Druze – started coming to the Rav and kissing his hand.*"

"*Another time, I came to visit the Rav together with another lawyer, and we decided to start singing with the Rav, because the Rav really loves to sing. So we're singing and dancing together, when the Rav suddenly tells us that we need to come and be his guests [in his prison cell].*

Now, the distance from the lawyers' room to the Rav's cell was at least 100 meters, and there are prison wardens everywhere, and CCTV cameras, and everything else. I asked him very politely: 'How are we meant to get there?', but I had no doubt that it was completely impossible.

The Rav took his tallis, put it over our heads, and then took us with him to his cell. We entered his room, and it's full of holy books, literally piles upon piles of books. The Rav looked through a couple of his books, poured us a couple of drinks that we made the blessing over and drank, and then told us: 'Now, I've performed the mitzvah of having guests'. The Rav then told us: 'Now, you can return to the Attorney's Room.' And we returned."

Suddenly, we see the head of that prison section running towards us, and he's all stressed-out and shouting at us: 'Where were you?! I can't see you on the CCTV!' We told him that we'd been with the Rav in his cell, but he insisted that this was impossible. "I didn't see you on the CCTV!" he tells us, as the Rav is just standing there and smiling at him.

Attorney Dimri concluded his words by saying: *"There are other stories that can only be told once the Rav has been freed, God willing. If we breathe a word of these stories too soon, the whole of the Israel Prison Service will be up in arms; they'll have no explanation for how these things occurred. We saw some truly miraculous things there in prison."*

Hot on the heels of the plea bargain, two of Rabbi Berland's main persecutors flew over to the US and scheduled meetings with a large number of well-known rabbis, to start peddling their slanders and lies wholesale on the other side of the Atlantic.

Thankfully, their trip met with very little success, and most of the American rabbis they met with saw straight through their lies and refused to get involved in their deception. Meanwhile back in Israel, more and more leading

Rabbis were putting out statements publicly supporting Rabbi Berland.

One such statement again came from the Kabbalist Rav David Abuchatzeira of Nahariya, who told one of his students: "It's impossible to touch the Tzaddikim, even by as much as a hair's breadth. It's impossible [for them] to harm Rabbi Berland, shlit"a.'"

Rabbi Meir Shmueli was even more direct and warned of the terrible dangers involved in speaking badly about Rabbi Berland. He said:

"*Throw away your own ideas (sechel) and tell yourself: 'What do I know, anyway, about the actions of the leaders of Israel? Why do I need to speak about these things?'*

"*But he admitted it!!! And it was written up all over the media!!!*"

"*It's all nonsense and futility...! [In the case of Rabbi Berland], they told him: 'if you don't go along with us, you're going to stay in prison for a long time, so it would be wise for you to say that you did these things, so you don't end up in an even worse situation.'*

"*Today, there are many people who are busying themselves by commenting on affairs involving Rabbis. The late Rav Elyashiv said that at least a third of the cancers affecting the Jewish community are being caused because people are disgracing Torah scholars... Don't speak! Do you really want to be playing with this type of fire?!*"

★ ★ ★

In the meantime, the Rabbi Berland's situation continued to be extremely serious, as his health steadily continued to worsen during his stay behind bars. His family, attendants and lawyers continued to hope that the Israeli courts would start acting with more clemency towards him and agree to release him after he'd served two thirds of his sentence, which would fall sometime in the spring of 2017.

Now that the State had got its show trial and public confession of wrong-doing out of the Rav, it was hoped they'd see no further point in dragging out his incarceration. But yet again, Rabbi Berland's persecutors continued to argue in court that the Rav should stay locked up for as long as possible.

The Rav and his team of lawyers found themselves repeatedly getting called back to court for hearing after hearing, and still there was no end to the ordeal in sight. At the end of December 2016, during the festival of Chanukah, Shuvu Banim organized an emergency fundraising appeal to try to cover the astronomical legal costs involved in trying to get the Rav out of prison that had now surpassed the million shekel mark.

As the court proceedings continued to drag out, the Rav's lawyers finally managed to force the Israel Prison Service to release the information about the Rav's current state of health that had been withheld from his family and attendants.

As soon as they saw his health records, it was clear to the Rav's attendants that Rabbi Berland needed serious, immediate surgery to deal with a number of potentially life-threatening growths that had been left untreated for months. While the lawyers continued to argue for the Rav's early release in court, his attendants mobilized to find the best doctors in the country to operate on the Rav.

The first operation took place on February 13, 2017, where three separate growths and part of the Rav's prostate were removed. At the same time the surgery was taking place in Hadassah hospital on the outskirts of Jerusalem, thousands of his followers gathered at the Tomb of Rachel to pray for the Rav's speedy recovery.

Despite the short notice and the lack of time to really organise the event, people arrived at Kever Rachel from all over the country, quickly filling it up to saturation point. The crush of people was so great the police were forced to close off the main corridor leading to the tomb, leaving a crowd of people standing outside.

Immediately after the prayer gathering ended, the good news arrived that the Rav's surgery had been successfully concluded, and that the Rav was in a good state and recovering.

Despite the fact that he'd just undergone a very complicated and serious procedure, immediately after the operation, the Rav asked to be brought three holy books so that he'd be able to continue to learn. Not even a serious operation could cloud his mind or pull him away from his Torah learning and religious devotion.

In typical overkill fashion, the State of Israel posted a large number of guards around the Rav's hospital bed, and even handcuffed him to the bed frame, while his lawyers continued to argue that the Rav should be freed on grounds of ill-health. Just as it looked as though the courts were finally coming around to the idea, Rabbi Berland's persecutors struck again.

On February 5th, 2017, Rabbi Moshe Kramer, head of the Breslov yeshiva in Meah Shearim, was attacked in public and had his shtreimel knocked off. A police investigation later affirmed that Rabbi Kramer's attacker was a young individual who had a personal grudge against Rabbi Kramer.

But, ever on the look-out for new ways of slandering Rabbi Berland and his followers, the Breslov zealots immediately started spreading the story that Shuvu Banim was behind the attack on Rabbi Kramer.

The media again quickly fanned the flames of these latest baseless slanders and lies. Headlines from the *Yeshiva World News* website screamed out:

SHOCKING VIDEO: Breslov Mashpia HaRav Moshe Kramer Attacked On Shabbos By Chasidim Of Rabbi Berland

February 5, 2017 4:45 pm

The story then continued: "The followers of Rabbi Eliezer Berland who was convicted of offenses have taken to attack [sic] his opponents. In the opening scene, a prominent Mashpia who dared to speak against Rabbi Berland was attacked violently. In the second you see followers of rabbi Berland covering their heads with Taleisim as they destroy HaRav Kramer's central air conditioner outside his home."

All the videos actually showed is that Rabbi Kramer was attacked by someone wearing the traditional garb of a Meah Shearim chassid, and that three hareidi men with prayer shawls over their heads were attacking an air-conditioning unit. There was nothing to link the attacks to Shuvu Banim, or Rabbi Berland – except the statements made by Rabbi Berland's persecutors.

When news of the attack reached Rabbi Berland, he immediately put out a recording condemning it, and encouraged his students at Shuvu Banim to attend the gathering being organized by members of the Breslov shul in Meah Shearim, to protest the outrage done to Rabbi Kramer.

In the meantime, the zealots wasted no time pasting posters up in every Hareidi city in Israel, falsely blaming Shuvu Banim for the attack. Then, they printed up more than 100,000 pamphlets containing a slanderous account of a 'pogrom' that they falsely claimed followers of Shuvu Banim had perpetrated on the Breslov Shul in Meah Shearim and distributed them to every Hareidi city in Israel, as well as to every media outlet.

ARAB ISRAELI CONFLICT   ISRAEL NEWS   OPINION   MIDDLE EAS

Jerusalem Post > Israel News >

'POGROM' IN BRESLOV SYNAGOGUE, RABBI BERLAND FOLLOWERS BEAT WORSHIPERS

Berland was the leader of one of the largest communities belonging to Breslov Hasidism.

BY YVETTE J. DEANE / SEPTEMBER 26, 2018 13:19

2 minute read.

All this was occurring at the same time Rabbi Berland was being rushed into hospital for his serious, emergency operation. When he was told about the pamphlets, the Rav told his followers not to fight back, and not to respond to the ongoing provocations of the Breslov zealots, even though the police had already announced that the original assault on Rabbi Kramer had nothing to do with Shuvu Banim.

But amazingly, more was still to come. As Rabbi Berland was being wheeled in for surgery, huge billboards appeared in a large number of hareidi towns, from Bnei Brak to Elad and Beit Shemesh, bearing the headline (paraphrased from the Hebrew): "A protest about the attack against Rabbi Moshe Kramer carried out by low-lifes from Shuvu Banim" - and which then segued into yet more horrible, slanderous lies about Rabbi Berland.

At the end of this horrible rant, came a long list of names of prominent Breslov rabbis, who'd apparently signed on this terrible statement.

Very quickly, many of these Rabbis put out public statements explaining how they'd been tricked by the Breslov zealots, who'd asked them to put their names to a protest against the attack on Rabbi Kramer, but never mentioned a word about Shuvu Banim or Rabbi Berland.

When news of this terrible desecration of God's name reached the ears of Rabbi Morgenstern, he immediately put out a statement decrying the terrible actions of the Breslov zealots, and also urged his followers to do everything they can to start publishing books - including in English - that would tell the true story of who the Rabbi Berland really was.

A number of other rabbis also publicly spoke out against this terrible public desecration, including Rabbi Yehuda Yosefi, who said:

"*Someone once told me, in the name of Jerusalem's Tzaddikim of the past generation: 'You should run away from every controversy, but when it comes to a conflict for the sake of Heaven - you should run away eight times faster.' Even*

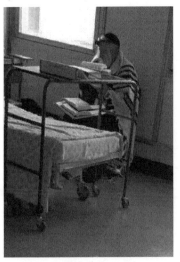

the biblical Korach believed he was arguing solely for the sake of Heaven…. it's so unfortunate, because people are going to pay a very big price for it.

Even if you want to take vengeance on someone else, do you really want to bring so much evil down upon yourself?!"

A few days' after his first, successful surgery to remove cancerous growths from his prostate the doctors discovered that the cancer had also spread to Rabbi Berland's kidneys, and another, even more serious, surgery was scheduled to remove the tumors.

Ultimately, the surgeons discovered that the disease had progressed so far in one kidney, they couldn't save it and had to be removed.

Within a few hours of the surgery, the Rav was sitting up in the chair next to his bed, poring over a number of holy books that were spread out on the small table in front of him. If that wasn't stunning enough, he continued to spend hours standing in prayer, as per his usual custom of serving God with every ounce of his strength.

Despite his advanced age (Rabbi Berland was 79 years old, when all this was happening), and the severity of the two surgeries he'd just undergone, including having a kidney removed, when the courts were informed that the Rav was standing up and praying next to his bed, they ruled he'd recovered enough to be sent back to prison within a week of having his surgery.

Given that most patients take between two and three months to recover from such serious procedures, the court's decision is very hard to understand. Back in prison, the Rav wasn't receiving even the basic medical care someone in his fragile situation really required, prompting his legal team and attendants to make a super-human effort to have the Rav released, at least to home arrest.

When Rabbi Berland's lawyers informed the courts they were preparing to sue the Israeli Prison Service for failing to treat Rabbi Berland's illness in a timely and humane fashion, finally things started to move.

* * *

On April 6, 2017, the Israeli court finally announced that they were freeing the elderly, ill Rabbi Berland to house arrest - with a twist. The Rav would be freed to the Hadassah hospital hotel, and he would also be accompanied by a team of court appointed security guards 24/7, that he would have to pay for himself.

The news of the Rav's partial release was greeted with very mixed feelings. On the one hand, there was a palpable sense of relief that Rabbi Berland would finally get the care he needed to really recover from his illness, and that he was out of prison.

But under the initial terms of his release to the Hadassah hospital hotel, the only people who'd be able to see him were his immediate family and attendants. The Rav himself released a statement asking his followers to stay away from the Hadassah hospital, so that the court wouldn't try to use that as grounds for sending him back to prison.

Still, as the pictures started to circulate of the Rav spending his first Passover with his family in Israel in more than four years, there was a feeling that maybe, the worst was finally behind the Rav and his followers. The Rav was joined by 12 of his family members for Seder night, and one of his grandsons shared the following:

"This Seder night was very similar to the one that I attended with the Rav, shlit"a more than four years' ago, [his last Seder] in Israel. I almost didn't see any differences between them. Yes, we could see that the Rav was still suffering from pain throughout the Seder, but apart from that, The Rav continued to serve God as normal, with great strength and tenacity."

Rabbi Berland's grandson continued: *"The doctors told the Rav it was absolutely forbidden for him to eat matzah, under any circumstances. But Rabbi Berland, shlit"a still ate them with great self-sacrifice."*

As the Rav's health slowly started to improve, his lawyers continue to fight for the court to ease the conditions they'd placed on his house arrest at the Hadassah hotel. Fairly quickly after Seder night, they received court approval for Rabbi Berland to start receiving visitors of importance, other than his family.

A steady stream of Rabbis and Rebbes started literally queuing up outside the hospital, often having to wait hours on end before being notified that the court had approved their visit, just to pay their respects to Rabbi Berland.

Breslov activist Aharon Boymill accompanied the Rebbe of Strapcov to visit the Rav at the Hadassah hotel, and he recalls: *"The Rebbe of Strapcov was waiting there with me for hours before they'd let us in, but I explained to him that there was nothing we could do [to speed things up], and that in the meantime you need a lot of official approvals to get through all the procedures set up by the State of Israel. But ultimately it was all worth it, in order to get the holy [Rebbe of Strapcov] inside."*

Rabbi Boymill continued: *"People wouldn't believe which [Torah] greats have been queuing up here simply in order to enter and see the Rav. Everyone wants to receive a blessing from Rabbi Berland.*

I stood outside for 14 hours, and I saw something amazing: Even the guards, who aren't from a Torah background, were sharing words of Torah with each other, and telling each other stories about the Tzaddikim. One of them told me that the Rav recited the morning blessings with him, and also told me that the Rav was praying with him.

I asked him, 'Tell me something, are you religiously observant?' He replied: 'What does it mean, 'religiously observant'? Every day, we're hearing words of Torah, until we got to a stage where we got a new soul.'"

Most of the Rav's well-known visitors kept a very low profile, but as time went on, word started to leak out that a number of prominent figures in the hareidi world were beating a path to Rabbi Berland's door.

On April 18, 2017 two prominent Israeli politicians, the Health Minister Yaakov Litzman and Rabbi Meir Porush, came to visit Rav Eliezer Berland, in a highly-publicized visit. As word of their visit spread, some MKs from the radical 'Meretz' party to launch yet another vicious verbal attack on the Rav and those who were visiting him.

The Health Minister, Rabbi Litzman, came under particular scathing attack from members of the ultra-left Meretz Party and other leftist MKs, and was vilified in the secular press after his visit to the Rav. The Rav's attendant, Natan Besanson picks up the story:

"The same people who have been behind the persecution of the Rav up until now are continuing to look for more ways to attack him," he said. *"As we all know, Rabbi Berland loves criticism, and looks for ways [that people] will shame and disgrace him. He even tried to calm me down, and he told me: 'Natan, relax! After all, you know that I like being shamed and disgraced, and that I even encourage it!' But while it's permitted for the Rav to forgo the honor that's due to him, we won't give up on it.*

They are so obsessed with their persecution of Rabbi Berland, that they are taking it to the furthest extreme. Everyone who hears them, and then who afterwards really looks at who the Rav is, he can clearly see that everything is lies. We all see that they're talking about a Tzaddik who simply learns Torah all day long and serves God.

One great Tzaddik told me: *'Rabbi Akiva had his flesh scraped with combs of iron, but this only happened once, right before he died. By Rabbi Berland, they're scraping his body, his soul, his honor, his character - and not only for one second, or one single day, but for year after year. And we're not talking about Romans, here, like the people who [tortured] Rabbi Akiva, but about people who claim to be engaged in Jewish outreach."*

Rav Besanson continued: *"It's insane, it's like a bad dream, we're talking about a level of wickedness that's diabolical, and that doesn't end. I'm waiting for the day when their web of lies will finally be exposed. [This injustice] is crying out up to the Heavens! They said they had hundreds of witnesses [against the Rav], but when it came down to it, they didn't have anyone or anything. Their lies simply didn't stand up [to any scrutiny].*

God will avenge the blood being spilled here. Usually, a man is only murdered once, but they haven't calmed down, and they are still thirsting for the tzaddik's blood. Rabbi Litzman [and the other visitors] have known Rabbi Berland for many years. They certainly don't regret their visit. We know the truth, and we understand what is going on here."

Given the unremitting attacks that were continuing in the press against Rabbi Berland and his followers at this time, other leading rabbis also came to publicly show their support. On May 3, 2017, the leading Sephardi Posek and head of the 'Toherah Ve Chaim' kollel in Bnei Brak, Rabbi Shimon Badani, arranged the first of what became many visits, firstly to the Shuvu Banim Yeshiva in the Old City, and later in the month, to Rabbi Berland himself.

Then in January 2019, Rabbi Badani made another trip to Jerusalem to pay his respects to Rabbi Berland and to ask the Rav for a blessing for a shiduch for his grandson. Afterwards, he explained some of the tactics the Rav's persecutors had been using to try to smear his name, which included setting up their own false Beit Din. In an interview he gave at that time[i], Rabbi Badani explained to one of Rabbi Berland's attendants what they had told him:

"I had three or four Breslovers by me who had beards longer than yours. [I said to them]: 'What are you saying [about the Rav]? We need to hold a Beit Din!' [They told me] 'You told us that there needs to be a Beit Din - here! We made ourselves a Beit Din!' I said, 'You made yourselves a Beit Din?! What did you decide?' They said, 'We brought the plaintiffs...' I said 'you brought the plaintiffs? Did you bring Rabbi Berland too?' [They replied]: 'No!'"

Rabbi Badani continued: *"How can this be?! How can you judge someone when he's not even there [to defend himself]?! This is a sin. [They told me] He is 'a dangerous person'[ii]. What*

---

[i] Which you can see: https://youtu.be/Nq43nweDRbA

[ii] Gavra Alma, or 'dangerous person' is a halachic term that applies in rare cases when someone is a known murderer. Then, a Beit Din will be afraid to bring him to court as he might take people's lives if he's

sort of 'dangerous person' is this?! He's a physically unwell man aged 80 years old. And this is a dangerous man?!"

apprehended. So in those cases, they are allowed to judge and hold the court case without the defendant being there.

[Rabbi Badani laughs, and then continues:] "*What is this nonsense?! There's no such thing! I said to them 'now he's a free man, take him to the Beit Din of the Eida Hareidis that they will be the judges!' They said, 'we're not going, we are going'. It's all nonsense!*"

"*I told them, Who appointed you? Breslov Rabbis? Who appointed you? Ok, let's suppose that's true [that they were really appointed by Breslov rabbis]. Why didn't you invite him [Rabbi Berland] to attend? [They told me] He's a dangerous man.* "*Who are you?! You are the judges and also the deciders?.... All of this is [coming from] you! Who gave you the right to do this?...*

Rabbi Badani concluded: "*I go according to the Shulchan Aruch (the Code of Jewish Law), and according to the Torah. I don't go according to my emotions. They said they went to this Rabbi and that Rabbi. I don't care, this Rabbi that Rabbi - if there is no Beit Din, then there is nothing! It's all nonsense. Even though the Gemara says that when there is a voice (rumor) that doesn't stop so we suspect the person, but that's on the condition that the person doesn't have enemies. So what do you want! You are all his enemies! God should help!*"

Another early visitor to Hadassah hospital was Rabbi Shalom Tzaddok, the head of the Ariel and Ayish settlements in the Shomron. Rabbi Tzaddok's connection with Rabbi Berland stretches back across 60 years, when they shared a room together at the Kfar Chassidim yeshiva for four years, until the Rav's marriage.

"*I was at his engagement and also attended his wedding (wedding),*" explained Rav Tzaddok. "*I remember Rabbi Berland's very unusual devotion to God back in the yeshiva. His diligence in learning was really only for its own sake. He used to rise early in the mornings and go to pray in holiness and purity. He would pray out loud, and then afterwards he'd be learning the whole rest of the day, until the end of the night.*

He was always the last one to return to our room, and then the next day he'd do it all over again."

Rabbi Tzaddok concludes: "I couldn't see any trace of concern on the Rav, despite everything he's gone through. The happiness of learning Torah is still lighting up his face. His whole being is immersed in Torah, he's got a big table there, and it's full of holy books, and he's radiating [holiness and happiness] to everyone who's coming to visit him. It's really a delight to see him.

I told him that all the suffering that he endured; it was an atonement) for the Jewish people. All those people who saw how much success he was having with the non-Torah observant public, did everything they could to try to torpedo it."

Other voices within the wider hareidi world were also speaking out in support of the Rav and deriding the intimidating and slanderous tactics being employed against him, including the well-known kabbalist Rabbi Gamliel Rabinowitz.

In a conversation with Rabbi Yosef Frank in Meron, Rav Rabinowitz told him: "Fortunate are you, that you have such a Rebbe, Rabbi Berland. He's a huge person, he's a huge individual, and the fact that he has all of this opposition only serves to testify about his true greatness. There is no doubt about this."

Still under house arrest, Rav Eliezer Berland returned to his home on HaChoma HaShlishit Road, in the Meah Shearim (Morasha) district of Jerusalem on May 24, 2017, after a five and a half year absence that saw him traveling from one continent to the next, jump from one country to another and move from one temporary dwelling to another, before spending well over a year in prison.

Immediately upon his return to his home in Jerusalem, Rabbi Berland issued the following statement:

"No-one is allowed to harm any of the complainants.

No-one is allowed to turn their nose up at them. We need to help them financially and give them monetary assistance. [We need] to lift them up higher and higher, and to give them every honour and every form of help. If you meet them in the streets, only smile at them and shake their hand [cordially]."

Rabbi Berland continued: *"Dance with them in the street and accord them all the honour they so richly deserve, because everything is in their merit. Everything that we managed to achieve, [like] giving three hour Torah classes on the Ketzos HaChoshen, and all the prayers, and praying the afternoon and evening prayers for four hours every evening, everything is in their merit.*

Just strengthen them, and encourage them, and give them all the honor and respect in the world. Also, help them financially, if you see that they are lacking something, give them some money. Give them money for their gatherings[i], encourage them, motivate them to hold more gatherings, and more gatherings - because all of this is big vessels full of [spiritual] diamonds.

All of Shuvu Banim's success is in their merit. All of the success that we had in Holland, and in Johannesburg [here, the Rav also mentioned other cities outside of Israel] - everything is in their merit. Just encourage them, and strengthen them, and Shuvu Banim will completely transform the face of the country."

And just like that, after five long, torturous years of exile, pain and imprisonment, Rabbi Berland returned to his community. The court stipulated that he was unable to leave his home in Morasha, and that he would still need to continue to pay to have a security team with him 24/7 - but suddenly, it was possible to pray with the Rav in the small

---

[i] The people within the Breslov community who were behind the slander and persecution of Rabbi Berland held a number of public gatherings against him.

courtyard next to his apartment building again, and to see him in the flesh.

Every day, hundreds and hundreds of people, including men, women and children, started flocking to the Rav's Jerusalem neighborhood. The makeshift *shul* where the Rav and his community prayed was full was always packed to capacity and beyond standing room only.

Rabbi Berland was back in business.

★ ★ ★

YOU CAN TELL A LEADER BY HIS FOLLOWERS

It is impossible to understand the Tzaddik himself since his intrinsic essence is beyond our grasp. Only through the followers of the Tzaddik is it possible to understand the Tzaddik's greatness. People are nearer to the Tzaddik's followers than they are to the Tzaddik himself and so they can understand them, at least a little, when they see that they are mature, hardworking, God-fearing people. One who sees the truth can thus know the greatness of the Tzaddik from his followers.

This is similar to a seal. The writing on the seal is unreadable because the letters are back to front. Only when one takes the seal and stamps it on wax can one understand the letters and designs inscribed on the seal, and one then sees what is written on the seal. Similarly, through the Tzaddik's followers one can come to understand something of the Tzaddik himself.

Likutei Moharan I, 140

On Shabbat August 19, 2017, around 12pm, Shuvu Banim student Nachman Lerner was walking back to his home after visiting the Kotel, around 12pm.

Just as he was leaving the Damascus Gate on Shabbos,

a female terrorist holding a knife suddenly ran directly at him and tried to stab him with all her might. Somehow, Nachman Lerner managed to evade the female terrorist, and then calmly continued home to where his family was waiting for him to begin their Shabbat meal.

Back at home, Lerner casually mentioned that he'd been involved in a minor altercation with an unbalanced women. But when the police later reviewed the video footage of the area, they realized that an attempted murder had taken place, and they decided to track down the victim, to get more details about what had happened.

Early Sunday morning, the police contacted some of the students from the Shuvu Banim yeshiva to try and find the student who'd been involved in the attempted stabbing the day before. Lerner had already gone to learn in the yeshiva and was out of contact, so one of the students went to go and tell him that he needed to head over to the police station to give a witness statement about the previous day's terror attack.

Lerner had no idea what he was talking about. It's only when he viewed the police footage that the penny dropped that he'd been attacked by a female terrorist intent on murder. "The police said that it's impossible to explain what happened to me, other than to say that I experienced an open miracle," he said. "There is simply no connection between what I experienced myself, and what I saw happening on the police footage, i.e. what was actually happening in reality."

★   ★   ★

At age 79, Rabbi Berland appeared to have more stamina, more strength, and more ability to stand on his feet non-stop for the very lengthy prayer service than many men less than half his age. Never complaining, always smiling at his community, often holding the hand of one of the teenage boys who thronged to be close to him, an outside observer wouldn't think for a moment that Rabbi Berland had any troubles or health problems.

But behind the scenes, the Rav was dealing with some enormously challenging circumstances on a number of fronts. Most of these difficulties continued to be hidden from the public, but on July 31, 2017, his health situation became so grave that he took the highly unusual step of publicizing his plight.

His community already knew that the Rav's health was in a precarious state, because he'd recently been forced to cancel his prayers with the community, which had never happened before.

Then, came the shocking report that two veins had burst in the Rav's leg as a result of a very serious infection, and that the doctors were advising the Rav to amputate it. The situation became so serious, the Rav himself recently wrote an unprecedented letter, asking the community, the nation, to help him in his hour need:

"To every Breslov chassid, to every chassid of Shuvu Banim, and to all of the nation of Israel," began the Rav's letter. *"This is a fateful cry [for help], to all of the Jewish people, before the amputation of [my] leg.*

Today, the Rav was in Hadassah Ein Kerem, and the doctors observed that there was an extremely toxic infection. At the moment, there is a whole discussion about whether the Rav's leg should be amputated or not, so they need to bring in all the specialist doctors both from within Israel and from abroad.

They need to fly in doctors from Boston in order to try to heal the Rav's leg, without having to amputate it.

We are talking here about a huge expense… that's accumulating in order to pay for the security team over eight months. *The security team was ordered by the State and by the Police.*[i]*"*

The letter concluded: "The Rav can't pray and can't do 'melava malka' with the community. He has to sit down, because of the terrible pain and suffering he feels throughout his whole leg."

Barely a day after the Rav's plea for help was publicized on Shuvu Banim's English and Hebrew websites, both sites were maliciously hacked and went down within a few hours of each other – leaving the online fundraising campaign effectively dead in the water.

The hackers did such a professional job that it took Shuvu Banim almost three weeks to get their websites operational again, as they had to rebuild them from scratch. However, as frequently happened throughout the five years of persecution, the more his opponents tried to harm the Rav, the more it rebounded in their faces. After the malicious hacking, many people started to realize that Rabbi Berland *was* being persecuted in an extremely unusual manner and were moved to donate to help save his leg.

On August 7th, 2017, a number of American specialists flew out to Israel to try to save the Rav's leg from amputation, and with God's help, they were successful.

At the behest of the Rav's persecutors, the Israeli court had decided that Rabbi Berland's prison sentence would end two weeks' after Rosh Hashana, on October 5th, 2017, which would prevent him from going to Uman.

So when the news first leaked out that on Monday, September 18, 2017 that the Israeli court had decided to give Rabbi Berland permission to travel to Uman for Rosh Hashana, 5778, the decision was very unexpected – not least

---

[i] Who also ordered that the Rav should be forced to bear the burden of paying for this astronomical expense out of his own pocket.

by the Rav's main persecutor, who quickly scrambled to try to overturn the court's decision.

When the Rav got to Ben Gurion Airport on Tuesday September 19th, together with his wife and a large contingent of court-appointed security guards, he was told that he wouldn't be able to board the plane to Uman after all. The Breslov zealots had struck again. Newspaper accounts spoke of a 'former pupil' of Rabbi Berland, who had filed an appeal with the Central District Court to prevent the Rav from leaving the country.

But this time, the persecutors didn't get things all their own way. Rabbi Berland's legal team appealed, and by some miracle, the court decided the Rav could fly out to Uman after all – but only after posting a massive bail of almost a million shekels. Two of the Rav's followers were prepared to put up the money – and the Rav was on his way to Uman, for the first time in three years.

The Rav arrived on a flight to Uman with his wife, Tehilla, his attendant, plus a large number of court-appointed security guards.

When news got out that the Rav was in Uman for Rosh Hashana after all, a strong feeling rippled through the crowd that Rosh Hashana 5778 marked some sort of turning point in the redemption of the Jewish people. But no-one had any idea what was actually going to happen next.

UMAN, 5778

"Kim Jong-un vows to wipe the US 'OFF THE FACE OF THE EARTH' in chilling WW3 threat."
 - Headline in the Daily Express, April 23ʳᵈ, 2017[i]

"The United States has great strength and patience, but if it is forced to defend itself or its allies, we will have no choice but to totally destroy North Korea. Rocket Man is on a suicide mission for himself and for his regime."
 - President Trump speaking at the UN General Assembly on 19 September 2017.[ii]

"MIAMI -- Hurricane Irma is churning across the Atlantic Ocean as a dangerous Category 5 storm and in preparation the City of Miami is warning residents near construction cranes to avoid staying in a building next to one. Tuesday evening city officials released a letter saying cranes in downtown Miami cannot withstand a Category 5 hurricane."
 – CBS Miami, September 6, 2017[iii]

[i] https://www.express.co.uk/news/world/795281/Kim-Jong-un-North-Korea-Donald-Trump-United-States-China-Russia-South-Korea

[ii] https://countercurrents.org/2017/10/us-north-korea-face-off-escalates

[iii] https://www.cbsnews.com/news/category-5-hurricane-irma-avoid-construction-cranes-miami/

As the holiness of Rosh Hashana began to descend on the tens of thousands of Jews in Uman, rumors of the Rav's imminent appearance at the Kloiz (the main shul in Uman) electrified the town.

Crowds of people accompanied the Rav every place he went in Uman, and his attendants and court-appointed security guards had their hands full trying to protect the Rav, amidst all the pushing and shoving as hundreds of people tried to come close enough to see him, speak to him and try to hold his hand.

There was a distinct feeling in Uman and beyond that the winds of change were blowing through the world, and that something big was looming on the horizon. Meanwhile, over in America, the winds of change had started blowing in a much more literal sense.

Hurricane Harvey was a Category 4 storm that slammed into Texas on August 25th, 2017, causing $125 billion worth of damage and causing 'apocalyptic' flooding in the Houston metropolitan area, displacing more than 30,000 people and killing 107.

The storm was hailed as a 'once in a decade' event, but the unsettled feeling that something unusual was occurring with the weather continued when barely two weeks later, the forecasters started urgently warning Florida, and particularly the city of Miami, to batten down the hatches as another massive storm, Hurricane Irma, started to approach the US.

As the hurricane drew closer and closer to Florida's east coast on Friday, September 8th 2017, all the weather models were predicting a direct hit on the city of Miami – with devastating consequences.

Before Rabbi Berland went into exile, he'd set up a branch of the Shuvu Banim yeshiva in Miami which has now grown to encompass many hundreds of people and includes a kollel and synagogue. Students at the Miami yeshiva called the Rav up on September 9th, 2017, to ask the Rav to pray for them.

The Rav immediately asked his followers in Jerusalem to recite a *Tikkun HaKlali* specifically for Miami, and to especially have Miami in mind the verse in Chapter 32:6 which reads: "Just that the mighty, flooding waters shouldn't reach to him."

Next thing the forecasters knew, Hurricane Irma hung a sharp left, skipped past Miami and Florida's East coast – and smashed straight into the state's West coast instead, which hadn't seen a hurricane of any real size since 1921. Irma completely destroyed twenty five percent of the houses in the area.

Meanwhile, back in Miami the winds were starting to pick up again and the authorities issued a warning for the residents to evacuate the area. Again, the worried students at the Shuvu Banim yeshiva in Miami called back the Rav for more *chizuk* and advice.

The Rav told them that the winds – which were becoming increasingly wild and dangerous – wouldn't get stronger than 75 mph (120 km/h), and that the hurricane would pass over all the houses of Torah learning in Miami. Meanwhile, the official forecasts for Miami were estimating that the wind speed would reach a much higher velocity, and were also forecasting a tornado to hit the area, that would see winds of up to 185 mph.

In the end, the winds in Miami never topped 72 mph – exactly as the Rav had promised. While Florida still sustained enormous damage, especially on its West coast, Miami and the East coast missed the 'eye of the storm' and came through the ordeal in relatively good shape.

Throughout the two days of Rosh Hashana 5778, the Rav was in a very serious mood and, uncharacteristically, he didn't so much as smile at another human being throughout the whole holiday. There was speculation that perhaps the Rav was busy trying to sweeten the judgments he'd spoken about shortly before the new year began, when he'd said that North Korea would try to fire a nuclear weapon at the United States of America on Wednesday, the first day of Rosh Hashanah. By Shabbos morning, though, the Rav was in a completely different mood.

After the Shabbos morning prayers, Rabbi Berland spoke about the storms in Florida. The Rav explained that: *"All the storms and hurricanes are sent away from a place where Torah is being learned and from where people travel from there to Uman."* The Rav then added: *"Because the storm got to Miami on Shabbat, it broke windows and sent floodwater only into the upper stories, but by the Jews who were living on the lower levels, nothing happened to them, because it was Shabbat.*

"We really saw the Divine providence that was happening. Houses were destroyed in Baton, whilst in Miami, nothing really happened."

Rabbi Berland then stunned the audience by continuing: *"Now, we've arrived at the time of Gog and Magog, the time of geula, and the end of days. North Korea is going to launch a nuclear weapon, but it's not going to reach to Miami, because there are synagogues there, and people who keep mitzvos. Perhaps it will fall into the sea. But North Korea has some very unique ideas. But despite all this, there's no need to worry. Just sit in the succah, and don't leave it. Anyone who sits in the succah will be protected and will survive."*

In the meantime, the confrontation between the United States and North Korea was coming to a head.

RAV LEVI SA'ADIA NACHMANI PREDICTS
NORTH KOREAN NUCLEAR PROBLEMS IN 1994

Rav Levi Sa'adia Nachmani was a well-known Israeli kabbalist.[i] In 1994, while the State of Israel was neck-high in it's failed 'peace accord' negotiations with Yasser Arafat and the PLO, Rav Nachmani was recorded as saying the following:

"Do you think there will be peace? Do you think it will be peaceful one day? [You are] total fools! Parshas Ha'azenu is talking about us today. It says: 'O, foolish and unwise people. A generation that's crooked and perverse.'

"Do you know what will happen, God forbid? Korea. Do you know who Korea is? Not Syria, not Persia, not Babylon (Iraq) not Qadafi (Libya). Korea will arrive here, God forbid, may the Lord save us.

"And anyone who pays any attention to what's going on in Korea today[ii], it's for us. The nukes. It will be very hard for us if we don't do teshuva. Understand this! Know that it's worse than the holocaust! 'For a fire is kindled in My nostrils, and will burn unto sheoul[8].' Do you know what 'sheoul' is? It's the capital of Korea.

"It will get to here, and 'devour the earth with her produce and set ablaze the foundations of the mountain. I will heap evil upon them. I will spend My arrows upon them[9].'

"What does this mean? We have left God, we think we belong to ourselves, and the PM[i] sits and does what he wants, as if God doesn't exist, if the land of Israel is his, and he does whatever he wants with it, as if the people are his.

"And the Torah says: 'For the portion of God is his people.' You don't belong to yourselves, you're His!... We have no dispute with the Arabs. We have a dispute with the God of Israel. If we won't listen to Him, we will have more and more troubles, and the situation will get worse. Don't believe these fools! You must beware of them, you must beware of the bad, foreign culture that they brought here.

"You are Jews, sons of Abraham, Isaac and Jacob, who received the Torah, your Torah. You must appreciate it and respect it and fight for it. Not with violence, but peacefully, by making teshuva...

"If we make teshuva, then we won't need to go and fight in the army at 18 instead of getting married. Instead of letting you 'rejoice in your home' they take you off to fight. Instead of letting our girls find peace, they take them as soldiers...? I don't understand this silence! Why don't we make some teshuva?

"Why do we keep quiet, and give the power to these fools who kill us? The yetzer hara is not you. It's a separate force that enters through the ears. You are brainwashed by the media, brainwashed by the press, brainwashed everywhere...

"How long will we be fools? How long will we be naïve and indifferent? How long? We must do one thing, and nothing else. Not violence, and nothing else. Only teshuva, that's the answer for them And then we'll receive the very best thing, life and peace."

More than two decades later, the world's media was full of worrying headlines about Pyongyang's growing nuclear capabilities and the threat their nuclear arms posed to the rest of the world.

---

[i] In December 1994, North Korea had just shot down a US Army helicopter, killing one pilot and taking the other captive for 13 days. Earlier in the year, the North Korean leader Kim Il-Sung had died, and been succeeded by his son, Kim Jong-Il, who was succeeded by his son, the present leader of North Korea, Kim Jong-Un in 2011. Kim Jong-Un has been notable for aggressively pursuing the development of nuclear weapons.

★ ★ ★

In the meantime, daily life started to settle down into something of a routine. Every day, the Rav could be found *praying* with his community at the temporary shul that had been created as a makeshift addition at the back of the Rav's building, when he was still under house arrest.

Every day, it was standing room only, and often barely that, as hundreds upon hundreds of people tried to cram themselves into the small hall to have the privilege of praying with the Rav. Even though the Rav continued to be under house arrest, a number of big rabbis and other names would come and publicly pray with him on the Rav's small stage, or *bima*, while many, many more came to see him privately, away from the prying eyes of the media and the Rav's persecutors.

In October 2017, Rabbi Berland welcomed the Chassidic singer Mordechai Ben David on to his small stage, and also gave a blessing to the well-known kabbalist and head of the 'Kiryat Baal Shem Tov' institutions in Netivot, Rabbi Tzvi Hori. Other visitors around this time included Rav Reuven Elbaz, the Spinka Rebbe of Bnei Brak, and Rav Aharon Stern, the son of the famous kabbalist from Bnei Brak, Rav Chaim David Stern, and head of the *Tzvi* Yehuda Torah institution. At the request of his father, who was too poorly to travel at that time, he came to visit the Rav at the beginning of October, very shortly before the Rav was formally released from house arrest. Rav Aharon made the following remarks to the community:

"Our Sages teach that in the end of days truth will be absent, it will be completely lacking and absent in all sorts of ways, and that every lie will be called 'the truth'. I want to tell you something about my teacher, Rabbi Yehuda Zeev

Leibowitz[i], *who once decided to go to sleep when it was time for the Kol Nidrei prayer service on Yom Kippur, instead of going to pray in the synagogue.*

Afterwards, he revealed to us that there had been a decree in Heaven on the Jews because so many of them were going to sleep on Kol Nidrei instead of going to synagogue. 'So, I decided to also go to sleep,' said Rav Zeev Leibowitz, 'so in shamayim they cancelled the decree.'[2]

We can see that the Tzaddik is doing something, but we don't really understand that whole picture of what's really going on with the Tzaddikim. We really have no idea about what their actions are doing. But, every act done by the Tzaddik is being done to sweeten the judgments on behalf of the Jewish people."

Rabbi Stern continued: *"When I first came to Rav Leibowitz to care for him, I said to myself: 'What are all these weird actions and different types of behavior?!' Once, I was thinking to myself about why the Tzaddik was conducting himself in ways which meant that sometimes, it appeared as though he was doing things that were contrary to Jewish law, but without saying anything about it.*

Then, Rav Leibowitz raised his eyes from his Gemara and said to me: 'Aharon, did you know Rebbe Aharon of Belz?' I told him that no I didn't, because he died before I was even born. Rav Leibowitz continued: 'Do you know, that he used to show up five minutes before the afternoon prayers and only then start praying the morning prayers? How can this be? But did anyone speak out against him? The Lelover Rebbe used to show up on motzei Shabbat, and begin shacharis then – did anyone speak out against him? Rav Shach didn't give in to

---
[i] Rav Yehuda Zev Leibowitz was a hidden Tzaddik who died just a few short years' ago and was rumored to be the head of the 'Lamed Vav' Tzaddikim in whose merit the world is sustained. He's buried in Bnei Brak.

— 317 —

anyone whose halacha he didn't agree with. So why didn't he come out against the Rebbe of Lelov?!'"

"Rabbi Berland is a Tzaddik who comes from the aspect of 'law', and no-one can touch him. Our Rabbi is holy and awesome, and all of his behavior – even if it seems to us to be strange, in truth, it's all for our own sake. Because he's taking our illnesses upon himself and he's suffering for our sake."

Rabbi Stern then struck a very somber note, saying: "We are currently in a period of time similar to that which occurred before the holocaust, but we have nothing to fear, inasmuch as we are sheltered under the *tallis* of Rabbi Berland."

Rav Stern continued: *"It gives me great sorrow that my father is so ill that he can't come to this gathering himself, and that the Satan is preventing the Tzaddikim from meeting. But when I came here, I met Rabbi Berland, and he said to me: 'Rav Stern, don't worry! Everything is on my shoulders. From the 25th of Elul, motzei Shabbos (September 16, 2017), you're going to see the beginning of the salvation of the Jewish people!' I ask you, where else can you find a rebbe like this?"*

Rav Aharon Stern concluded his remarks by saying*: "I'd like to request just one on thing, that we should have unity and love between us, which will bring us the redemption. Before his death, Rav Leibowitz ordered me to make the following announcement about America, so I repeat this every opportunity I get.*

"He told me that the anti-Semitism in the United States is only going to continue to grow, until it gets to the point where the Jews will be forced to flee. We can also see how the forces of nature are going crazy there, and this is because we see how the people there are overturning everything, and no longer know who their Mother and Father is ....The same is true in Tel Aviv, which is why Rav Leibowitz told me: 'Tel Aviv will be destroyed.'

Rabbi Berland is fighting against the head of the snake, in direct combat. Rabbi Berland is gouging out it's eyes and he's taking upon himself all our troubles. I heard from my teacher and father who told me: 'I'm scared... I don't know how Rabbi Berland is doing this! There is no other rabbi in Israel, there is no other rosh yeshiva in Israel, there is no other rebbe in Israel who knows how Rabbi Berland is able to fight this war, and to fight against the head of the snake itself."

Around the same time that Rav Stern came to visit the *Beit HaRav*, Rabbi Rachamim Bracha, the editor of Shuvu Banim's *Knishta Chada* newsletter happened to meet a young man there, who asked him when the Rav was expected to come out to join the community for the prayers that evening.

Rabbi Bracha continues: *"We carried on talking a while, and this young man told me that he came from Bnei Brak, and that this was his first time traveling to pray with Rabbi Berland in Jerusalem,"* he recounts.

"So, I asked him what had brought him to the Rav, and he told me that he'd come because of a dream he'd had. 'A dream?' I asked him, a little surprised. 'Yes, a dream!' he told me, completely serious.

'I had a dream about Rabbi Berland, and in the dream I saw that the Tzaddik was bigger than the whole of Israel, and that he was standing and looking over the whole of the country. I was still trying to figure out the meaning of what I was seeing, when suddenly a total war exploded in my dream,' continued the avreich.

'Immediately, the Tzaddik spread his tallis over the whole of Israel, while continuing to hold onto it, but the whole of Israel was covered by it.'"

Rabbi Bracha continues: *"I was amazed, after all, I knew that the Rav has spoken on many occasions about his efforts to sweeten the decree of the rockets and missiles and, here, this avreich was telling me in all innocence about his dream, and he'd never even heard the words of the Rav.*

So, I had to ask him, what happened at the end of the dream? He told me: 'All the missiles were caught by the tallis that the Tzaddik had spread out[i]. I went to my Rosh Kollel, and told him about my dream, and he told me: 'The tzaddik Rabbi Berland is protecting the whole of Israel.' So, I came to see for myself who this tzaddik really is,' concluded the young."

★ ★ ★

On October 8, 2017, on the anniversary of Rebbe Nachman of Breslov's passing, Rabbi Berland ordeal at the hands of Israel's 'justice' system was finally over. The Rav

---

[i] Painting by Yehoshua Wiseman: www.yehoshuawiseman.com, Tel: 054-844-1131.

was formally released on the intermediate days of Succot, and thousands of his followers flocked to Jerusalem, to celebrate his freedom in the biggest public Succah ever erected.[i]

Given the Rav's poor health at this stage, his advanced age, the many years he'd spent wandering around the world and the tremendous stress and suffering he'd recently undergone at the hands of the Israeli Prison Service, you might think that after being formally released from his ordeal, the Rav would want to just put his feet up a little, and relax.

But 'relaxing' was the last thing Rabbi Berland had on his mind. Within a few short days of being formally released from house arrest, he'd already made plans to visit a number of the country's holiest sites to continue praying for the safety and welfare of the Nation of Israel. Despite all the suffering and persecution, Rabbi Berland was sending a very clear message that he was back, and that from now on, it would be business as usual, his age, ill-health and ongoing opposition notwithstanding.

The first grave the Rav went to was Joseph's Tomb in Shechem (Nablus), on October 11, 2017. He was joined by a very large number of his followers, making it one of the biggest private visits to the tomb in modern times.

A few days' later, Rabbi Berland and a few hundred of his followers next visited the grave of Joshua bin Nun, located in the radicalized Arab town of Kifl Haris. And then, on October 31st, Rabbi Berland visited Rachel's Tomb, on the outskirts of Jerusalem - which coincided with the worst terrorist attack in New York since the Twin Towers, when an Islamic terrorist used his truck to mow down eight people in cold blood.

---

[i] You can see clips of the celebrations at: https://www.youtube.com/watch?time_continue=8&v=NrOtJlvb2Aw
https://www.youtube.com/watch?time_continue=28&v=3tKHYef0S5I

★   ★   ★

While few people were that surprised that Rabbi Berland would immediately return to visiting the holy kevarim upon his release, they were a little shocked by another of the projects that the Rav embarked on immediately after being freed: criss-crossing the country to renew his visits and appearances in homes and venues across Israel.

40 years ago, Rabbi Shalom Arush used to give Rabbi Berland a lift to Eilat on the back of his motorbike, where the Rav was headed in order to try to bring some of the Jews there back to God and an observant lifestyle. Many tens of thousands of Jews returned to the path of their forefathers in the merit of Rabbi Berland's cross-country trips.

But that was back when the Rav was a much younger man. No-one expected an octogenarian who'd been through such severe health issues and other recent challenges to renew this type of outreach work. Not for the first time, the Rav surprised everyone – but why was he doing it?

Rabbi Yosef Assulin spent many years as the Rav's personal attendant. He recalls: *"Already back in 1989, the Rav said that the Iranians were investing billions in weapons that were going to be aimed at Israel, and that every square metre of Israel would have a rocket aimed at it."* While the immediate threat from an Iranian nuke had started to noticeably recede, the Israeli security establishment was starting to publicly voice concern over the growing Iranian presence in war-torn Syria.

So, Rabbi Berland took it upon himself to being an 'exile within an exile', and embarked on a grueling schedule of visits, to try to encourage more people in Israel to make teshuva – this time at the age of 79. Initially, the visits started small, and were kept low-key. But as word started to spread that the Tzaddik was coming to town, more and more people started clamoring for a chance to see Rabbi Berland for themselves.

As more and more communities started requesting the Rav to come and speak to them, and as the crowds of people attending these events quickly mushroomed from tens to hundreds and even a couple of thousand people, Rabbi Berland's persecutors couldn't believe what was happening.

After all the time, effort and money they'd put into blackening the Rav's name, hounding him all over the world and imprisoning him on trumped-up charges, the last thing they expected to see was the elderly Rav pulling in massive crowds all over the country as soon as he was released. The Rav's persecutors weren't prepared to let such a development occur without trying to put another spoke in the wheel, so a new campaign of intimidation and threats was begun against the Rav, this time spear-headed by another group of Facebook activists.

The group's tactics were very simple; any events hall who agreed to host the Rav would be bombarded with threats and intimidation until they would be forced to cancel the event. And if the events hall themselves continued to stand strong against these strong-arm tactics, then the local politicians would be called in to cancel the event 'from the top'.

At the same time, a very small group of protesters would come and demonstrate outside the Rav's events with loudspeakers and signs, and to make every effort to try to provoke the Rav's followers into some sort of confrontation with them would make some sensational headlines. To their credit, none of the Rav's followers and students got drawn into a fight with the anti-Rabbi Berland activists, even when the protestors taunted and goaded them.

The Rav's persecutors started their latest round of bullying tactics at one of his first events in Bat Yam, where a very small group of protesters managed to generate some enormous headlines in the secular Israeli press. Buoyed by their success, they turned their sites on a big event that the Rav's followers had organized at the Mann Auditorium in Beer Sheva, to take place on December 28, 2017.

After posting up a number of inflammatory and abusive Facebook posts, this group then organized a harassment campaign over the telephone, where they put enormous pressure on the hall's management to cancel the event. The Rav's followers managed to find another events hall in Beer Sheva last minute – but then the persecutors also intimidated that hall into pulling out of their agreement as well.

Finally, the event took place in the industrial area of Beer Sheva, in two enormous marquees that had been hastily erected on the premises of a tiling warehouse. Despite all the obstacles and last-minute changes of venue, hundreds of people still came to the event, while 10 'enlightened' protesters with bull-horns stood across the way yelling insults and abuse at them.

Other cities who saw their events cancelled thanks to the Rav's persecutors included Ma'alot Tarshiha in the North and Dimona in the South, with many other events either being moved 'in-house' to private residents and synagogues, or occurring only thanks to the incredible *emunah* of the hall owners who continued to host them.

In January 2018, Rabbi Berland was scheduled to speak at a synagogue in Rehovot. As soon as his opponents got word of the event, they quickly mobilized to get the Mayor of Rehovot involved in pressuring the synagogue to cancel the event. The synagogue bowed to the pressure tactics, and the event was moved to a hall in the industrial area of Rehovot instead.

But the demonstrators didn't stop there and continued to apply pressure tactics to try to force the hall owner to cancel the event there, too, including making all sorts of threats about getting his business closed down.

After all these threats had been made against him, the owner of the hall in Rehovot said that he'd been contacted by a number of journalists who were trying to get his reaction to the situation. The hall owner told the Breslov Information Line that he'd told the persecutors point blank that:

"I'm going to close the hall, and open up a kollel there, where the Torah of Rabbi Berland will be studied instead. How is it possible for someone to be scared of people, but not to fear God?!" The owner of the hall continued: *"I will open six kollels in Rehovot, and one of them will be for Rabbi Berland, and I'm not going to bow to the pressure I'm coming under from his opponents."*

Despite the demonstrators' aggressive efforts to disrupt the Rav's Torah classes, the Rav continued undeterred, holding back-to-back events up and down the country in Tel Aviv, Nahariya, Holon, Ashkelon, Ashdod and Eilat, amongst many other places.

"Rabbi Berland is a Jew who simply can't live without being disgraced," explains Rabbi Yosef Assulin. "The Rav explained to me once that if a person works hard to serve God properly. Slowly, slowly, everyone in his environment is going to start challenging him, until ultimately, everyone is challenging him. When you get to the biggest of the big, like Rabbi Berland it just has to be that the whole country is going to be against him."

★ ★ ★

Throughout the next few months, stories of the Torah luminaries who were meeting with Rabbi Berland were interspersed with yet more lurid headlines, as the Rav's persecutors continued their vendetta against him via the media.

On February 4th, 2018, media outlets started published more scandalous headlines announcing that a 'shocking video' of Rabbi Berland touching a woman's throat had surfaced. Again, none of the journalists involved in peddling this latest scandal actually spoke to Klara Hammer, the woman in question, to get the real story of what was happening. After the video surfaced, Klara Hammer agreed to be interviewed by the Shuvu Banim website, where she explained that she'd been suffering with life-threatening throat cancer – and the tumor had shrunk after she'd seen the Rav.

"I've known Rav Eliezer Berland since I was a little girl," she began. *"The Rav loves everyone. Anyone who knows the Rav, they see miracles. I'm the mother of 11 children, and I discovered that I was very sick with cancer around Rosh Hashana time [in 2014].*

Shortly before Rosh Hashana, the Rav had spoken to me on the telephone, and he'd told me that I was very ill - that I only had a month left to live, and that I needed to come and see him, so he could help me. At that time, I had no idea what the Rav was talking about, because I still hadn't discovered that I was sick.

Two weeks after that, I went to Hadassah hospital, because I was really starting to feel unwell. There, they confirmed my worst fears, and they told me that I had a very serious illness, and that my chances of making it through were very small. The next day, I was already in the operating room. By this point I'd already lost 15 kilos in weight, and I decided that I just had to go and see the Rav.

I knew what this illness was, I'd already experienced it elsewhere in my family, both with my relatives and with my friends. The agreement I made with the hospital was that if I decided to go through with the operation, then afterwards I'd need to have a series of 40 radiation treatments.

The Rav contacted me and told me to come to him in Amsterdam. I came for two days, with my husband. When you see the Rav, it's truly like seeing an angel of God. From the moment I saw him, I started to feel a bit more emuna and hope.

"The Rav gave me a soup to eat. Up until that point, I hadn't been able to swallow any food, but suddenly I found myself asking for another bowl. I told the Rav that I just had to have the operation. The Rav told me not to worry, and that he would send me the best experts."

Klara continued: "You could say that my recovery actually started there, in Holland, when I saw the Rav. Every day that I was in Holland, the Rav blessed me. I used to cry, and ask the Rav to pray for me - because who else can pray like the Tzaddik? By the time I got to the Rav, my tumor had already grown tremendously. When I returned home, it was already smaller. I also had two metastased tumors growing in the direction of my lungs that had already bypassed the cartilage." But three years' later, Klara's cancer had become a thing of the past.

On March 6th, 2018, there were headlines of a different kind when the grandson of the late Baba Sali, Rabbi David Abuchatzeira, met with Rabbi Berland for the first time at Rav Abuchatzeira's home in Nahariya.

Despite the very warm feelings these two tzaddikim had for each other, they had never actually met each other face-to-face before. Throughout the visit, Rav Abuchatzeira showed Rabbi Berland the greatest respect, including stopping his audiences with the general public at his home for 15 minutes, during which time he only spoke with the Rav.

After these two tzaddikim left the room where they'd been conversing and studying the deepest secrets of the Torah privately together, Rav Abuchatzeira then asked

Rabbi Berland to step into the adjoining beit midrash, to learn something in the merit of Rav Abuchatzeira's holy forefathers, including the Baba Sali and the Baba Meir.

Then, Rabbi David asked Rabbi Berland's attendant to enter the room, while he continued to praise Rabbi Berland very highly. Rabbi Abuchatzeira said: "He is entirely Torah! We have merited having a completely pure person come to visit with us."

★　★　★

At the beginning of the book, we explained how three of the Jewish nation's biggest tzaddikim, the Baba Elazar, Rabbi Dov Kook of Tiberius and Rabbi Berland agreed to forge a spiritual 'pact' that would see each of these holy man experience tremendous suffering and mesirus nefesh, in order to sweeten the harsh decrees that were gathering over the heads of the nation of Israel.

The Baba Elazar was brutally murdered shortly afterwards, and the rumors and exile of Rabbi Berland began a few months later. Throughout the more than four years of exile, Rabbi Dov Kook gave periodic messages of hope and inspiration to the Rav and his followers, each one a beacon in a very dark night.

But it would only be on March 24th, 2018, many months after Rabbi Berland was finally released, that these two Torah luminaries would actually meet again face-to-face. The two tzaddikim met to share the melava malka meal together, and then went outside together to recite the blessing over the new moon.

Just before reciting the blessing, Rabbi Berland started talking to the small group of people gathered around: "*Now that Rav Kook came, we're going to bring the redemption by Seder night. Rav Kook is going to bring the light of redemption, the light of Moshiach, and the light of the exodus from Egypt. Like the days when we left Egypt, God is going to show us wonders. We're going to see wonders that have never been seen since the creation of the world, with God's help."*

Rabbi Berland concluded: *"Now is the moment of the redemption." Later on during the meal, Rabbi Berland leaned over to Rav Kook, and said: "He's bringing Moshiach, he's opening the way for Moshiach now."*

After the meal ended, Rabbi Dov Kook said the following:

"I merited understanding a little bit of what he said; it's the deepest of the deep. I'm amazed how the people who follow him and listen to him, how they understand what he's saying. I understood only a little bit. He's a genius, he's a computer [of Torah], he's an angel. He went through terrible, terrible suffering. I just wish I (was on such a level that) could understand everything he says."

It sounded as though the redemption of the Jewish people was imminent. But over the next few months, at least from the outside, the process of redemption looked like it had gotten stuck.

TUNNELS AND TRICKSTERS

"Israel Is On The Brink Of War With Hamas, Hezbollah, Syria And Iran All At The Same Time"
– Headline from the True Conservative Pundit website, March 19th, 2019[i]

"The Lebanese terrorist group Hezbollah's arsenal of missiles and rockets has grown to 150,000, Internal Security Minister Gilad Erdan (Likud) revealed Sunday."
- Arutz Sheva, October 21st, 2018[ii]

"Our strategy is to erase Israel from the global political map."
– Iranian Brig. Gen. Hossein Salami, speaking in Tehran on January 28th, 2019[iii]

"A recent political ad from Israel compared ultra Orthodox Jews to terrorists. 'It makes no difference if one is subjugated by someone with raised weapons,' the ad proclaims, to images of masked, ominous

---

[i] https://trueconservativepundit.com/2019/03/19/israel-is-on-the-brink-of-war-with-hamas-hezbollah-syria-and-iran-all-at-the-same-time/
[ii] How many missiles does Hezbolla have aimed at Israel? - http://www.israelnationalnews.com/News/News.aspx/253558
[iii] https://www.timesofisrael.com/iran-general-says-tehran-aims-to-wipe-israel-off-the-political-map-report/

Hamas militiamen with mortars,' or by someone who isn't prepared to raise a weapon.' Cue shots of a haredi Jew next to a dumpster fire, and a gathering of haredi rabbis on a dais protesting the conscription of yeshiva students. This ad, put out by Avigdor Lieberman's Yisrael Beiteinu party ahead of the April election, is shocking in its comparison."

– Avi Shafran, writing in The
Forward, February 4th, 2019[i]

"*I want to emphasize another time: We are in favor of a Jewish state, we are against a halachic state,*"
- Avigdor Lieberman, May 27th, 2019

★ ★ ★

Over the next few months, Rabbi Berland continued to criss-cross the country appearing at synagogues and private homes across the country, while his persecutors continued cranking up fresh allegations against him, most notably now in the in the English-language media.

The pattern was predictably the same each time: the Breslov zealot who was the main figure behind the persecution of Rabbi Berland would give another 'exclusive' interview, and the journalists would unquestioningly reprint and embellish every lie they were told.

In the meantime, on April 29th, 2018, Rebbetzin Tehillah Berland was awarded three million shekels in damages – the maximum sum permissible – against one of the persecutors. This astronomical sum was awarded to underline the terrible pain and humiliation this man had caused the Rebbetzin, by secretly recording conversations he'd had with her while he

---

[i] https://forward.com/opinion/418734/why-does-the-world-hate-haredi-jews/

was posing as a 'mediator', which he later edited and splashed all over Youtube.

★ ★ ★

And so, the Jewish year of 5778 gave way to the new year of 5779, and Rabbi Berland returned to Uman, where he spoke of the great need for the Jewish community to be unified. Upon his return, the Rav continued his grueling routine of making house visits and attending speaking engagements the length and breadth of the country – sometimes, speaking in 5 or 6 different locations a night, before returning to Jerusalem to pray the morning prayers with his community.

Then, shortly before Chanukah 5779 (November 2018), the Rav started to give over a number of disturbing messages about the security situation in Israel, and urged his attendants to organize another big prayer gathering in Hebron, for the last day of Chanukah.

In a statement that he put out a few days beforehand, Rabbi Berland said:

"The whole of the nation is currently facing a terrible, threatening situation. Every part of Israel is now under threat of being deluged with rockets. After we saw 400 rockets falling on Ashkelon and the surrounding cities, including Beer Sheva, Netivot, Ofakim and Sderot, now they are preparing thousands and thousands of rockets, which will reach to Tel Aviv and Jerusalem.

And we have no possibility of stopping this from happening, because the whole world is against us. They can launch 10,000 missiles, and if we fire back even just one, they will say that we are the aggressors, and they are the victims.

They will say that we began [hostilities], and that they are simply defending themselves. We have no [military] might, we only have the power of Psalms. All of the State of Israel's efforts to stop the missiles of Hezbollah and Hamas ended in failure. Every day, we are threatened with thousands of new rockets. They can reach any target precisely...

The nation of Israel is in the greatest danger, and our only possibility of coming through this lies in our mouths: "The voice is the voice of Jacob, and the hands are the hands of Eisav[10]."

We are now at the final moments that we can stay in Israel, in the State of Israel, because the goal of the Arabs is to destroy everyone here. They don't care if its religious Jews, secular Jews, hareidim, Neturei Karta – they aren't interested.

They want to annihilate every single Jew, until the very last one of us – regardless of whether he's secular, or religious, or national religious, or has a knitted kippah. It's written: "And I will divide them, into the light and into the dark.[11]"

They are not going to distinguish between the 'light' and the 'darkness'. Right now, we are all in the gravest danger. So, we need to really urge people to attend this Prayer Gathering, so that almost 50,000 thousand people will come. And everyone should read the whole of the Book of Psalms.... and so, every single person is obliged to complete the book of Psalms at the Prayer Gathering, and to make good use of this opportunity for 50,000 people to say Psalms together.

This will (be considered in heaven) as though a billion people are saying Psalms, and this will certainly stop the rockets. Only prayers can stop the rockets – not the IDF, not weapons, not tanks, not Patriot missiles, no Iron Dome – none of these things can stop the missiles. Only the Psalms that we will say at this Prayer Gathering can stop the missiles."

Although many thousands of the Rav's followers from across Israel made the effort to attend, the number fell far short of the 50,000 people the Rav had requested[i]. And it

---

[i] Rabbi Berland privately commented at the end of the prayer gathering that while it had been big enough to defer the decree until

wasn't long before the Jews in Israel realized why the Rav had been so concerned.

The prayer gathering in Hebron was called for motzei Shabbos, Saturday night on December 8, 2018 and it continued well on into the small hours of the morning, until around 4.00 am, when the crowds started to disperse and the Rav returned to Jerusalem for the morning prayers.

★ ★ ★

At the same time that the Rav and his followers were lighting the Chanukah candles and beginning their recitation of the book of Psalms in Hebron, at a bus stop just outside the town of Ofra, North of Jerusalem, Hamas terrorist Salih Omar Barghouti was loading his weapons, and taking aim.

His target was a group of young Jews, including Shira Ish-Ran, a heavily-pregnant first-time mother, and her husband Amichai. Despite firing 15-20 bullets at a large group of Jews crowded together at the bus stop at close range, Barghouti injured only seven people, and most of them were lightly wounded.

Shira's husband Amichai had been shot three times in the legs – but one of the terrorist's bullets had entered Shira's lower abdomen, and her life, and the life of her unborn baby, were in serious danger as she was rushed to hospital.

Speaking to reporters afterwards, Shira's mother Liora Silberstein said: "The bullet went through her body. It's a complete miracle that it missed all her major organs." In another interview, she said: "We want to thank God for all the miracles that took place. So many bullets were fired at a large group of people, crowded together."

Nissan, another prayer gathering would would be needed on 1st of Nissan – April 4th, 2019.

Sadly, Shira and Amichai's newborn son, Amiad, died three days after he was born.

On December 12, Salih Barghouti was shot dead by the IDF while conducting a gun battle with the soldiers who'd been sent to arrest him. But the terror wasn't over yet. The next day, December 13, 2018, Barghouti's brother Asem carried out another terror shooting at the bus stop on Route 60 near the West Bank town of Bet El, where he murdered two soldiers in cold blood, and badly injured another soldier and a civilian young woman.

And this time, the murderer's bullet fell even closer to home, for the Shuvu Banim community.

★   ★   ★

That Thursday, December 13th, 2018, Yosef (Yossi) Cohen, 19, Yuval Mor Yosef, 20, and Nathaniel Felber, 20 were guarding the Givat Assaf hitch-hiking point on Route 60 when the terrorist drove up and started firing at them. Yosef and Yuval died on the spot, while Nathaniel survived being shot in the head at close range but was critically injured.

Yossi and Yuval were serving in the 'Netzach Yehuda' brigade of the IDF, part of the Nahal Haredi Division that enables hareidi young men to serve in the army.

Very quickly after the terror attack, word spread that one of the victims was the step-son of Rav Eliyahu Meirav, a leading figure within the Shuvu Banim community and one of Rabbi Berland's oldest students.

Shortly after the murder, Rav Meirav was interview by the Israeli media, and he gave over an anguished plea for unity to finally take the place of division, and for Am Yisrael to come together in times of peace, instead of only in times of war.

"Yossi was a pure soul. He was on a spiritual mission. We sent him [on that mission] with very great love. At every Shabbat meal, we sit together as a family, and everyone says 'thank you' for something that they're grateful for. Last Shabbat, Yossi said the following: 'I'm grateful to God that I have the merit of using my body to protect the people of Israel.'

That's who this soul was. He didn't really know what he was saying, but these were the last words that he said in our home. Now, all of us understand what he was really saying."

A clearly distraught Rav Meirav continued:

"Yossi was a pure soul. He was a child full of self sacrifice, a child who only wanted to help other people – right from the time he was small. And now, God has taken him. We need so much strengthening...

We were very proud of Yossi, and he was proud of us, too. We sent him [to the army] with love, from a very deep sense that he had a mission to do. We believe that the Jewish people is one unit, indivisible. We believe that everyone is joined together. Everyone, in whatever place they find themselves, needs to help others, and to give to others."

"This is how I was raised," continued Rav Meirav. *"I grew up on Kibbutz Beit Alfa, of the Shomer HaTza'ir, and these were the eternal values [we were taught] about loving another human being, loving humanity. No politics can sway these values, this feeling of eternal unity.*

It's so unfortunate that bereavement is what brings us together. Perhaps, we'll actually start to win when we are joined together by love. Alavai. Why can't we come together on happy occasions?! It hurts me so much. It's hard to speak."

A journalist asked Rav Meirav about his own career with the army, and he responded:

"I served in the IDF, and then made teshuva after the Yom Kippur War. I've been hareidi for 45 years already. But first and foremost, I am an Israeli. I am a product of the breakdown of secular Israeli society. It pains me tremendously that there are families who don't accept their children after they enlist [in the IDF]. I understand that everybody has to follow their own beliefs, and to walk in their own path. But we have to maintain our respect for the other person. We have to maintain the mutual respect between us!

We have to put an end to the awful hatred between us. It's impossible to build a home, to build a state, in this way. Yossi was a young, Israeli, Hareidi man. He had a heart of gold, and he was the crowning glory of the Jewish people. He wanted to finish the army, and then continue to give to the nation of Israel by becoming a dentist. And now, he's above. He's watching over us."

Just that Thursday morning, another student from the Shuvu Banim community called David HaLevi had narrowly missed being injured in a terrorist attack in the Old City, when the assailant had tried to stab him, but somehow just managed to push him roughly to the ground, instead. A couple of seconds later, the terrorist ran over to two Israeli Border police standing close by, and stabbed the policeman in the face, and the woman police officer in her leg, before he was shot dead.

Afterwards, HaLevi explained what had happened: "*In the early hours of the morning, I'd been in the yeshiva. I'd learnt some Torah, immersed in the mikveh, and when I came out of the mikveh, another student came over to me, and asked me for some charity.*

I have never, ever had such a difficult time persuading myself to take out a few coins to give for charity. But in the end, I got a hold of myself, and I gave him the last 10 shekels that I had in my wallet. It was only afterwards that I remembered the Sages' dictum that" "*Charity saves from death.*" *I really felt that I'd had such a hard struggle with myself to give that money, but that in the end, it had saved my life.*"

Thursday evening after the deadly murder at Givat Assaf, another Palestinian was shot dead after trying to ram his car into a group of soldiers near Bet El. And then that Friday, another Palestinian terrorist broke into a military outpost near Bet El, where he managed to seriously injure an Israel soldier by clubbing him in the head with a large rock, and also stabbing him, before he was shot and wounded.

After months of relative calm, it suddenly felt as though the West Bank had been plunged into another cycle of awful, murderous violence – just as Rabbi Berland had foreseen. But there was still more revelations to come.

The Rav's first call to gather people together for a prayer rally at Hebron was publicized on the Shuvu Banim English website on December 2, 2018. That story explained that: "The stated aim of this gathering is to sweeten the wars that the Rav can see looming both in Israel's south, but also in Israel's north – which has been relatively quiet since the Lebanon II war, which occurred well over a decade ago."

Two weeks' earlier, Southern Israel had come under a barrage of over 400 rockets from Gaza, which had residents in the South scurrying into their security rooms and fearing that a full-blown war had begun. Twenty four hours later, a fragile peace had been renewed – which struck many observers as unusual, in and of itself, given the ongoing boiling tensions on the Gaza border.

So, no-one was surprised that the Rav had called for a prayer gathering to avoid war and rockets from the South. But Israel's Northern border had been relatively quiet for years, so that part of the Rav's statement raised a few eyebrows. But not for long.

Just two days' later, on December 4, 2018, the IDF announced the start of Operation Northern Shield and revealed to the stunned Israeli public that Hezbollah had built a number of huge terror tunnels underground, crossing the Lebanese border into Israel, which the IDF was about to start locating and dismantling.

Two weeks and four tunnels later, Israeli Prime Minister Bibi Netanyahu gave an English-language press conference at the Knesset where he said that the purpose of Hezbollah's tunnels were to: "penetrate our territory, kidnap our people, including civilians, murder civilians, and conquer the northern piece of the Galilee. This is not merely an act of aggression. It's an act of war. It's part of a war plan."

When Operation Northern Shield formally concluded in the middle of January 2019, six tunnels had been found. Netanyahu gave another press conference where he said: "I think everyone understands that a very serious threat was averted here. Hezbollah's operational plan was to use the tunnels weapon to infiltrate many fighters, between 1,000-2,000 terrorists, into the Galilee, to seize communities here. Everyone understands how the war would look if Hezbollah battalions were in the Galilee, and with the Iranian army opposite the Golan Heights."

It's amazing to remember that no-one was even really talking about the Lebanese border when the Rav first asked for the prayer gathering to be organized in Hebron. But that's not all that was happening.

On December 19th, 2018, US President Donald Trump surprised the world – and by all accounts, most of his own administration, too – when he put out a message over social media that: "We have defeated ISIS in Syria, my only reason for being there during the Trump Presidency."

A few days' later, in response to a question about how the American withdrawal from Syria would impact Israel, Trump reportedly said: "we give Israel $4.5 billion a year. And they are doing very well at defending themselves." At the end of March 2019, the Trump administration announced that they were recognizing Israel sovereignty over the Golan Heights, which was hailed as a major 'breakthrough' by many in Israel.

But others were not so optimistic about what the future might hold, when it came to preventing terror from Syria spilling over the border and drawing Israel into a serious confrontation with the Iranian forces stationed in the country. The Israeli air force had been flying a number of missions over Syria for years, trying to disrupt, destroy and otherwise hamper the free supply of Iranian weapons and soldiers into the country, and Iran's influence in Lebanon, Syria and Gaza continued to keep Israeli officials up at night.

On January 13, 2019, PM Netanyahu made a highly unusual public admission that Israel had been behind hundreds of 'ambiguous' bombings of Iranian weapons' depots in Syria, and other Syrian targets, over the last few years. This was the latest in a series of boastful statements the Israeli government was making about how strong, and efficient, and successful the Israeli army really was, in keeping all the enemies on its borders in check. But not everyone agreed with that assessment.

One vocal critic was Major-General (res.) Isaac Brick, the outgoing IDF Ombudsman, who had been making public statements for months that the IDF was nowhere near as strong, or as prepared for war, as the public was being told.

Brick's concerns were repeatedly mocked and ignored by army and government officials alike, with an IDF panel headed by IDF comptroller Brigadier General (res.) Ilan Harari, and a Knesset committee both releasing reports which stated that the Israeli army was in the best shape it had been for years.

Harari's report stated that: "the IDF's ground forces are unequivocally prepared for war." While the Knesset report said the level of war preparedness had "significantly improved since Operation Protective Edge," with "a dramatic increase in readiness by almost every indicator — whether in the number of training drills, whether in munitions stocks, spare parts inventory and more."

But Brick wasn't convinced. In October 2018, he drew a lot of flack by publicly claiming that the situation with the IDF was "worse than it was at the time of the Yom Kippur War", when Israel was caught badly off guard by a surprise attack by its Arab neighbors, which almost lead to an unmitigated disaster for the Jewish people.

As he was publicly smeared as an 'alarmist' and fear-mongerer, Brick refused to back down from his warnings, and even continued to turn up the heat.

In a statement he put out on December 26, 2018, he had the following to say: *"Israeli citizens will pay a heavy price for the serious cover-up by the system and no one will be able to say I didn't warn them. This is the first time in my ten years as ombudsman that I've met members of the IDF General Staff who are unable to accept criticism. I advise the senior command to stop playing games of ego and immediately get into the thick of things to correct the failures before it is too late."*

But as usual, this warning was also rebuffed.

Immediately after Chanukah's prayer gathering in Hebron, Rabbi Berland told his attendants to begin preparing for the next prayer gathering, to be held on April 8th, 2019 – shortly after Rosh Chodesh Nissan.

The week after Chanuka, Israel's governing coalition finally toppled over on December 24, 2018, when party heads announced new elections would be held on April 9th, 2019 – the day after the Rav had called for the next prayer gathering.

With a raft of allegations swirling around the PM, open hostilities on almost every border, the ongoing problem of a nuclear Iran and ongoing terror attacks within Israel's border, within a few short weeks of the prayer gathering it had become crystal clear that the Rav had been right, when he warned about the terrible dangers facing the Israeli people.

No-one knew if enough had been done to sweeten the judgments hanging over the Jewish people, or if more suffering was in store. What was clear is that the fate of Am Yisrael was once again hanging in the balance – and that was being reflected in the Rav, himself.

After his major surgery and leg problems, Rabbi Berland's health continued to be precarious throughout 2018. On December 30, 2018, during the celebrations for his 81st birthday, he took the unusual step of writing a very short, but very disturbing note, asking his congregants to pray for his continued good health. The handwritten note said the following: "Please pray for the Rav, that he shouldn't be taken before Passover. Rather, his days should be lengthened until 210 years. Signed, Eliezer Berland."

The scene was eerily reminiscent of what had occurred four years' earlier, in Holland, just prior to when the Rav had suffered the cardiac arrest that had nearly claimed his life.

Then, too, he'd asked the community to fast and pray for him. Then, too, the Rav's health had taken a very serious and sudden turn for the worse. At that time, too, other tzaddikim had suddenly passed away, and it's known that when these holy souls are taken, judgments are sweetened.

Was the same thing about to happen again?

On December 31st, 2018, the Breslov community was rocked by the news that the leader of the Breslov community in Tzfat, Rav Elazar Mordechai Koenig, zt"l, had passed away at the age of 73.

In his eulogy for Rav Koenig, Rabbi Berland crisply summed things up: "Rav Koenig was the greatest in the generation. He was well learned in both the revealed and the hidden Torah. He was the Rebbe *mamash*. The fact that there are hareidi Jews in Tzfat is all in his merit. He was the last of the *tzaddikim*."

A day after Rav Koenig's passing the Shuvu Banim community was galvanized into action by reports that Rabbi Berland had been taken ill during one of his regular Torah classes in Tel Aviv. Very unusually for the Rav, he'd asked his attendants to take him back to his home as soon as the class was over, and to cancel his other Torah classim and house visits that were planned for the rest of the night.

The Rav gave over a brief recorded message, where you could clearly hear how weak he was, and how every word required an enormous effort:

"Already, I can't speak for two days," he said. "I'm asking everyone to do 2,000 tikkun haklalis, and to reach saying 2,000 tikkun haklalis [altogether], so that the Rav can start to speak again today at the evening prayers, mincha and ma'ariv...

Because if not, the Rav won't even be able to say the Kaddish. Everyone is needed to save the Rav, and to return the power of speech to him, which was taken from him, as a result of [Am Yisrael's] many sins. Only reciting the Tikkun

HaKlali can rectify everything. So, we need to recite 2,000 Tikkun Haklalis – the entire community, and anyone else who wants to help the Rav."

Thousands of people stepped up to pray for the Rav, and the organizers at Shuvu Banim estimated that at least 11,000 Tikkun HaKlalis were recited in the merit of the Rav's recovery, over the next 24 hours. Thankfully, the Rav's health took an immediate, and significant, turn for the better.

The next day found the Rav driving down to the Southern-most city of Eilat, where he jumped straight back into visiting communities, synagogues and private homes all over the region. But health wise, things were still touch and go. After returning from Eilat again asked his followers to recite a minimum of 1,000 Tikkun HaKlalis every day, in the merit of his full recovery.

The Rav's exile had begun more than six years' earlier, with a spiritual deal to suffer disgrace, humiliation and persecution, as a kapparah, or atonement for Am Yisrael's sins. As 2019 began, full of possible wars, freak weather and enormous political unrest across the planet, the question of whether all the self-sacrifice and prayers and teshuva to date would be enough to tip the balance in Israel's favor was the unspoken thought in so many people's minds.

And the coming months were about to answer that question, decisively.

★ ★ ★

The following weeks saw more and more Jewish blood being shed. On February 7th, 19 year old Ori Ansbacher was raped and brutally murdered by a Palestinian terrorist in broad daylight, in the Ein Yael forest on the outskirts of Jerusalem. The attack shook the country to its core.

Then, on March 15th, 2019, terrorists in the Gaza strip

launched two rockets at Central Israel, which miraculously landed in empty spaces in the heavily-populated city of Holon, near Tel Aviv. Hamas claimed the launch had been an 'accident'. Two days later, another terrorist stabbed Sgt. Gal Keidan, 19, at the Ariel Junction in the Shomron, then stole his gun and shot him, and other civilians, including Rabbi Ahiad Ettinger, a 47 year old father of 12, who died of his wounds the next morning.

Just before the Fast of Esther, (March 20th, 2019), the Rav put out another hair-raising message asking his followers to spend the next three days praying that he would live to see Passover 5779.

Emergency prayer meetings were swiftly organized at the Kotel, and despite the hustle and bustle of the busy Purim holiday, hundreds of people still turned up each night at *chatzos*, to read through the whole book of Psalms, in the merit of the Rav's speedy recovery.

Three days later, there was another 'accidental' rocket attack from Gaza, which this time almost totally destroyed a house on Moshav Mishmeret, near Kfar Saba, while the family was sleeping in it. In another open miracle, the family of 7 only sustained very light injuries.

But as Rabbi Berland had warned at Chanuka time, the rockets were back, and this time, they were striking to the heart of the country.

The following day, March 26, 2019, another 60 rockets were launched at Israel, but most were intercepted by the Iron Dome, or fell harmlessly in empty areas. Even when a rocket crashed through the wall of a house in Sderot, it miraculously didn't explode. God was still watching over the nation of Israel, He was still doing miracles for the Jewish people every moment, and every second.

As Rosh Chodesh Nissan approached, most of the world remained in a state of turmoil. There was a feeling in the air that so many things were hanging by a thread, and that the slightest nudge could tip the planet headlong into chaos.

In Israel, there were so many questions, so many concerns. The next few weeks could bring all-out war with the Arabs; a US-imposed 'peace' plan, a new government run by the same anti-hareidi politicians who did so much damage to the Torah world five years earlier. So many things were up in the air, there was so much to pray for.

Back in Jerusalem, Rabbi Berland re-iterated the importance of getting as many people as possible to Hebron, for the prayer gathering on April 8th, 2019. The stakes had never been higher.

Epilogue

Taken from a recording of a Lesson Rabbi Berland gave on Likutei Halachos, *in February 2015.*

"The more falsehood there is, the more truth will be revealed in a clearer way. The truth will be revealed in the end. As much as the lies will be spread in the world, more falsehood to fool everyone, that's the degree that the truth will be revealed in the end. They didn't tell all of the lies yet. It's only the beginning.

There are a still a lot of Tzaddikim in the world, in every generation, that aren't listening to the lies, they're not letting themselves be fooled by the deceit. There's not enough deception. As long as we see that there's still Tzaddikim in the world so it's a sign that the falsehood didn't take over enough. Therefore, we need the deception needs to be victorious. Until the lies win, there can't be the redemption. Once the falsehood is victorious, then the people will go through a clarification process, they'll be sifted out, according to all of the strong truth that's inside of them.

And that's how Moshiach is going to be revealed. Moshiach needs to be revealed from the epitome of falsehood, Moshiach and his people. They're not going to be pulled by the deception. The deception wants to take everyone. The falsehood says: "I didn't say enough lies. Maybe I'll say a little bit more, maybe I'll succeed in saying something else, a different way.

In every generation there are new lies. The deception makes up things that never existed from the creation of the world. But specifically through this spreading of the lies, the falsehood will take over the whole world and there won't be even a drop of truth. Only a small number of people will hold strong to the truth, but the *sheker* will take over everyone... And everyone will be taken over by the falsehood and everyone will be fooled, and only then will the truth be revealed and Moshiach will come. Only through the deception increasing.

Therefore, we need to strengthen the people saying the lies. Don't go against them, give them strength. We need to strengthen them even more, so they should make up more lies and do more articles. Only when the falsehood reaches its end and is completely satisfied, only then will the truth be established.

Moshiach will come when he sees there are some people who aren't being pulled and who know that it's all falsehood and nothing is able to fool them or confuse them.

Because as long as it's possible to change people's minds, to brainwash them to go for the lies, and then brainwash them again and convince them to go against the lies, Moshiach won't have anywhere to go. Because then Moshiach will come and also convince people to come after him... No! We need that the people will be able to convince everyone until it's no longer possible for them to change their minds again.

If there's even a minyan left, 10 people left whose minds haven't been turned by the lies, then the Moshiach can be revealed, and he'll reveal himself to this group of people. And from here, it will go on and spread throughout the whole world.

Therefore, we shouldn't try to stop it, we shouldn't go

against it. We shouldn't do articles against articles to prove that they're wrong. Why do we need more articles? We don't need more articles against articles. The falsehood has the strength to fool the whole world. The strength that it has, it got from the the holy side.

So why did God let it happen? God let it happen so that the truth, a person's truth that he has within him, should be so strong, should be so burning strong, and should get stronger the more he sees that the deceit is winning. That real truth from within him, the pure truth from within him, should get so strong they can't brainwash him [anymore]. And then, they'll reach a very high spiritual level, and then Moshiach will be revealed."

★ ★ ★

When Rabbi Berland was in South Africa during the summer of 2015, he gave a *Torah class* where he explained that the revelation of the Moshiach wouldn't change anything at all in the world. Until everyone did *teshuva*, there simply couldn't be a true redemption, and the real work of the Moshiach would be to bring everyone in the world back to God.

Around that same time, in a different Torah class he said: "*These next six years, from 5775 to 5781 (2014-2021), are the years of redemption. These are the years when the whole of the Jewish people will do teshuva. Even the biggest criminals and thugs are going to do teshuva. There are no criminals in the nation of Israel, there are no wicked people in the Jewish nation. It's all just stages of the redemption process. It's all just stages in the evolution of the soul, in receiving the different stages of the soul. The biggest criminal is going to end up being the biggest tzaddik...*

We also need to bring the 70 nations back in repentance.

The King Moshiach is going to return all the nations back to God, because God forbid that even a single non-Jew should die! We don't want any non-Jews to die, except for [exceptionally evil] people like Hitler, may his name be erased, *but even common murderers can do teshuva."*

Rabbi Berland was sending a clear message that redemption is a process, and that the process that will culminate in true peace, and the coming of the Jewish redeemer, is already occurring right now, however it may look externally.

Moshiach, "the son of Jesse," is likened to a sprout for a very good reason. For many long weeks, months and even years, the seed of Moshiach lays underground, hidden from public view, apparently decaying and rotting away. Until… that first sprout of redemption finally bursts forth.

ADDITIONAL RESOURCES

I f you would like to learn more about Rav Eliezer Berland, **One in a Generation - Volume I** contains hundreds of hours of interviews, stories and first-hand sources.

In Hebrew, there are many additional books available about Rabbi Berland, including collections of his Torah lessons, miraculous stories of the people he's helped and compendiums of his advice and prayers. A good place to start is the **www.ravberland.com** bookstore, which can be found here:

https://ravberland.com/product-category/english-books/

★ ★ ★

LEARN MORE ABOUT RAV ELIEZER BERLAND AND SHUVU BANIM

Latest news and updates about Rav Eliezer Berland and Shuvu Banim (in English) can be found at:

www.ravberland.com

Real-time updates, announcements and stories (in Hebrew) are available over the telephone on the Shuvu Banim hotline.

THE SHUVU BANIM HOTLINE:

In Israel call:	*9148 or 02-800-8800
In the USA call:	845-640-0007
In the UK and Europe call:	+44-203-807-3333

To send a name to receive a blessing from Rabbi Berland, visit: ravberland.com/contact

To make a pidyon nefesh, visit: ravberland.com/pidyon-nefesh

To make a donation, visit: www.ravberland.com/donate

GLOSSARY

Ahavas Chaveirim	To love our fellow Jew (literally, to love our friends).
Achdus	Unity.
Admor	A Rebbe in a Chassidic court.
Al Kiddush God	In order to sanctify God's name.
Aliyah	Literally, 'going up' - both to the Torah, and to the land of Israel.
Am Yisrael	the nation, or people, of Israel.
Am Ha'aretz	An unlearned man; a boor.
AN"SH	Abbreviation of *Anshei Shelomeinu*, or 'our people', used in reference to other Breslov chassidim.
Atik Yomin	A kabbalistic term referring to higher worlds.
Aufruf	A celebration held by the groom on the Shabbos before his wedding.
Aveira (pl: aveiros)	Sin, wrong-doing.
Avodah Zara	Idol worship.
Avodas God	Literally, 'God's work' - refers to any holy endeavours, prayers or mitzvos, etc.
Avodas HaTefillah	Literally, 'the work of praying' - refers to praying.
Avreich	A married student who's serious about learning Torah, often full-time.
B'Iyun	In depth.
Ba'al Teshuva	(plural: *ba'alei teshuva*) A person who returns to God (repents).

Baal Tokei'ah	The one who blows the Shofar in synagogue on the High Holidays.
Baalei Batim	Householders who work instead of learning Torah full-time.
Bachor (pl: bachorim)	An unmarried student who's learning Torah in a Yeshiva.
Baki	Knowledgeable.
Baraisa	Tannaic statements that are found in the Gemara, but that have a lesser status than mishnayos.
Baruch God	*Literally*: Bless God. *Colloquially*: Thank God.
Bat Kol	A voice from heaven.
Bein Hazmanim	Literally, 'between times' - refers to the period between the 9th of Av and the first of Elul, when Torah institutions are closed for the summer.
Beis Din	A religious, Jewish court of law.
Beis HaMikdash	The Temple in Jerusalem.
Beis Midrash	*Literally:* The house of learning. Colloquially, the yeshiva's main study hall.
Bentch	To bless - usually refers to reciting the grace after meals.
B'ezras God	With God's help.
Birkas HaMazon	The blessing after meals.
Birkas HaShachar	The blessings recited in the morning, from the prayer book.
Bitachon	Trust (usually refers to trust in God).
Bitul	Self-nullification.
Biyas HaMoshiach	Hebrew for: The coming of the Moshiach.
Bnei Torah	*Literally:* Sons of Torah. Refers to Torah observant Jews.
Blessing	A blessing.
Bris Mila	The circumcision ceremony typically held eight days after a Jewish boy is born.

Cheder (pl: chadarim)	Religious pre-school.
Chaburah	A Torah study group.
Chai V'kayam	A biblical expression usually used to refer to a dead Tzaddik, as being still 'alive' spiritually, and present and acting in the world.
Chalakah	A celebration where a three year old Jewish boy has his first haircut.
Chalban	The Milkman. Referring to the kabbalist, Rav Chaim Cohen.
Chas v'shalom	*Colloquially:* God forbid.
Chassid (pl: chassidim)	A group of religious, orthodox Jews who usually follow their own 'Rebbe' (or '*Chassidim*') Devout students or followers of Rabbi Nachman of Breslov.
Chassidei Breslov	
Chassidus	The spiritual path originated by the Ba'al Shem Tov, and followed by his students, including Rabbi Nachman. A sect of Judaism which emphasises joy in its practice and teaches that every Jew, no matter his level, can get close to God.
Chatzos	The time of halachic midnight.
Chavrusa	A one-on-one study partner, when learning Torah.
Chazal	The initial letters of the following expression in Hebrew: **Ch**achameinu **Z**ichronam **L**'vracha. *Literally:* "Our Sages, may their memory be for a blessing."
Cheshbon Nefesh	taking a self-reckoning or personal accounting of our own deeds.
Chessed	Kindness.
Chevrah Kaddisha	The organisation responsible for preparing a Jewish body according to halacha, before burial.
Chizuk	Strengthening, spiritual encouragement.

Chol HaMo'ed	Refers to the intermediate days between the first day (or days) of Yom Tov, and the last day (or days) of Yom Tov, of either Sukkos or Passover.
Wedding	The marriage canopy used in Jewish weddings.
Chutz L'Aretz	*Literally:* Outside the land. Refers to anywhere outside of Israel.
Chutzpadik	Brazen, shameless, cheeky.
D'Oraisa	Refers to a commandment or mitzvah that's derived directly from the written Torah, as opposed to the Oral Torah.
Da'as	Godly awareness, knowledge or wisdom.
Daf Yomi	The daily study of a specific, set page of the Gemara.
Dam (pl: damim)	*Literally:* blood, or bloods. Refers to 'blood money'.
Darshan	Someone who gives over a Torah class or lesson in public.
Dati Leumi	*Literally:* National-religious. Describes a group of more modern orthodox Jews in Israel.
Davka	On purpose, specifically.
Derech Eretz	Good manners. *'Derech Eretz kadma le Torah'* literally means that you have to put practical considerations before learning Torah.
Deveikus	Closeness or clinging to God.
Ein Od Milvado	*Literally:* There is only Him (i.e. God).
Eis Ratzon	A favourable time.
Emunah	Trust, faith and belief in God. *Emunas Tzaddikim:* believing in the words of our Tzaddikim.
Erev	*Literally:* The eve of. *Erev Shabbos* refers to the time before candle-lighting on Friday.

Es HaMoshiach	The time of Moshiach.
Gabbai	Responsible for managing the services within synagogue, and / or attending a rabbi or Rebbe, in a capacity similar to a private secretary.
Gadol HaDor	*Literally:* Great one of the generation. Refers to the senior, leading figure in the Torah world.
Galus	Exile.
Gaon	Torah genius.
Gashmiyus	Materialism, materiality.
Gedolim	*Literally:* Great ones. Refers to the leading Torah personalities of a generation.
Gehinnom	Purgatory.
Gemilus Chassadim	Acts of kindness, good deeds.
Gemach	A free loan fund for money or other items.
Geula	Redemption.
Gog and Magog	The last war that's meant to occur at the end of days, ushering in the time of Moshiach.
Hachnassas Orchim	The mitzvah of hosting guests.
HaKadosh Baruch Hu	*Literally:* The Holy One, blessed be He. Another term for God.
Hakafot Shniyos	Referring to the custom to dance with the Torah all night long on the night after Shmini Atzeres.
Hakaras HaTov	Gratitude.
Halachah (pl: halachos)	Jewish law.
God	G-d.
God Yisborach	G-d, may He be blessed.
Havdalah	*Literally:* separation. The service performed at the conclusion of Shabbos, before returning to the mundane activities of the rest of the week.
Hilulah	Anniversary of a person (usually a Tzaddik's) passing.

Hishtadlus	One's own personal or physical effort.
Hisbodedus	Personal prayer to G-d in one's own words.
Ibburim	Refers to containing sparks of a particular soul, or souls.
Kabbalas Shabbos	Welcoming the Shabbos.
Kapparah	*Literally:* Atonement. Often refers to a financial or material loss that occurs instead of something worse happening.
Kavanah	Intention.
Kedusha	Holiness.
Kehillah	Community.
Keitz	The end, usually specifically referring to the end of days.
Kesubah	Marriage contract.
Kiddush God	Something that sanctifies God's name.
Kiddush Levanah	The monthly blessing recited over the sighting of the new moon.
Kibbutz	Often secular agricultural settlement in Israel founded on socialist principles. *Kibbutznik:* Member of a kibbutz.
Kippah	Skull-cap.
Kisei HaKavod	*Literally:* The holy throne. Refers allegorically to God's throne in the Heavens.
Kivrei Tzaddikim	Plural of *kever Tzaddik*, or the grave of a holy, righteous person.
Kloiz	The main synagogue in Uman, originally built by Rabbi Natan.
Korbanos	*Literally*: The Temple sacrifices. Here, it means the recitation of the sacrificial service in the morning prayers, in lieu of actually performing the sacrifices in the Temple.
Kotel	The wailing or Western wall of the

	destroyed Temple, that still stands in Jerusalem.
Kriyah	The Jewish custom of tearing the clothing upon being told of the death of a close relative, as a sign of deep mourning.
Kvitlach	A note requesting a blessing that's sent to a Tzaddik.
Kvod HaRav	*Literally:* The honour of the Rav. A respectful greeting offered to rabbinic figures.
Lashon Hara	Evil speech, gossip.
Likutei Moharan	The main work of Rebbe Nachman of Breslov.
Limud Torah	*Literally:* Torah learning.
Lishmah	For its own sake, or for God's sake, without any other ulterior motives.
Ma'ariv	The evening prayers.
Machlokes	Strife, trouble-making, discord.
Malach	Angel.
Maseches	Tractate - usually referring to the Gemara.
Mashgiach (also, Mashgiach Ruchani)	
Masmid	Someone who is constantly engaged in learning Torah.
Masorti	Traditionally religious.
Mattan Torah	The giving of the Torah.
Mechitzah	The barrier between the men and women's section of a hall or synagogue.
Megillah	Scroll.
Melava Malka	*Literally:* The queen's meal. Refers to the meal that occurs after the end of Shabbos, to bid farewell to the Shabbos Queen.
Menahel	Head teacher.
Meraglim	Spies.
Meshugga, Meshugganer	Yiddish terms for craziness, a crazy person.

Mesirus Nefesh	Self-sacrifice.
Midda Keneged Midda	A measure for a measure.
Middos	Character traits.
Midrash	Stories and explanations from the Gemara and other holy books.
Mikveh	A pool of ritually pure water that cleanses a person from their spiritual impurity.
Milah D'Shtusa	*Literally:* Foolish words.
Milchama (pl: milchamos)	War, wars.
Minchah	The afternoon prayers.
Minyan	A quorum of at least 10 men required for Jewish communal prayers.
Mishnayos	Plural of *Mishna*. Refers to the Tannaic statements that are part of the Oral Torah.
Mitzvah	(plural: *mitzvos*) Commandment(s), good deeds.
Morenu	*Literally:* Our teacher.
Motzei Shabbos	The night after Shabbos has ended, Saturday night after nightfall.
Navi	Prophet.
Ne'ilah	The final prayer service on Yom Kippur.
Neshama	The Divine soul.
Netz	Sunrise.
Ovdei God (also 'ovdim)	*Literally:* God's workers, people who are continually engaged in mitzvos, prayer and learning Torah.
P'gam HaBris	*Literally:* A blemish in the covenant. Refers to physical immorality.
Parsha	Refers to the Torah portion for each week.
Parnasa	Livelihood.
Pashut	Simple, in all simplicity.
Pasul	Halachically invalid / not kosher.
Payos	Side-curls.
Pidyon HaKlali	The general redemption payment

	which sweetens all the judgments over a person. *Pidyon HaKollel:*
Pidyon Nefesh	A redemption of the soul (a payment made to a Tzaddik that is used to redeem the person's soul from where it is trapped).
Pirkei Avos	Ethics of our Fathers - a collection of aphorisms from Chazal.
Poskim	Halachic decisors. A *psak* is a halachic decision or ruling.
Protekzia	Influence, nepotism (often a by-product of endemic corruption).
Prutah	A coin of very low value.
Rabbeinu	Rabbi Nachman of Breslov (but also means 'our teacher' when used in reference to other Rabbis).
Ratzon	Will or desire.
Refua sheleimah	*Literally:* A complete recovery, or healing.
Ribono Shel Olam	*Literally:* Master of the World. Another term for God.
Rosh Yeshiva	The head Rabbi of a yeshiva.
Ruach Hakodesh	Divine intuition.
Ruchniyus	Spirituality, spiritual matters.
Samech Mem	Refers to the head of the forces of evil.
Sandek	An honourable position given at a bris, refers to the person who holds the baby.
Seforim	Holy Jewish books.
Segulah	A practice which results in a spiritual or material benefit, which is not logically derived.
Seichel	Wisdom, intellect, brains.
Seudah shlishis	The third Shabbos meal.
Shacharis	The morning prayers.
Shalom Bayis	*Literally:* Peace in the home. Marital peace.
Shamash	Attendant.
Shamayim	Heaven.

Shechinah	The Divine Presence in this world.
Shefa	Bounty.
Sheker	Lies, untruths.
Shemittah	The seventh year of a seven year cycle, in which the land is left unworked.
Shemoneh Esrei	The central prayer, consisting of 19 blessings, that is said three times a day.
Sheva Brachos	The seven blessings that are recited for a newly-married Jewish couple on each of the first seven days after their wedding.
Shidduch (pl: shidduchim)	Marital match, a date with a view to getting married.
Torah class	Torah class or lesson.
Shaliach Tzibbur	The one leading the prayer service.
Shlichus	Going out to do outreach, some other mitzvah.
Shlit"a	An honorific term appended to the name of holy men during their lifetime.
Shmiras Einayim	*Literally:* Guarding the eyes. Refers to the mitzvah of not looking at immoral, spiritually damaging things.
Shtreimel	A round fur hat typically worn by chassidim on Shabbos, festivals and to other communal celebrations.
Simchah (pl: simchas)	Happiness. Also used to refer to a happy occasion like a wedding, for example.
Sinas Chinam	Baseless hatred.
Sitra Achra	*Literally:* 'The other side'. The dark side or source of negative spiritual forces, also an aspect of the yetzer hara.
Si'ata d'Shemaya	Heavenly help, Divine providence.
Smicha	The process of conferring rabbinic status on an individual.

Sofer Stam	The practice of writing mezuzahs, sefer Torahs and other holy texts. (Also called '*safrus*'.)
Sugya (pl: sugyos)	The section of Torah being learnt, usually refers to Gemara.
Tallis	Four-cornered prayer shawl.
Talmid Chacham	A wise Torah student.
Techiyas HaMeisim	The revival of the dead, that will happen in the times of Moshiach.
Tefach (pl: tefachim)	A biblical unit of measurement, approximately 8-10 centimetres.
Tefillin	Black boxes containing holy texts that are worn on the arm and the forehead.
Psalms	Psalms.
Teshuva	Repentance.
Teshuvos	Responses to halachic questions.
Tikkun	(plural: tikkunim) Spiritual rectification. *Tikkun Olam* - rectification of the world. *Tikkun Chatzos* - Midnight prayer, said to rectify / lament the destruction of the Temple.
Tikkun HaKlali	*Literally:* The General Rectification. The Ten Psalms (numbers: 16, 32, 41, 42, 59, 77, 90, 105, 137, 150) prescribed by Rebbe Nachman as a powerful spiritual remedy.
Tisha B'Av	The ninth of Av, the date on which we remember the destruction of the Beit HaMikdash.
Toivel	To immerse in a mikveh.
Tosafos	One of the more famous groups of commentators on the Gemara, dating from approximately the 12th century.
Tumah	Spiritual impurity.
Tzaddik	(plural: *Tzaddikim*), The righteous one.
Tzedaka	Charity.

Tzitzis	A four cornered garment normally worn by Jewish men under their clothes, with fringes / strings at each corner.
Tziyun	The grave of a Tzaddik, e.g. Rebbe Nachman's grave.
Vasikin	Dawn minyan.
Yeshiva	Religious Jewish institution for learning Torah.
Yetzer Hara	The evil inclination.
Yirah; Yiras Shamayim	Fear of Heaven.
Yishuv HaDa'as	A settled mind.
Yom HaAtzma'ut	Israel's Independence Day.
Zechus (also Zocheh)	Merit, to merit.
Zemiros	Jewish songs, usually containing biblical verses, that are typically sung on Shabbos, and on other Jewish festivals and happy occasions.
Zman	Period of time.
Zt"l	Stands for: **Z**ichron **H**aTzaddik **L'**vracha: *Literally:* May the tzaddik's memory be for a blessing.

END NOTES

1   *Isaiah* 2:2.

2   Baal Shem Tov al HaTorah Parshas Korach and Komarno Rebbe in the name of the BESHT brought in Netiv Mitzvosecha Path of Unification, 6th path, 5th passage.

3   FOOTNOTE OF RAV ROMPLER: If someone can even begin to entertain a suspicion of this sort about a man like this, that is a sign that the person is on an extremely low level and very far from anything spiritual. He has absolutely no conception of the nature of spirituality, or how a spiritual person who is far from anything mundane [behaves], and he himself should be checked in regard to his own behavior in the matter of [adultery].

> For it is known that which our Sages teach: "kol haposel b'mumo posel – 'Any person who behaves in a disgraceful manner always accuses others of his particular fault." See what it says in the responses of the RaShDan (Yoreh Deah 215, and the Chofetz Chaim in Hilchos Lashon Hara, klal 6 in Be'er Mayim Chaim 31 mentions this RaShDan) about a story similar to ours. There, it says that whoever believes in the Torah of Moshe, it is forbidden for them to believe in the rumors, and anyone who is not sure (that is, he suspects that the rumors may be true) is someone who himself is infected with this disease (i.e. he does those things which he suspects the righteous of doing). These are the words of the RaShDan.

> It is known what the Tzaddikim said, that if those who go after physical pleasures and desires would know the pleasure that we feel when we say "Nishmas" on Shabbos kodesh - which is a thousand times more pleasurable than the physical pleasure that they feel when indulging in pleasures and sins - they would

abandon all of their physical pleasures, and they would return in teshuva to become sincere servants of God and the Tzaddikim. Behold, this pleasure is felt by anyone who is engrossed in the service of God and the study of the Holy Torah, and therefore, whoever occupies himself with Torah and avodas God, it will not even enter his heart to begin to believe any of these stories about another servant of God, for he knows that it's just not possible.

> And just like it is against all logic to say about someone who is enjoying the taste of sweet honey that maybe he would prefer to leave it, and desire the 'sweetness' of salt, instead, so we know what the Rambam says, that the evil inclination and sinful thoughts are only found in a heart that is empty of Torah. (And when someone studies Torah, but his heart is not yet fully engrossed in it, that is also considered as if his heart is 'empty', because the Torah has not yet engulfed his heart. Rather, his Torah learning is still only in his mind).

[4] FOOTNOTE OF RAV ROMPLER: In our case, his intentions are clear to those who know his way of speaking and understand his nature, that his intention in purposely causing himself disgrace is to atone for the entire Nation. It's written in Sha'arei Teshuva by Rabbeinu Yona that disgrace and insult are kinds of suffering that are considered to be more severe than death, and it is known from the holy books that the Tzaddikim would accept on themselves death in order to atone for the entire nation [and save them] from harsh decrees.

> And those idiots who spread these rumors [aren't aware that] there are high tikkunim involved, that we have no idea about. This rumor was either invented by the [Rav's] persecutors with the evil intention of making it sound as though his followers believe the stories, but have a strange way of explaining it away, i.e., by saying that a tzaddik is allowed to do these things, in order to make [the Rav] and his look bad, by saying that they believe these horrible things happened, and they even believe that its allowed etc.

> Or, these things were actually said by crazy people. But whatever the case is, let it be known that these ideas are complete heresy against the Torah of Moshe and those who reveal these false Torah ideas have no share in the World to Come. These sorts of ideas were spread by the Shabsai Tzvi cult, may their names be

erased, and in the end they all converted [out of Judaism], as is known, and that was the end of them, but only after many people were fooled by them.

> Even though there is no need to write all this, nevertheless, I mentioned it because today there are so many crazy, insane ideas in the world, as we mentioned previously. This is because we are at the time of the final birur, or clarification process, before the complete redemption, therefore every evil and klippa that ever existed in the world is coming up again, in order for it to become reattached to the evil that still exists in the world, which is still mixed up with the good. In this way, it will be separated from its good, each will find its type, and the good will be left pure and clean, sifted from all evil, and that is the way that the evil can be abolished and destroyed completely, soon, together with the sitra achra and Amalek and all the other parts of evil. And then there will be room for the revelation of the Kingdom of Heaven and the complete redemption will be revealed very soon, in our days.

5   Isaiah 59:15.

6   Psalms 119:165.

8   Devarim 32:22

9   Devarim 32:22

51207046R00227

Made in the USA
Middletown, DE
30 June 2019